Being an Adult Learner in Austere Times

Ellen Boeren · Nalita James
Editors

Being an Adult Learner in Austere Times

Exploring the Contexts of Higher, Further and Community Education

Editors
Ellen Boeren
Moray House School of Education
University of Edinburgh
Edinburgh, UK

Nalita James
School of Education
University of Leicester
Leicester, UK

ISBN 978-3-319-97207-7   ISBN 978-3-319-97208-4 (eBook)
https://doi.org/10.1007/978-3-319-97208-4

Library of Congress Control Number: 2018951561

© The Editor(s) (if applicable) and The Author(s) 2019
This work is subject to copyright. All rights are solely and exclusively licensed by the Publisher, whether the whole or part of the material is concerned, specifically the rights of translation, reprinting, reuse of illustrations, recitation, broadcasting, reproduction on microfilms or in any other physical way, and transmission or information storage and retrieval, electronic adaptation, computer software, or by similar or dissimilar methodology now known or hereafter developed.
The use of general descriptive names, registered names, trademarks, service marks, etc. in this publication does not imply, even in the absence of a specific statement, that such names are exempt from the relevant protective laws and regulations and therefore free for general use.
The publisher, the authors and the editors are safe to assume that the advice and information in this book are believed to be true and accurate at the date of publication. Neither the publisher nor the authors or the editors give a warranty, express or implied, with respect to the material contained herein or for any errors or omissions that may have been made. The publisher remains neutral with regard to jurisdictional claims in published maps and institutional affiliations.

Cover image: © StudioM1/Getty

This Palgrave Macmillan imprint is published by the registered company Springer Nature Switzerland AG
The registered company address is: Gewerbestrasse 11, 6330 Cham, Switzerland

Contents

1 Adult Education in Austere Times: An Introduction 1
Nalita James and Ellen Boeren

2 Being an Adult Learner in Europe and the UK: Persisting Inequalities and the Role of the Welfare State 21
Ellen Boeren

3 The Message or the Bottle? Community, Associationism and Adult Learning as "Part of the Process of Social Change" 47
Sharon Clancy

4 Keeping Going in Austere Times: The Declining Spaces for Adult Widening Participation in Higher Education in England 71
Lindsey Fraser and Kerry Harman

5 Mature Students and Social Isolation: Being Excluded or Choosing to Be Alone? 97
Charlie E. Sutton

6 Subjects in Formation: Women's Experiences
   of Access to Higher Education Courses and
   Entering Higher Education   123
   Sherene Meir

7 Further Educations: Transformative Teaching and
   Learning for Adults in Times of Austerity   151
   Vicky Duckworth and Rob Smith

8 Adult Education in Community Organisations
   Supporting Homeless Adults: Exploring the Impact
   of Austerity Politics   179
   Katy Jones

9 Conclusions and Recommendations   199
   Ellen Boeren and Nalita James

Index   211

Contributors

Ellen Boeren Moray House School of Education, University of Edinburgh, Edinburgh, UK

Sharon Clancy University of Nottingham, Nottingham, UK

Vicky Duckworth Edge Hill University, Ormskirk, UK

Lindsey Fraser University of Leeds, Leeds, UK

Kerry Harman Birkbeck, London, UK

Nalita James School of Education, University of Leicester, Leicester, UK

Katy Jones University of Salford, Greater Manchester, UK

Sherene Meir City of Bristol College, Bristol, UK

Rob Smith Birmingham City University, Birmingham, UK

Charlie E. Sutton University of Leicester, Leicester, UK

List of Figures

Fig. 2.1	Participation rates by educational attainment per country (*Source* Eurostat Labour Force Survey)	28
Fig. 2.2	Participation rates by employment status per country (*Source* Eurostat Labour Force Survey)	31
Fig. 2.3	Participation rates by age per country (*Source* Eurostat Labour Force Survey)	32
Fig. 2.4	Participation rates per country (*Source* Eurostat Labour Force Survey)	33
Fig. 2.5	Investment in R&D (*Source* Eurostat indicators R&D)	35
Fig. 2.6	Material deprivation (*Source* Eurostat EU-SILC)	36
Fig. 2.7	Life statisfaction scale (*Source* Eurostat Quality of Life)	36
Fig. 2.8	Expenditure on education as part of GDP (*Source* Eurostat Government Finance Statistics)	38
Fig. 2.9	Levels of employment (*Source* Eurostat Labour Force Survey)	39
Fig. 2.10	Literacy levels (*Source* PIAAC)	39
Fig. 2.11	Tracking index (*Source* Bol and Van de Werfhorst [2013])	40

List of Figures

Fig. 4.1　Number of UK domiciled mature and part-time entrants in English institutions (*Source* Higher Education Statistics Agency: Widening participation performance indicators, Tables T2a and T2b)　77

Fig. 5.1　Mature first degree entrants (*Source* HEFCE, 2016. *Note* UK-dominated students at Hefce-funded HEIs only)　102

List of Tables

Table 5.1   Age of Access to HE students, on enrolment   103
Table 5.2   Participation in the interview and diary phase   108

1

Adult Education in Austere Times: An Introduction

Nalita James and Ellen Boeren

Introduction

Adult education is known to be able to transform lives and can especially be powerful for those individuals who missed out on educational opportunities earlier in life. Participation in adult lifelong learning activities are linked to economic and social benefits, both at the level of the individual and the level of society (Field 2012). Many governments have highlighted the significance of learning for both economic gain and as a mode of social inclusiveness, in attempt to bridge the learning divide between those who have benefited from education and training and those who have not. However, in an economic and political climate dominated by austerity, support for adult learning

N. James (✉)
School of Education, University of Leicester, Leicester, UK
e-mail: nrj7@leicester.ac.uk

E. Boeren
Moray House School of Education, University of Edinburgh, Edinburgh, UK
e-mail: Ellen.Boeren@ed.ac.uk

© The Author(s) 2019
E. Boeren and N. James (eds.), *Being an Adult Learner in Austere Times*,
https://doi.org/10.1007/978-3-319-97208-4_1

is significantly decreasing. This problem strongly present in Britain and around the world, is acerbated by neoliberal policies that have constrained the practice of adult education (Mclean 2015). Rose (1999) has argued that neoliberal rationalities of government has also depended on the construction and regulation of people who see themselves as individuals with the responsibility to shape their lives through their own actions and choices. In short, a high level of individual autonomy, in contrast to a high level of social engagement, is seen to characterize the ideal–typical, neoliberal citizen (Ginn 2013). The widespread existence of such forms of subjectivity have substantially constrained the forms of practice in which adult learners can engage in continuing education.

Research specific to, and explicitly naming austerity, is much more scarce in the field of adult education. The title of this book, *Adult Learners in Austere Times* aims to address this issue. The chapters in this book, of which some have emerged from papers presented at the 2016 Standing Conference for University Teachers and Researchers in the Education of Adults (SCUTREA) (James 2016), have been selected to specifically focus on adult education in austere times and to show how the political and economic contexts that adult education operates in, can impact on adult learners. They also highlight how adult education pedagogy and practice can be deliberately designed to challenge austerity measures arising out of neoliberalism.

This introductory chapter will discuss why adult education matters, and the impact of austerity measures on the delivery of adult education, as well as individuals' opportunities to access and participate in adult learning. The chapter also refers to a range of current policy actions that demonstrate the declining support for adult education. As well as setting the scene, the introductory chapter will signpost the rest of the book, which has been divided into two sections. The first section focuses on the context, history and classed nature of austerity and adult education, and positions the current state-of-art of participation in adult education in Britain against other countries in the EU-28. The second part of the book focusses on experiences of adult learners, reporting on findings from empirical research. Chapters in the second part of the book focus on adult education settings in higher education, further education and the community.

Adult Learning–Does It Matter?

Lifelong learning, traditionally conceived as learning for adult and mature students, can also be applied to the multiplicity of contexts through which people engage in learning across different phases and stages of their lives (Schuller et al. 2002). Adult learning can be a route to gain or maintain employment, and the means to sustain livelihood. It can offer second chances to people who missed out in their earlier education, and have been previously excluded from formal learning opportunities, and first chances to people who never had the opportunity to go to school (Coffield 2009). Many researchers have argued for the wider benefits of learning beyond the level of the individual, from family and household, through to community and wider society (Schuller et al. 2002; Tuckett 2017; James and Busher 2018). There is also powerful evidence that adult learning has positive mental health and well-being effects (Feinstein et al. 2009), as those who participate in learning are healthier, happier, and better paid than those who do not (Taylor 2014, p. 4). Further, the benefits of learning, particularly for adults in terms of the growth of human, social and identity capitals as proposed by Schuller et al. (2002) are evident in the key components of adult education and its positive impacts as presented in the European Association for the Education of Adults (EAEA) Manifesto for Adult Learning in the Twenty First Century. These include:

- **Active citizenship, democracy and participation**: People who participate in adult education have more trust in the political system, participate more in society, by voting, by volunteering or taking active roles in communities.
- **Life skills for individuals**: Adult learners feel healthier, lead healthier lifestyles, build new social networks and experience improved well-being.
- **Social cohesion, equity and equality**: Adult education provides many opportunities to equalise societies on a larger scale and to create fairer societies as well as more economic growth.
- **Employment and enhanced career prospects**: Workplace learning is one of the key drivers for adults' participation in lifelong learning.

- **Migration and demographic change**: Civic education and intercultural learning can create integration-friendly cultures. Language and basic skills training can enable migrants to become active citizens in their new home countries.
- **Sustainability**: From environmentally friendly consumption and transport to energy efficiency, citizens need a lot of information and innovative spaces to develop new lifestyles, new projects, and new approaches. Adult education can help provide the information, the debate spaces and the creativity.

(Extract taken from the EAEA [Manifesto for Adult Learning in the Twenty First Century], Brussels, December 2015).

Governments have presented lifelong learning as a social good that opens up both social and economic opportunities to adult learners. Both Britain and Europe have responded to the challenge of changing economic climates by trying to create better access to qualifications and skills training because 'learning benefits individuals, the economy and society as a whole' (Taylor 2014, p. 4). For example, a rapidly changing economy, and the process of population ageing, means that wider access to higher education are priorities for many European nations (Field and Kurantowicz 2014). The European Commission (2011) called on member states and higher education institutions (HEIs) to encourage participation of disadvantaged adults, for example by attracting a broader cross-section of society into higher education and minimizing drop-out rates, and ensuring that financial support to potential students is better targeted. Across Europe, HEIs have been encouraged by policy interventions to create mass higher education that will satisfy the need of European economies for high-skilled labour in a global market (Field et al. 2010). However, in the current economic climate, gaining higher education qualifications does not always guarantee a greater likelihood of employment compared with people with lower qualifications (Holmes and Mayhew 2016). The high likelihood of people finding a job whatever level of skill they have and however well paid they are for the skills they possess, is likely to diminish people's enthusiasm for pursuing the risky route of returning to formal education as a mature learner (Mannay and Morgan 2013). Yet the opportunities for pursuing a career which they cherish can be the expected non-financial reward to encourage people to pursue lifelong education, despite the risks and the potentially limited financial rewards on offer.

The economic imperative for adult education is that learning in the form of continued education provides a crucial resource that learners can take into the labour market (Tomlinson 2013). All adults beyond school age should have the chance and encouragement to start accumulating skills and qualifications that will lead to better, more fulfilling life chances, and be better equipped to support their families and local communities (Hughes et al. 2016). Yet the hollowing out of the labour market also has considerable implications for individuals hoping to improve the quality of their opportunities for employment through continuing education, and ignores the socio-economic contexts of such adult learners. This includes wider facets of their lives and identities that impact on the constraints and opportunities that facilitate their participation in adult learning (Busher et al. 2014). The choices that individuals make will be shaped by the parameters within which they make choices and understand their wider position both within the education system and beyond in the labour market (Tomlinson 2013).

Providing adult learning opportunities has the potential for transformation, however without a combination of public investment and effective targeting, it can also reinforce inequality, and the marginalisation of disadvantaged groups (Tuckett 2017). The importance of adult learning is clearly recognised both nationally through successive British government White Papers, and globally via UNESCO, European Commission and OECD policies and research findings (Boeren 2016). While such reports demonstrate the positive impact of adult participation in learning, further analysis of participation patterns and statistics also demonstrate that participation is unequal and varies between individuals and countries (Boeren 2011). A review of the participation rates in adult education commissioned by UNESCO (see Desjardins et al. 2006) provides evidence that those with high skills and education are more likely to participate in adult lifelong learning activities. While there is a global recognition for more adults to be economically and educationally active for much longer than in previous generations due to changes in state pensions and increased lifespans (Eurostat 2014) there is evidence of a decline in adult participation in skills training and broader credit and non-credit bearing provision, and a decline in the broader programmes of adult education, notably those offered by local authorities and university lifelong learning departments, many of which have been closed in the last decade (Hughes et al. 2016). Despite the massive promotion of lifelong learning since the launch of *The Learning Age*, a Government Green Paper published in the 1990s, the policy initiatives the Labour government introduced at that time (which included individual learning accounts, neighbourhood learning development, and a national literacy, numeracy and ESOL strategy) (Tuckett 2017), and the idea individuals need to gain or upgrade their qualifications to obtain, or sustain, employment in any kind of job, the January 2016 House of Lords debate devoted to adult learning reported evidence telling the opposite story (Bynner 2017).

An Age of Austerity?

The notion of a country gripped by an age of austerity is not new. David Kynaston (2007) details the impact of an earlier age of austerity on the ordinary people of Britain, a time of huge hardship and want in the aftermath of the struggles of wartime and post-war Britain. Austerity is a highly contested concept in terms of both its necessity and its effect. Governments have claimed that austerity is the inevitable consequence of the global financial and economic crisis of the late 2000s, and the subsequent recession. However, liberal adult education in Britain became seriously vulnerable to attack from the early 1980's when the then Conservative government, bent on neoliberal reform, began to assert a strongly instrumentalist and individualised vision for education and training and to tighten funding controls on adult education (Bowl 2010). The logic of neoliberalism is underpinned by a conviction that the market is paramount and that the state should take a minimal role in the social realm. In the field of adult education and training, this logic places the responsibility for educational participation or non-participation, success or failure on the individual, rather than on government. In this formulation, the valid outcome of education is the development of human capital (Becker 1975).

Today, across Britain and Europe austerity is viewed as a neutral, almost technical phrase, simply referring to a period of economic stringency and constraint, driven by government strategies to greatly reduce public spending (O'Hara 2014). The political choice following the financial and economic crisis has shifted between austerity and stimulus, with Britain and many European countries choosing the former. As such, the term 'austerity' is especially prominent in European discourses to represent severe government cutbacks of social services. In Britain, the Liberal/Conservative coalition government of 2010 announced the biggest cuts in state spending since the Second World War (Farnsworth and Irving 2015, p. 2). Austerity then, can also be defined as 'enforced or extreme economy' (Sanburn 2010).

O'Hara (2014) argues that the 'age of austerity' is a fallacy, at least in terms of which individuals/groups in society are experiencing it. There is mounting evidence (see, for example, Hills 2015; Lansley and Mack 2015; Sayer 2015) that both Britain and Europe have become a more unequal society and that the gulf between the rich and the rest of society is increasing dramatically (Blyth 2013). In the past decade, the reach of neoliberalism has deepened as the post-crash austerity mode of governance has legitimated the discourses and practices of new managerialism throughout public services. Its impact has disproportionately affected certain sectors of the population in Britain and Europe, especially those who are more vulnerable, marginalised and precarious (Hills 2015). It is the most disadvantaged who rely the heaviest on such services and other amenities that are publicly provided—the national health services, social housing, state provided education, local authority health centres, leisure amenities, libraries etc. It can be argued that austerity is not 'fair' in its impact (O'Hara 2014), which has been profound and devastating for many in society. In Britain and across Europe, particularly in Greece, Portugal and Spain, austerity policies are not only dismantling welfare benefits and public services, but also the very mechanisms that have worked in the past to ameliorate the impacts of inequality. These policies have been used to forward a managerialist agenda to the point of the '…denigration of a whole host of public sector workers', including the targeting of educators (Coulter 2015, p. 13).

Not everyone suffers from austerity of course, reinforcing the Mathew effect (Desjardins et al. 2006; Boeren 2016) in which those who have, receive more. Those who have already been successful learners in the past are more likely to continue their education and training. Adult education participation is unequal, and especially in austere times, the gap between those who have and those who do not have can widen instead of narrow. Austerity policies are consistent with the ideology of the three major political parties in Britain, alongside the mantra of 'personal responsibility', implying that those who are poor have brought their situations on themselves (Ginn 2013). Shaw and Crowther (2014, pp. 398–399) also argue:

> the new hegemony that there is no policy alternative to austerity reaches deep into cultural life, reinforcing its veracity as it goes. The inclusiveness trope that "we are all in it together", despite vast differentials in power, wealth and agency, can all too easily become internalized by those who have most to lose – and the persistent demonization of the poor acts to reinforce the myth. So it is that neoliberalism hollows out the collective social and political imagination.

The austerity policies that have been rolled out in many European countries have brought all the pain of economic stagnation but hardly any of the promised benefits of debt reduction, renewed growth and prosperity (Schui 2014, p. 1). The combined austerity measures put in place by the current and previous British governments have resulted in generalised reductions in spending on adult education. The European Commission (2014) reported a 33% reduction in spend-per-student in post-secondary non-tertiary education, and a 12% reduction in spend-per-student in tertiary education (p. 2). The Association of College's Funding Survey (2014–2015) similarly reported reductions in adult skills funding (outside of Apprenticeships) of up to 23%.

Austerity has been a useful hook for successive governments to hang ideologically driven policies so as to blame 'outside' factors for 'cuts'. Adult learning has been seriously affected by these cuts and consequently learning opportunities for adults have been particularly restricted (James and Busher 2018). Since the coalition government of 2010–2016, more than a million publicly funded adult learning opportunities have disappeared (Bynner 2017). Recent downturns in the global economy have resulted in significant cuts to adult education programmes and spiraling costs for higher education. The learning opportunities available to adults both in higher and further education have declined. Universities prefer to focus on first generation students while other adult education providers suffer from lack of resources and are challenged to deliver learning that has 'economic value' (Biesta 2006, p. 168). In the context of lifelong learning, adult learners must therefore constantly invest in a long string of credentials to continually adapt to the fluid market (Grace 2007). This investment is seen through a neoliberal lens as the product of an individual's hard-earned personal and professional efforts. In other words, within a neoliberal context, the responsibility for attaining educational credentials has become an individualized responsibility, as noted by Kopecký (2011, p. 256)

> Lifelong learning is expected to make a positive contribution to economic growth, innovation, and competitiveness or social coherence, but at the level of the individual, these certainties are transformed into (mere) opportunities.

During austere times, it is perhaps unsurprising to learn that 'employability' becomes a major focus for adult learners. However, wider issues are at play. For example, it has been demonstrated that employability programmes which are instrumental in their design and enactment serve to 'churn' unemployed people around a system that fails both individuals and communities (Forster 2015). Austerity is operationalised in this scenario through the impact of broader macro-level economic changes related to the global economic meltdown and through governments' short-sighted vision for the role of adult education, particularly in the higher education context. In both Britain and Europe, universities are encouraged to adhere to a primary mission of providing 'educated citizens' (albeit with an emphasis on those aged 18–24) for the marketplace (European Commission 2011). Yet, two million part-time adult learners in Britain have been lost since 2007 as a consequence of the fees increase for university degree courses, while full-time undergraduate numbers have increased (Butcher 2015). Moreover, over the same period, adult participation in further education has gone down from 50% to 15%, a drop of over 500,000 aged 24 or more. This has been paralleled by a fall in the adult skills budget of 35% (Hughes et al. 2016). In view of the many ways in which part-time adult education supplies the foundations for extended learning through adulthood that the economy is said to need, the retreat from it is therefore significant. The collapse coincides with a number of shifts in British government policy towards adult education including:

- Students bearing the costs of adult education rather than the state
- Prioritising the Leitch skills agenda against the wider mission of adult learning in terms of personal development and well-being
- Raising the price of engaging in non-award-bearing courses coupled with ever rising university fees for both full-time and part-time study
- Restricting support for students taking award-bearing courses below degree level if not demonstrating progression in qualification terms. (Bynner 2017, p. 72)

Such factors provide a range of powerful disincentive for adults to sign up for learning, as researchers continue to argue (see, for example, Biesta 2006; Coffield 2009; Field 2012; Tuckett 2017; James and Busher 2018).

Adult Education: Moving Beyond Austerity?

Wolff (2010) has argued that there exists 'some alternative "reasonable" kinds of austerity', such as collecting incomes taxes from huge multi-million corporations. His point is that '…(even) if governments have no choice but to enforce austerity, it does not then follow that austerity itself is something other than a series of choices' (Veck 2014,

1 Adult Education in Austere Times: An Introduction

p. 778). While austerity may not solely provide the background for the cuts behind adult education (Sen 2012) it has certainly created barriers to individuals accessing and participating in adult education. The first section of the book, including this introductory chapter, further analyses this argument by looking both conceptually and theoretically at the nature of adult education participation from both a British and European perspective. Chapter 2, authored by Boeren, discusses this in more detail by examining the level and variability in adult learning participation in both Britain and Europe, drawing on evidence from the Labour Force Survey, data officially used by the European Commission to monitor participation in adult education and training. This chapter will focus on the situation within Britain, but will compare this with statistics from other European (EU28) countries drawing on research on adult learning and political economies (Desjardins et al. 2006). It examines the different determinants of participation at the individual level and focusses on bounded agency approaches to highlight the role of welfare state regimes. The chapter demonstrates that, although participation rates in certain countries (e.g. the Scandinavian ones) are higher than in other countries, generally those with the lowest educational attainment and the weakest positions in the labour market are least likely to participate. However, variation in participation rates also correlates with a number of system level characteristics, including the investment in research and development, in education and in the strength of the labour market. Given these findings of inequality, it is argued that not investing in adult learning will widen gaps in society, instead of narrowing them.

Chapter 3, authored by Clancy, further explores the historical context of adult education, and the strong relationship between class, knowledge dispossession and austerity. The chapter provides examples of traditional adult education practices, such as those that tend to take place in residential adult education colleges, with four of these colleges still being operational today. Clancy's work heavily draws on work by Welsh Marxist theorist Raymond Williams and puts a strong critical lens on the failed promises of opportunities of social mobility to be generated through the education system. The chapter makes a strong point for the need of a stronger reclaim for adult education as a way to strengthen communities and society in general.

The second part of this book bundles five chapters highlighting the role of adult education in the age of austerity. These chapters are written around stories told by adult learners themselves, and also identify the experiences of those working with adult learners in education practice. As hinted at in the subtitle of this book, chapters in this second part focus on a range of diverse adult learning settings, more specifically higher education, further education and the community. The first three chapter (Chapters 4–6) focuses on being an adult learner in higher education.

Chapter 4, written by Harman and Fraser, explores the declining spaces for adult widening participation in higher education, the ongoing decline in part-time undergraduate education and the decrease in the number of mature full-time learners in the English higher education context. The chapter critically reflects on the recent Green and White Papers outlining the future of higher education. It draws on a range of concrete statistics from HEFCE (Higher Education Funding Council England), OFFA (Office for Fair Access), and HESA (Higher Education Statistics Agency), to highlight how adult learners, in particular those from disadvantaged social backgrounds represent a key but all too invisible example of a group under-represented in higher education. This includes students from white working class, specific black and ethnic minority groups and disabled students (OFFA 2017). The chapter will draw on two leading widening participation programmes in England (one in Leeds and one in London) in which the authors are involved in their own teaching practice. Their narrative strongly highlights how successful programme interventions can attract adult learners to higher education in spite of HEI cultures which can work against the needs of adult learners. Recommendations for a gentler policy agenda in relation to higher education part-time and mature students in times of austerity are discussed.

While adult learners can experience challenges in accessing higher education, often caused by a lack of or accurate information, advice and guidance, stringent admissions criteria, poor academic support, and/or high tuition fees, it is also important to generate insight into how adults who do participate, experience their learning process in order to help them succeed in the system. Chapter 5, authored by Sutton, highlights the difficulties experienced by mature students undertaking an undergraduate degree level programme. This chapter aims to formulate recommendations towards policy makers and practitioners on how to support mature learners to survive in higher education in austere times. Specifically, this chapter generates more insights in how to prevent mature students from dropping out from the education system, as they are more likely to leave without a degree compared to younger students. Drawing on qualitative research data obtained through in-depth interviewing and diaries from one university, findings will indicate that mature students tend to feel more isolated than younger students and that these feelings are generated through either uncomfortable feelings towards being mixed with younger adults or through the need to strictly focus on study-related aspects in order to combine studying with other life domains. This chapter highlights the importance of supporting adult learners to find their place within the social fabric of university so they can easily self-identify as a fully legitimate student and member of the learning community (Lave and Wenger 1991).

Chapter 6, authored by Meir, offers more insight in how to attract mature learners in higher education in austere times, unfolded through in-depth engagement with narratives from working-class women's changed life experiences through participating on an Access to Higher Education Diploma course. The Access to HE Diploma is an important route for mature students and has been the focus of a new book by James and Busher (2018). Meir's chapter starts from the assumption that working-class adults who failed in the initial education system often lack a strong level of agency and are unaware of the learning they have acquired through non-formal and informal learning outside academic settings. It highlights, based on very in-depth experiences of three female adult learners, their socio-economic backgrounds and contexts, as well as their experiences of educational transitions. This includes their educational beginnings and experiences, which are often very negative. This chapter will bring out the message of increased empowerment, resilience and agency as a result of participating in the Access to HE course. Meir achieves this goal through a critical discussion of both feminist and adult education theories. The chapter also confirms that investing in Access to HE courses for the most disadvantaged adults can generate a wide range of personal and social benefits. This message generated through timely empirical academic research is translated into a set of concrete recommendations for both policy makers and practitioners at the end of the chapter.

Chapter 7 of this book has been authored by Duckworth and Smith, and provides a critical discussion on the role of further education in transforming adults' lives. Their project 'FE in England: Transforming Lives and Communities', funded by the UCU (the Universities and Colleges Union) has received widespread attention in the wider adult education community in Britain. The chapter focuses on the role of the knowledge economy, and timely consequences of neo-liberal policies, such as the replication of social inequalities, further stratification and marketization of education systems. Duckworth and Smith then use powerful narratives of adult learners in further education to underline the transformative nature of participation, including aspects like confidence and self-value. The chapter critically discusses the current state of adult education in relation to class and austerity, the persistent role of social, cultural and education capital, and the important role of communities. It ends with a specific set of policy recommendations, intending to avoid future situations in which further education is being hit hard, mostly at the expense of the most disadvantaged adults.

The last chapter of this book, Chapter 8 authored by Jones, provides an insight into what is happening more generally within the wider adult and community education landscape in which arguably, both austerity and resilience operate in tandem. As argued earlier in the chapter, austerity is operationalised through the impact of broader macro-level economic changes related to the global economic meltdown and through governments' short-sighted vision. The funding base for adult and community education has never been lavish, so the reductions/removal of funds can mean it is more restricted, privatised and instrumental in purpose (Findsen 2014). Drawing on results from her doctoral thesis, Jones focusses on the impact austerity policies can have on homeless adults and community education. Jones explains that homeless adults are often excluded from mainstream education, but that specific third-sector community organisations do pay attention to this group.

These organisations help homeless adults to build confidence, reduce their social isolation, as well as help them find a place to live, and also a job. In this chapter, Jones shares the narratives from the in-depth interviews undertaken with practitioners working with homeless adults in the Greater Manchester area. The findings will give insight into how learning opportunities for the homeless population are structured, and how funding arrangements and policy interventions can support this type of provision. This chapter will also show how austerity politics has impacted on adult education in third sector organisations and how they have responded to welfare reforms. Jones will end with a set of recommendations for policy and practice, specifically targeted towards the government, the adult education sector and the homelessness sector.

Within the final chapter of the book, as editors, we will engage in a critical reflection on the previous chapters and will focus on the need for a continuous support for both research in the field of adult education as well as for the existence of learning opportunities for adults. This chapter will highlight the many positive empirical findings of the previous chapters as well as the remaining challenges to be tackled in the sector. It will therefore end with a specific set of recommendations for policy and practice, as well as future research. It will provide a comprehensive analysis of findings from each chapter with a specific focus on how to take the field forward.

Conclusion

The book will demonstrate both the policy impacts, challenges and successes of adult education initiatives and how the contemporary drive to redefine and re-orientate adult education in an era of austerity, along with the impact of professionalization and performativity measures of new managerialism on practice and learning has wider societal and justice implications. The deeply personal impacts of austerity cannot be understated. Austerity is unlikely to be temporary and long term strategies are required to assist in protecting education for adults, and specifically marginalised and excluded groups. The chapters of this book will identify key lessons and important challenges for adult education policy makers, providers and practitioners. As Tuckett (2017, p. 237) argues, '…you cannot be certain of the purposes of the learners, or of the benefits they derive, from the title or category of the courses they join. There is always an interplay between skills acquired, personal confidence and social engagement.' As the book will show, in austere times, there is a critical need to respond effectively to adults' appetite for learning.

References

Association of Colleges. (2014). *College Funding and Finance*. https://www.aoc.co.uk/sites/default/files/College%20Funding%20and%20Finance%201%20May%202014%20FINAL_0_0.pdf.
Becker, G. S. (1975). *Human Capital: A Theoretical and Empirical Analysis, with Special Reference to Education*. Chicago: University of Chicago Press.
Biesta, G. (2006). What's the Point of Lifelong Learning If Lifelong Learning Has No Point? On the Democratic Deficit of Policies for Lifelong Learning. *European Educational Research Journal, 5*(3–4), 169–180.
Blyth, M. (2013). *Austerity: The History of a Dangerous Idea*. Oxford: Oxford University Press.
Boeren, E. (2011). *Participation in Adult Education: A Bounded Agency Approach*. Leuven: Katholieke Universiteit Leuven.
Boeren, E. (2016). *Lifelong Learning Participation in a Changing Policy Context: An Interdisciplinary Theory*. London: Palgrave Macmillan.
Bowl, M. (2010). University Continuing Education in a Neoliberal Landscape: Developments in England and Aotearoa New Zealand. *International Journal of Lifelong Education, 29,* 723–738.
Busher, H., James, N., Piela, A., & Palmer, A. P. (2014). Transforming Marginalised Adult Learners' Views of Themselves: Access Courses in England. *British Journal of Sociology of Education, 35*(5), 800–817.
Butcher, J. (2015). *'Shoe-Horned and Side-Lined'? Challenges for Part-Time Learners in the New HE Landscape*. York: The Higher Education Academy.
Bynner, J. (2017). What Happened to Lifelong Learning? And Does It Matter? *Journal of the British Academy, 5,* 61–89.
Coffield, F. (2009). *Differing Vision for a Learning Society*. Bristol: Polity.
Coulter, C. (2015). Ireland Under Austerity: An Introduction to the Book. In C. Coulter & A. Nagle (Eds.), *Ireland Under Austerity: Neoliberal Crisis, Neoliberal Solutions* (pp. 1–43). Manchester: Manchester University Press.

Desjardins, R., Rubesnon, K., & Milana, M. (2006). *Unequal Chances to Participate in Adult Education: International Perspectives*. Paris: UNESCO.
European Association for the Education of Adults. (2015). *Manifesto for Adult Learning in the 21st Century*. http://eaea.org/wp-content/uploads/2018/02/manifesto.pdf.
European Commission. (2011). *Supporting Growth and Jobs—An Agenda for the Modernisation of Europe's Higher Education Systems*. Brussels: Office for Official Publication.
European Commission. (2014). *Education and Training Monitor Report*. http://ec.europa.eu/dgs/education_culture/repository/education/library/publications/monitor14_en.pdf.
Eurostat. (2014). *Eurostat Regional Yearbook 2014*. http://ec.europa.eu/eurostat/documents/3217494/5785629/KS-HA-14-001-EN.PDF.
Farnsworth, K., & Irving, Z. (Eds.). (2015). *Social Policy in Times of Austerity*. Bristol: Policy Press.
Feinstein, L., Kirpal, S., & Arévalo Sánchez, I. (2009). *The Wider Benefits of Learning: Handbook of Technical and Vocational Education and Training Research*. Berlin: Springer.
Field, J. (2012). Is Lifelong Learning Making a Difference? Research-Based Evidence on the Impact of Adult Learning. In D. Aspin, J. Chapman, K. Evans, & R. Bagnall (Eds.), *Second International Handbook of Lifelong Learning* (pp. 887–897). Dorderect: Springer.
Field, J., & Kurantowicz, E. (2014). Retention and Access in Higher Education. Implications for Policy and Practice. In F. Finnegan, B. Merrill, & C. Thurborg (Eds.), *Student Voices on Equalities in Europena Higher Education* (pp. 163–169). London: Routledge.
Field, J., Merrill, B., & Morgan-Klein, N. (2010, September 23–26). *Higher Education Access, Retention and Drop-Out Through a European Biographical Approach: Exploring Similarities and Differences Within a Research Term*. ESRA, Sixth European Research Conference, Reykjavik, Iceland.
Findsen, B. (2014). Older Adult Education in a New Zealand University: Developments and Issues. *International Journal of Education and Ageing, 3*(3), 211–224.
Forster, J. (2015). *Churning or Lifeline? Life Stories from De-industrialised Communities*. Proceedings of the 45th Standing Conference for University Teaching and Research in the Education of Adults, University of Leeds.
Ginn, J. (2013). Austerity and Inequality. Exploring the Impact of Cuts in the UK by Gender and Age. *Research on Ageing and Social Policy, 1*(1), 28–53.

Grace, A. P. (2007). Envisioning a Critical Social Pedagogy of Learning and Work in a Contemporary Culture of Cyclical Lifelong Learning. *Studies in Continuing Education, 29*(1), 85–103.

Hills, J. (2015). *Good Times Bad Times: The Welfare Myth of Them and Us*. Bristol: Policy Press.

Holmes, C., & Mayhew, K. (2016). The Economics of Higher Education. *Oxford Review of Economic Policy, 32*(4), 475–496.

Hughes, D., Adriaanse, K., & Barnes, S. A. (2016). *Adult Education: Too Important to Be Left to Chance*. https://www2.warwick.ac.uk/fac/soc/ier/research/adult_education/dh_adult_education_full_report.pdf.

James, N. (2016, July 5–7). *Adult Education in Austere Times*. Standing Conference for University Teachers and Researchers in the Education of Adults (SCUTREA) Conference Proceedings, Vaughan Centre for Lifelong Learning, University of Leicester.

James, N., & Busher, H. (2018). *Improving Opportunities to Engage in Learning: A Study of the Access to Higher Education Diploma*. London: Taylor and Francis.

Kopecký, M. (2011). Foucault, Governmentality, Neoliberalism and Adult Education—Perspective on the Normalization of Social Risk. *Journal of Pedagogy, 2*(2), 246–262.

Kynaston, D. (2007). *Austerity Britain. 1945–1951*. London: Bloomsbury.

Lansley, S., & Mack, J. (2015). *Breadline Britain*. London: OneWorld.

Lave, J., & Wenger, E. (1991). *Situated Learning: Legitimate Peripheral Participation*. Cambridge: Cambridge University Press.

Mannay, D., & Morgan, M. (2013). Anatomies of Inequality: Considering the Emotional Cost of Aiming Higher for Marginalised Mature Mothers Re-entering Education. *Journal of Adult and Continuing Education, 19*(1), 55–75.

Mclean, S. (2015). Individual Autonomy or Social Engagement? Adult Learners in Neoliberal Times. *Adult Education Quarterly, 65*(3), 196–214.

Office for Fair Access (OFFA). (2017). *Strategic Guidance: Developing Your 2018–19 Access Agreement*. www.offa.org.uk/wp-content/uploads/2017/02/Strategic-guidance-developing-your-2018-19-access-agreement-FINAL.pdf.

O'Hara, M. (2014). *Austerity Bites a Journey to the Sharp End of the Cuts in UK*. Bristol: Polity.

Rose, N. (1999). *Powers of Freedom: Reframing Political Thought*. Cambridge: Cambridge University Press.

Sanburn, J. (2010). *What Is the Definition of Austerity?* http://newsfeed.time.com/2010/12/20/what-is-the-definition-of-austerity/.

Sayer, A. (2015). *Why We Can't Afford the Rich*. Bristol: Policy Press.
Schui, F. (2014). *Austerity: The Great Failure*. London: Yale University Press.
Schuller, T., Brassett-Grundy, A., Green, A., Hammond, C., & Preston, J. (2002). *Learning, Continuity and Change in Adult Life*. London: The Centre for Research on the Wider Benefits of Learning.
Sen, A. (2012, July 3). Austerity Is Undermining Europe's Grand Vision. *The Guardian*. http://www.theguardian.com/commentisfree/2012/jul/03/austerity-europe-grand-vision-unity.
Shaw, M., & Crowther, J. (2014). Adult Education, Community Development and Democracy: Renegotiating the Terms of Agreement. *Community Development Journal, 49*(3), 390–406.
Taylor, C. (2014). On Solid Ground. *Adults Learning* (Spring), 4–5.
Tomlinson, M. (2013). *Education, Work and Identity*. London: Bloomsbury.
Tuckett, A. (2017). The Rise and Fall of Life-Wide Learning for Adults in England. *International Journal of Lifelong Education, 36*(1–2), 230–249.
Veck, W. (2014). Disability and Inclusive Education in Times of Austerity. *British Journal of Sociology of Education, 35*(5), 777–799.
Wolff, R. D. (2010, July 15). Austerity: Why and for Whom? *In These Times*. http://inthesetimes.com/article/6232/austerity_why_and_for_whom/.

2

Being an Adult Learner in Europe and the UK: Persisting Inequalities and the Role of the Welfare State

Ellen Boeren

Introduction

The European Commission's aims in relation to education and training have been expressed by a set of benchmarks and indicators (Ioannidou 2007; Grek 2009; Lawn and Grek 2012; Holford and Mohorcic-Spolar 2012). In relation to adult learning, it includes the benchmark that by 2020, 15% of the adult population between the ages of 25 and 64 needs to participate in at least one lifelong learning activity, measured on a four weeks basis (European Commission 2009). Data being used for this measure come from the Labour Force Survey (European Commission 2010; Boeren 2014). While 15% might not sound much, data used in this chapter will demonstrate that a wide range of adults do not participate in any learning activity and that many European

E. Boeren (✉)
Moray House School of Education, University of Edinburgh,
Edinburgh, UK
e-mail: Ellen.Boeren@ed.ac.uk

© The Author(s) 2019
E. Boeren and N. James (eds.), *Being an Adult Learner in Austere Times*,
https://doi.org/10.1007/978-3-319-97208-4_2

countries will likely fail to meet this target by 2020. Both in Europe and the UK, stimulating higher levels of educational attainment and skills is being strived towards because of the positive correlations between education and skills and income, employment, good health and active citizenship (Schuller et al. 2004; Campbell 2012; Field 2012). However, not all countries make adequate investments in adult lifelong learning and levels of provision are also not well established in a wide range of countries. In the United Kingdom, voices have been raised about adult education being in crisis, and statistics have demonstrated that the number of adult learners between 2010 and 2015 dropped significantly (Spellman 2017). Recent research (Callender and Thompson 2018) has also demonstrated the sharp decline in participation of mature students in higher education. Recently, proposed plans on the reduction of the number of courses and lecturers at the Open University led to the resignation of Vice Chancellor Peter Horrocks. The Association of Colleges, a sector responsible for a wide range of adult learning activities, has also raised the alarm that adult education is at risk of being wiped out (Howse 2015).

This chapter will explore the current state-of-art of adult lifelong learning participation in the EU-28 and will contrast the situation in continental Europe with that of the United Kingdom. It will start by discussing how participation in adult education has been conceptualised by the European Commission, influenced by work of UNESCO and the OECD. It will then zoom in on the persisting inequalities in participation between adults from different socio-economic and socio-demographic groups based on aggregated data from the Labour Force Survey. Countries in Europe will also be compared with each other focussing on the role of welfare states and the investments they make in education, but also in a range of other social policies. As such, this chapter aims to introduce the reader to the major determinants of adult lifelong learning participation and to increase understanding on why adults do or do not participate in learning activities.

Measuring Adult Learning Participation in Major Surveys

Being an adult learner can take place in a wide range of education and training settings (see Boeren 2016). Measuring participation in the major surveys starts from the classic divide between formal and non-formal education, referring to UNESCO's work in defining formal and non-formal education and informal learning (see UNESCO 1979; Colley et al. 2003). This is the case in the Labour Force Survey, but also in the Eurostat Adult Education Survey and the OECD's Survey of Adults Skills, part of PIAAC. In its traditional meaning, formal education refers to those activities that take place in organisational settings, and are credential based. When successfully completing the course, the adult learner will be awarded an official diploma, certificate or degree. As such, the formal adult education system mirrors the initial schooling system, divided into a range of different educational levels, typically a ladder structure in which lower levels need to be gained before one can start at the higher levels. In international surveys, these different levels of education are often expressed through ISCED levels—the International Standard Classification of Education (UNESCO 2011). Non-formal education is very important in the field of adult learning, as the majority of education and training activities for adults take place in non-formal settings (Boeren 2016). These follow organisational formats as well, but do not provide credential-based courses as is the case in formal learning settings. It can, for example, include participation in short courses organised at the workplace, attendance of seminars in local folk high schools or undertaking private tuition in learning a new language or how to play a musical instrument. That said, non-formal learning providers might hand out certificates for completing courses which might be used by adults to demonstrate their levels of knowledge and skills to future employers, but are mostly not recognised as official qualifications by ministries of education and accreditation boards. Informal learning has typically been defined as at random learning, mostly non-intentionally or incidentally, and is therefore something that happens on a day to day basis (see Coffield 2000). An example includes watching television without the intention to engage in a learning activity, but picking up a whole range of new knowledge. While this form of learning is thus very relevant in adults' lives, they are not included in the benchmark of 15% as set out by the European Commission. Statistics being monitored to follow up progression towards this target are thus a combination of participation in formal and non-formal participation. This will also be the focus of the statistics presented below.

Having surveys in place is useful for governments to monitor the situation of adult learning in their countries, however, it is important to note that the current approach has also been criticised by scholars in the field (Holford and Mohorcic-Spolar 2012; Ball et al. 2014; Boeren 2016). The current way of measuring fits into the Open Method of Coordination in which the European Commission does in fact have soft power only, as new policy implementations in the field of education and training are still the responsibility of the countries themselves (Dale and Robertson 2008). Publishing statistics on a regular basis is thus a matter of putting peer pressure on countries to compare and learn from others on how they are progressing towards hitting the target of 15%. Policy learning between countries is thus encouraged, but rather competitive in nature. While these statistics are useful to work with, a number of critical reflections need to be taken into account. First of all, the current approach of monitoring and the European Commission's discourse on adult learning in general, have been criticised as placing too much attention to the role of education and training for the purpose of competitiveness, innovation and economic growth (Holford and Mohorcic-Spolar 2012). The strong vocational orientation of both the European Commission and the OECD have moved away from the more humanistic view on adult learning and education as visible in the work by UNESCO (see Boeren and Holford 2016). As will be demonstrated below, inequalities in adult learning persist between adults from different socio-economic and socio-demographic groups. Recognising the needs of those who are mostly in need of compensating skill deficiencies encountered during childhood and teenage years need to be put into the picture as well, and it is hoped that new initiatives like Upskilling

Pathways will help from the most disadvantaged groups to find their place in the education and training landscape (European Commission 2016). As will be demonstrated below, this problem is also relevant to that of the United Kingdom. Secondly, data being used for monitoring purposes are cross-sectional in nature (Boeren 2018a). The Labour Force Survey, but also the Adult Education Survey and the OECD's Survey of Adult Skills as part of the Programme for International Assessment of Adult Skills (PIAAC), do not collect longitudinal data. The benefits of adult learning are often mentioned in lifelong learning reports, however, a longitudinal follow-up of learners has not yet been put in place at the European level (Boeren 2016). The United Kingdom is in fact a good example of a country that has implemented a range of longitudinal surveys, going back to birth cohort studies following the lives of those born in 1958 and 1970, but also a range of newer longitudinal measurements (see Boeren 2018a). In order to compare the situation in different countries, and to get a clearer picture on the universal benefits of learning, it is hoped international organisations will come up with a longitudinal survey that measures both participation and monetary as well as non-monetary benefits of learning. Thirdly, monitoring reports are rather descriptive in nature and do present little context information on the different countries they present data from. As policy learning is one of the aims of monitoring exercises, not providing enough information on how participation results need to be interpreted in relation to a wide range of social policies, we run the risk of implementing new policies which are in fact 'quick fixes' only (Phillips and Ochs 2003). Borrowing of education practices from abroad might not work if we do have enough understanding on what contributed towards their success factors. It is therefore important to explore a number of factors that relate to lifelong learning participation rates across countries, for example the investments they make in education (Groenez et al. 2007; Blossfeld et al. 2014; Desjardins 2017). This is therefore included in this chapter. Fourthly, and in relation to this third point, the nature of adult learning provisions in surveys is rather vague. While information on formal versus non-formal learning activities are available, survey data give little away on their institutional settings, access and retention policies.

This makes it difficult to judge in how far educational opportunities are truly available to adult learners. Where possible, references will be made to recent work by Boeren et al. (2017) to reflect on the role of educational institutions both in the United Kingdom and Europe.

Nevertheless, having acknowledged these survey limitations, it is still worthwhile to use these data in order to provide a general birds-eye picture on the current state-of-art of adult learners in Europe and the United Kingdom. The following sections will focus on both the individual micro level and country macro level determinants of participation. Data focussing on individual determinants are EU-28 data and come from the Labour Force Survey 2017.

Individual Determinants of Lifelong Learning

The literature on adult lifelong learning participation is rather clear. Being highly educated, being employed in white collar jobs and being young are the major individual determinants of higher participation rates in adult learning (Desjardins et al. 2006; Boeren 2016). Participation theories have a long tradition of focussing on the role of motivation and attitudes, on the role of generating benefits based on the initial investments made, and on the role of sociological attributes such as higher levels of social and cultural capital (see Courtney 1992). In short, these different viewpoints are strongly interacting with each other, making it easier for people from certain socio-economic and socio-demographic groups to recognise the value of adult learning. Those who are highly educated have experienced educational success in the past. They obtained a degree or relevant higher education qualifications and know they are capable of finalising a course successfully. They are also more likely to be employed in white collar jobs. These types of occupations tend to be less routine-type jobs undertaken by blue collar workers, and therefore demand a constant need to keep up to date on the newest developments in their field of work (see, e.g., Desjardins and Rubenson 2011; Kyndt and Baert 2013; Kaufmann 2015). As this is important for the success of the company they work for, their employers are more likely to invest in their continuous training, through for example paying for course fees and/or providing them with time to participate in these activities (see Hefler and Markowitsch 2012). Younger adults are also more likely to participate in learning activities. This strongly correlates with the dominant vocational orientation of lifelong learning nowadays. Those who are younger have a longer time to spend on the labour market and the time they can profit from the benefits on their initial investment is therefore longer than for older adults. Employers will also be more willing to pay for education and training of their younger employees compared to the older ones who might go on retirement soon. While lifelong learning for older learners is becoming an increasingly popular theme, given demographic changes and increased life expectancies, it should be noted that participation rates in official statistics as published by the European Commission only focus on those between age 25 and 64, and thus excludes adults beyond the traditional retirement age of age 65. It is expected that learning beyond the age of 65 shifts the focus onto learning for enjoyment, to engage in meaningful activities beyond retirement, as a way to maintain human relationships and to keep up with good health (Findsen and Formosa 2011).

It should be noted that other individual determinants of lifelong learning do exist as well, but that they are not as strong as the three core determinants discussed above. Recent analyses on the Survey of Adult Skills (PIAAC), conducted by myself, shed light on the lower participation rates of foreign-born adults and those who speak another language than the dominant language in the country they live in (Boeren 2018b). Controlling for factors like education and work, it was found that highly educated foreign-born adults participate much more in adult learning activities than those who are native-born and low-educated, however, foreign-born highly educated adults still participate less than those who are native-born and also highly educated. While educational attainment thus remains the major predictor, smaller effects are still in place for those who are foreign-born. Similar comments can be made in relation to parental education. Those who have low educated parents are

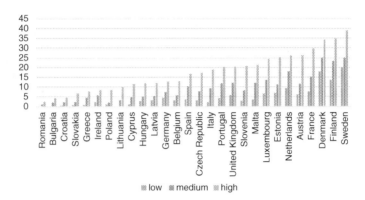

Fig. 2.1 Participation rates by educational attainment per country (*Source* Eurostat Labour Force Survey)

more likely to be low or medium educated themselves (see, e.g., Nesbit 2005; Raey 2010; Brookfield 2010), but once they succeeded in becoming highly educated themselves, it becomes the major predictor for their participation behaviour. As such, parental education has more of an indirect instead of direct effect on participation rates. Participation rates are usually in favour of women, although the employer support for workplace learning traditionally tends to be biased towards men, who succeed more in obtaining employment in senior management roles.

Having touched on the major individual determinants of participation, statistics are being shown in relation to the participation rates of the three main determinants in Europe. The situation of the United Kingdom will be highlighted in the interpretation of data (Fig. 2.1).

Educational Attainment

In international surveys, educational attainment is traditionally expressed through the use of ISCED levels, despite being criticised, a standardised way of engaging in comparative research (Schneider 2010). Data from the Labour Force Survey make a distinction between those who have 'less than primary, or primary or lower secondary education levels', 'upper secondary education levels' and 'tertiary education'. The ones classified as low qualified have below upper secondary education at this is the level of qualification that is perceived by Europe as the minimum qualification people should have to properly function in society. Exploring the participation rates by educational attainment, it is clear that in all European countries, the most educated adults participate most in adult education. There are no countries in which the highest educated do not generate the highest participation statistics, and the lowest educated have the lowest participation rates in all countries. This is thus also the case for the United Kingdom. However, as will be further explained below, looking into educational attainment in itself is not enough as, for example, highly educated adults in Romania and Bulgaria still clearly participate less than lower educated adults in Sweden, Finland and Denmark. Only 9 out of 28 countries in the EU have participation rates higher than 5% for low educated adults. While the UK is within this group, the gap in participation between the lowest and highest educated adults has remained consistently large in the past 10 years. In general, the United Kingdom tends to have a rather wide offer of learning opportunities available for adults, with a strong role for the College sector (Boeren et al. 2017). However, decreased government support for adult learners has made it more difficult for learners to sustain their participation. While apprenticeship schemes have been introduced and are currently receiving wide attention, their lack of focus on basic skills and general education has been highlighted by the OECD (2018). The argument for an increased need for basic skills training seems a valid and fundamental one in a rapidly changing society in which the knowledge based economy asks for continuous adaptations to new situations, often underpinned by good levels of literacy, numeracy and problem-solving.

Employment

Together with educational attainment, having a job or not strongly determines participation in lifelong learning activities. Statistics from the Labour Force Survey demonstrate that the pattern of participation according to whether someone is employed, unemployed or inactive differs among countries. In the United Kingdom, it is clear that adults in employment participate most, followed by those who are unemployed but searching for work. Those who are inactive and thus out of the labour market circuit have the lowest participation rates. This is in contrast to for example Ireland, where inactive people participate most, followed by unemployed adults. A 'peak' in participation rates among unemployed adults can be observed in Belgium and Sweden, and although also to a lesser extent, in a range of other countries. As will be discussed below, this is mainly the result of the work undertaken by public employment services as part of their Active Labour Market Policies (Boeren et al. 2017). Once adults are without a job, they might have to undertake training in order to keep their social benefits and to actively contribute to their search towards a job, underpinned by an effort to increase or update their skills and knowledge. The observation that adults who are inactive tend to have the lowest participation rates—although not in all countries—further underlines the dominant work-related nature of lifelong learning in Europe. Given the lower participation rates for adults who are unemployed and inactive, it is thus a valid question to ask whether the United Kingdom is doing enough for its unemployed population to engage in education and training. Furthermore, it is important to come back to the indirect determinants of participation as discussed above. While employment is a major determinant of lifelong learning participation, it is clear that not everyone gets the same chances to be employed in the most knowledge intensive jobs. Adults with disabilities, coming from lower socio-economic groups and those from minority ethnic backgrounds tend to be underrepresented in the higher white collar jobs. Women are still experiencing problems in breaking the glass ceiling into the best well-paid senior jobs. This is a problem that affects the United Kingdom as well and thus deserves further attention by policy makers. This should ideally include a focus on education and training for underrepresented groups, both in employment, and in education and training (Fig. 2.2).

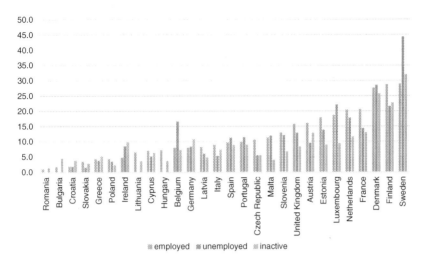

Fig. 2.2 Participation rates by employment status per country (*Source* Eurostat Labour Force Survey)

Age

Participation rates decline by age. This observation is clear in all European countries and thus also in the United Kingdom, where participation rates drop under 10% for those between the ages of 55 and 64, although this is still generally high in comparison to the participation rates of the older age groups in most other European countries. As discussed above, adults tend to make fewer investments in their work-related learning once they are closer to retirement age and both upskilling and retraining are thus more recognised by younger adults who want to make progress within their occupation. Adults in the oldest age groups are also more likely—on average—to be lower educated than the younger generation because of the increased democratisation of education. Psychologists have also focussed on the decreased functioning of the brain and the difficulties for many older adults to learn new things, especially if they did not continuously learn during the lifespan. Overall, the decreased participation during the lifetime is a rather universal trend and applies to the United Kingdom as well (Fig. 2.3).

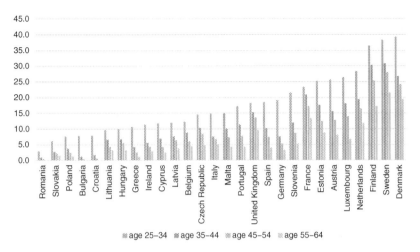

Fig. 2.3 Participation rates by age per country (*Source* Eurostat Labour Force Survey)

The Role of the Welfare State

Statistics above have demonstrated that adult learning participation rates are unequal between adults from different socio-economic and socio-demographic groups, but that significant differences are also present between the different countries. Participation is clearly highest in the Nordic countries. Participation rates are especially low in the Southern European countries and in the majority of Eastern European countries. The United Kingdom scores generally high, although not as high as the Nordic countries. The Western continental countries like Belgium and Germany have average participation rates. In further understanding why country differences exist, scholars in the field tend to refer to the role of welfare states and to how the different system characteristics of countries seem to correlate with participation rates (Desjardins 2017). Work by Groenez et al. (2007) focussed on a range of factors which they related to the role of the economy, the labour market, the strength of social security and labour market policies, the configuration of the initial and adult education systems, the changing demography in countries and the role of culture and values such as dominant ideologies and work ethic (Fig. 2.4).

2 Being an Adult Learner in Europe and the UK ...

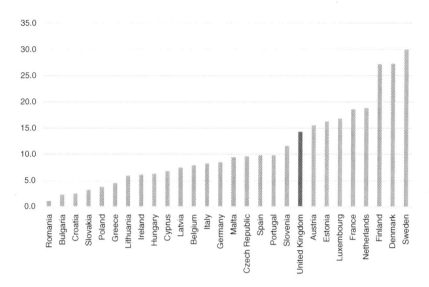

Fig. 2.4 Participation rates per country (*Source* Eurostat Labour Force Survey)

Much of this work flows from traditional groupings of countries, for example starting with the work by Esping-Andersen (1989). Based on levels of decommodification and stratification, referring to how much the state intervenes into the provision of social services and the levels of inequalities respectively, he created three groups. The first group refers to the Nordic social-democratic countries, the second to the Anglo-Saxon countries and the third one to the Conservative-Corporatist countries. Later on, other scholars, for example Fenger (2007), have extended this typology, taking into account the Eastern European countries, important after the enlargement of the European Union in 2004. These countries have also been labelled as 'catching up' countries, which are still adapting to their new role as being part of the European Union and it is still the case that these countries tend to perform weaker on a wide range of macro level indicators, as will be indicated below.

In the data shown below, the situation of the United Kingdom will be highlighted in comparison to countries who have both higher and lower participation rates, hence the different colouring of the bars in the Figures. The United Kingdom is typically seen as a country in which state involvement is low and which has high levels of stratification, characterised by a strongly classed society. This situation will now be discussed in relation to adult lifelong learning participation rates. The selection of indicators was inspired by work by Groenez et al. (2007), who focussed on the importance of indicators in relation to employment, education, the economy, social security, Research and Development, and general social and cultural characteristics of countries. The selected indicators will be discussed by their strongest correlation with lifelong learning participation rates in the EU-28 countries, based on the author's calculations, expressed by the R^2.

Investment in R&D ($R^2 = 0.5587$): Based on recent Eurostat data, in 2016, the United Kingdom invested 1.69% of its GDP in Research and Development. Out of the eight countries who have higher adult lifelong learning participation rates than the United Kingdom, six invested more in R&D. The two countries with higher participation rates who invested less in R&D are Estonia and Luxembourg, two of the smallest countries in the EU-28. With a high correlation between lifelong learning participation rates and the investment in R&D, it can be argued that the stimulation of innovation goes hand in hand with the need to continuously retrain and upskill employees in the labour market (see Virkkunen 2018). Germany and Belgium are two countries that invested more in R&D that the United Kingdom, but have stronger vocational systems in place as part of their initial education systems. Currently, the government in the United Kingdom has pledged to invest 2.4% of its GDP in R&D over the next ten years, with a longer term intention to increase this target to 3% (Reid 2018). Given the Brexit situation and the unclear situation in relation to accessibility of markets, it seems necessary to increase funding for innovation, and it is hoped this will be done in relation to the creation of learning opportunities for adults (Fig 2.5).

Material Deprivation ($R^2 = 0.5457$): The level to which households experience material deprivation can be used as an indicator on the effectiveness of the social security system and the way in which people are being supported in being able to set up a life in which they can afford basic goods and services (see Saltkjel 2017). This includes, for example, the purchase of food and the ability to pay once heating bills. Looking

2 Being an Adult Learner in Europe and the UK ...   35

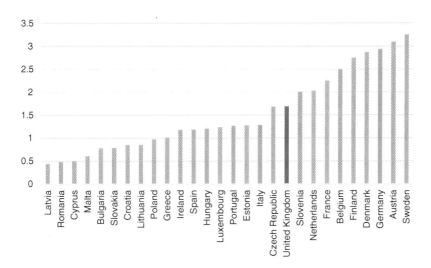

Fig. 2.5 Investment in R&D (*Source* Eurostat indicators R&D)

at the situation of the United Kingdom, it is clear that all countries with higher participation rates in adult education score lower on the material deprivation index. In the Scandinavian countries, but also in the continental-conservative countries like Austria, The Netherlands, Luxemburg and France, together with Belgium and Germany, material deprivation is lower. This result is not unsurprising as the United Kingdom is a typical example of a Liberal Welfare State, in which state support for social policies tend to be lower than in the rest of the Western European countries. Having a stronger involvement of the state in supporting people's day-to-day living, integrating a role for adult lifelong learning systems, thus needs to be encouraged (Fig 2.6).

Life Satisfaction ($R^2 = 0.4084$): General life satisfaction in the United Kingdom is on average higher than in the other EU-28 countries. However, it is not as high as in the Nordic countries and in a number of Western European continental countries such as The Netherlands, Austria and Luxembourg. These countries also have higher participation rates in adult lifelong learning activities. The Life Satisfaction Index focuses on subjective well-being and has been analysed in relation to the United Kingdom's Index of Multiple Deprivation (Armitage 2017).

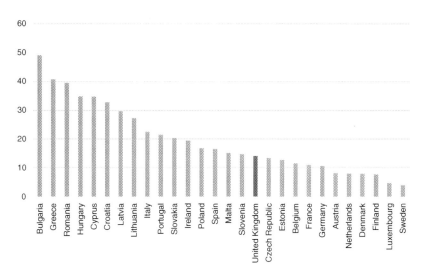

Fig. 2.6 Material deprivation (*Source* Eurostat EU-SILC)

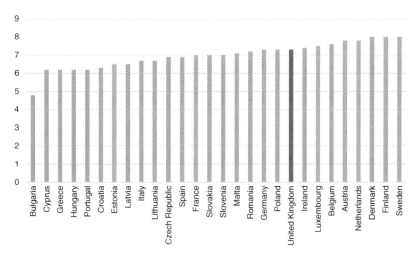

Fig. 2.7 Life statisfaction scale (*Source* Eurostat Quality of Life)

It is clear that life satisfaction is lower in neighbourhoods not only that suffer from material deprivation, but also from a wide range of other types of deprivation, including lower levels of health and higher levels of crime. Again, this is an indication of the functioning of social security and policy systems, and can be further increased, including a stronger role for education and training of those who are most in need of these activities (Fig. 2.7).

Expenditure on Education as part of GDP ($R^2 = 0.3905$): The United Kingdom's investment in education as part of their GDP is above average, and among those countries with higher participation rates in adult lifelong learning, only Finland and Sweden invest more. It is not only a matter of how much money gets invested into education, but how it is distributed among different levels of education. The United Kingdom has in recent years been criticised to have a too strong focus on young people only (Callender and Thompson 2018). Higher education for first generation students has increased despite the higher tuition fees being introduced in England. Investment in schemes like apprenticeships for those who do not go to tertiary education have been put in the picture (OECD 2018). However, part-time participation in higher education has significantly dropped and more money for adult education is being asked for by the sector. The focus on younger people is important as early years in life are vital in developing good levels of skills and knowledge on which they can build further in adult life. However, in the current situation, it is not enough to think about the accumulation of skills alone, as not everyone has basic levels of core skills. Compensation strategies for those who missed out earlier thus need to keep on having their place in the adult education landscape (Fig 2.8).

Employment ($R^2 = 0.3484$): Levels of employment in the United Kingdom are high in relation to other countries in the EU-28. Only in Sweden and Germany, employment levels in 2016 were higher. Of these two countries, only Sweden has higher participation rates than the United Kingdom. This indicates that a range of other countries with lower employment rates succeed in generating higher levels of participation in adult lifelong learning. The quality of jobs is important here too. Within the United Kingdom, there has been a steep rise in the proportion of workers who are self-employed. They traditionally face high levels

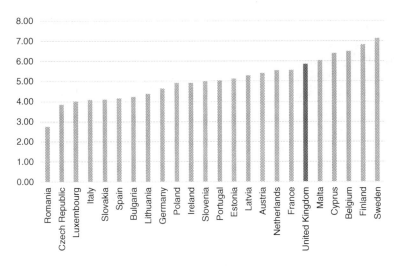

Fig. 2.8 Expenditure on education as part of GDP (*Source* Eurostat Government Finance Statistics)

of job insecurity. A 2018 report by the TUC highlighted the creation of new jobs based on low pay, insecure and zero hours contracts (Heyes 2018). The casualization of work and the increase in the number of self-employed adults is thus positive for the employment statistics, but does not automatically promises a high quality labour market in which workers get many chances to participate in education and training (Fig. 2.9).

Literacy ($R^2 = 0.2982$): Not all countries in the EU-28 participated in the OECD's Survey of Adult Skills (PIAAC), but among those who did, the United Kingdom scored rather average on the literacy measurement (272 points). Finland and The Netherlands scored above 280 and are two countries with high adult lifelong learning participation statistics. Estonia and Sweden, two other countries with higher participation rates, also generated higher scored on the literacy measure. While the correlation between literacy and the participation in adult lifelong learning is not as high as for a number of other indicators, as discussed above, it is still clear that there is—in general—a positive correlation between the two. It has been clear from PIAAC data that the UK has a proportion of low literature adults too (OECD 2013) (Fig. 2.10).

2 Being an Adult Learner in Europe and the UK ...

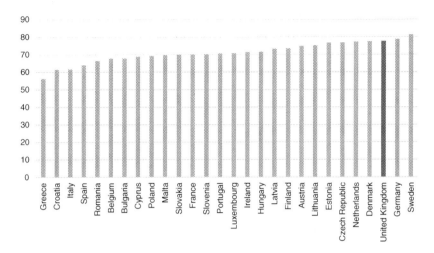

Fig. 2.9 Levels of employment (*Source* Eurostat Labour Force Survey)

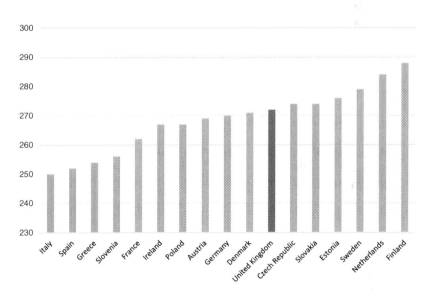

Fig. 2.10 Literacy levels (*Source* PIAAC)

Tracking ($R^2 = 0.1375$): Tracking is often discussed as a macro level indicator in relation to adult lifelong learning and refers to the age in which children in school have to choose between different education and training pathways (see Bol and Van de Werfhorst 2013). Generally, tracking happens at a young age in the Dutch and German speaking countries. It is also the case in Slovakia and the Czech Republic. The United Kingdom shows lowest on the tracking index and it thus means that young people stay together in the same track until a later age. This refers to choices pupils make in continuing to A-levels or taking alternative pathways after finalising their GCSEs. In countries like Belgium and The Netherlands, these choices are made when pupils are 11–12 years old. In general, the correlation between tracking and adult lifelong learning is weak. The Nordic countries also score low on the tracking index, but we know from the discussions above, they have different approaches in relation to for example social security and investments in Research and Development (Fig. 2.11).

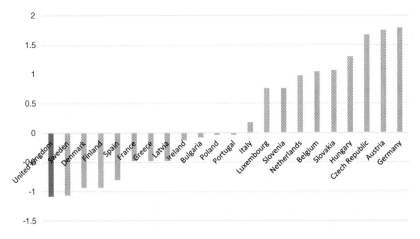

Fig. 2.11 Tracking index (*Source* Bol and Van de Werfhorst [2013])

Discussion

This chapter has demonstrated that in relation to adult lifelong learning participation, the United Kingdom scores above average, but not at the top of the class. The first part of this chapter demonstrated that it is normal to have lower participation rates for older adults and for those who are lower educated. These mechanisms seem core in explaining the determinants of participation in adult lifelong learning and are also found in the countries with the highest participation rates, which are located in Scandinavia. Employed adults in the United Kingdom score higher than those who are unemployed, which was not found in all countries and this might be explained through the lack of education and training opportunities targeted towards those who are unemployed, as is the case in a range of other countries.

While participation rates in the United Kingdom are clearly higher than in the majority of the Eastern and Southern European countries, the Nordic model is often presented as the ideal type of welfare state, with high levels of life satisfaction, subjective well-being and happiness. Looking into the macro level system characteristics, it is clear that measures in relation to social security and poverty reduction have been better developed in these Nordic countries than in the United Kingdom. While levels of employment and investments in education seem rather positive at first sight, a more critical engagement with breaking down the meaning of this indicators have revealed that employment in the United Kingdom tends to be precarious for a high proportion for adults, and the investment in education is mainly targeted towards young adults, not adults. While a focus on the accumulation hypothesis—wanting to guarantee a good start for every child so they can build further on skills and knowledge acquired during the first 25 years of their lives—is a valid one, policy makers need to create more awareness and sensitivity to the needs of adults too.

References

Armitage, P. (2017). *Indices of Multiple Deprivation in the UK*. https://socialvalueportal.com/indices-of-multiple-deprivation-in-the-uk/.

Ball, S., et al. (2014). OECD and Pisa Tests Are Damaging Education Worldwide—Academics. *The Guardian*.

Blossfeld, H.-P., Kilpi-Jakonen, E., Vono de Vilhena, D., & Buchholz, S. (Eds.). (2014). *Adult Learning in Modern Societies: An International Comparison from a Life-Course Perspective*. Cheltenham: Edward Elgar.

Boeren, E. (2014). Evidence-Based Policy-Making: The Usability of the Eurostat Adult Education Survey. *International Journal of Lifelong Education, 33*(3), 275–289.

Boeren, E. (2016). *Lifelong Learning Participation in a Changing Policy Context: An Interdisciplinary Theory*. London: Palgrave-Macmillan.

Boeren, E. (2018a). Cross-Sectional and Longitudinal Surveys. In L. Hamilton & J. Ravenscroft (Eds.), *Building Your Research Design in Education: Theoretically Informed Advanced Methods*. London: Bloomsbury.

Boeren, E. (2018b). *Native- Versus Foreign Born Adults' Participation in Education and Learning: Insights from PIAAC*. Paper Presented at the Conference of the Comparative and International Education Society.

Boeren, E., & Holford, J. (2016). Vocationalism Varies (A Lot): A 12-Country Multivariate Analysis of Participation in Formal Adult Learning. *Adult Education Quarterly, 66*(2), 120–142.

Boeren, E., Whittaker, S., & Riddell, S. (2017). *Provision of Seven Types of Education for (Disadvantaged) Adults in Ten Countries: Overview and Cross-Country Comparison*. Brussels: European Commission.

Bol, T., & Van de Werfhorst, H. (2013). *The Measurement of Tracking, Vocational Orientation, an Standardizationof Educational Systems: A Comparative Approach*. Amsterdam: GINI.

Brookfield, S. D. (2010). Theoretical Frameworks for Understanding the Field. In C. E. Kasworm, A. D. Rose, & J. M. Ross-Gordon (Eds.), *Handbook of Adult and Continuing Education* (pp. 71–81). Thousand Oaks: Sage.

Callender, C., & Thompson, J. (2018). *The Lost Part-Timers: The Decline of Part-Time Undergraduate Higher Education in England*. London: The Sutton Trust.

Campbell, M. (2012). *Skills for Prosperity? A Review of OECD and Partner Country Skill Strategies*. London: Centre for Learning and Life Chances in Knowledge Economies and Societies.

Coffield, F. (2000). *The Necessity of Informal Learning*. Bristol: Policy Press.

Colley, H., Hodkinson, P., & Malcolm, J. (Cartographer). (2003). *Informality and Formality in Learning: A Report for the Learning and Skills Research Centre.*
Courtney, S. (1992). *Why Do Adults Learn? Towards a Theory of Participation in Adult Education.* London: Routledge.
Dale, R., & Robertson, S. (2008). *Globalisation and Europeanisation in Education.* Oxford: Symposium Books.
Desjardins, R. (2017). *Political Economy of Adult Learning System Comparative Study of Strategies, Policies and Constraints.* London: Bloomsbury.
Desjardins, R., & Rubenson, K. (2011). *An Analysis of Skill Mismatch Using Direct Measures of Skills.* Paris: OECD.
Desjardins, R., Rubenson, K., & Milana, M. (2006). *Unequal Chances to Participate in Adult Learning: International Perspectives.* Paris: UNESCO.
Esping-Andersen, G. (1989). *The Three Worlds of Welfare Capitalism.* Cambridge: Polity.
European Commission. (2009). *Strategic Framework for Education and Training.* Brussels: European Commission.
European Commission. (2010). *Europe 2020: A European Strategy for Smart, Sustainable and Inclusive Growth.* Brussels: European Commission.
European Commission. (2016). *Upskilling Pathways: New Opportunities for Adults.* Brussels: European Commission.
Fenger, H. J. M. (2007). Welfare Regimes in Central and Eastern Europe: Incorporating Post-communist Countries in Welfare Regime Typology. *Contemporary IIssues and Ideas in Social Sciences, 3*(2), 1–30.
Field, J. (2012). Is lifelong Learning Making a Difference? Research-Based Evidence on the Impact of Adult Learning. In D. Aspin, J. Chapman, K. Evans, & R. Bagnall (Eds.), *Second International Handbook of Lifelong Learning* (pp. 887–897). Dordrecht: Springer.
Findsen, B., & Formosa, M. (2011). *Lifelong Learning in Later Life: A Handbook on Older Adult Learning.* Dordrecht: Springer.
Grek, S. (2009). Governing by Numbers: The PISA 'Effect' in Europe. *Journal of Education Policy, 24*(1), 23–37.
Groenez, S., Desmedt, E., & Nicaise, I. (2007). *Participation in Lifelong Learning in the EU-15: The Role of Macro-Level Determinants.* Paper Presented at the European Conference for Education Research. Retrieved from: https://www.academia.edu/attachments/3248407/download_file?st= MTUwMjcyMjIxNCwxOTQuODEuMjQ1Ljg2LDQyNzI2MjY5ands= swp-toolbar.

Hefler, G., & Markowitsch, J. (2012). Bridging Institutional Divides: Linking Education, Careers and Work in 'Organizational Space' and 'Skill Space' Dominated Employment Systems. In R. Brooks, A. Fuller, & J. Waters (Eds.), *Changing Spaces of Education—New Perspectives on the Nature of Learning* (pp. 160–181). London: Routledge.

Heyes, J. (2018). *Casualisation Leaves Workers Facing a Difficult and Uncertain Labour Market*. https://www.tuc.org.uk/blogs/casualisation-leaves-workers-facing-difficult-and-uncertain-labour-market.

Holford, J., & Spolar, V. A. M. (2012). Neoliberal and Inclusive Themes in European Lifelong Learning Policy. *Lifelong Learning in Europe: Equity and Efficiency in the Balance*, 39–61.

Howse, P. (2015). *Colleges Say 'Swathe of Cuts' Threatens Adult Education*. London: BBC.

Ioannidou, A. (2007). A Comparative Analysis of New Governance Instruments in the Transnational Educational Space: A Shift to Knowledge-Based Instruments? *European Educational Research Journal*, 6(4), 336–347.

Kaufmann, K. (2015). *AES from a Research Perspective*. Paper Presented at the DwB-Training Course: Working with Data from Official Statistics in Europe Particularly the Adult Education Survey (2011). Retrieved from: http://www.dwbproject.org/export/sites/default/events/doc/dwb_tc6_kaufmann_aes_research_perspective.pdf.

Kyndt, E., & Baert, H. (2013). Antecedents of Employees' Involvement in Work-Related Learning: A Systematic Review. *Review of Educational Research*, 83(2), 273–313.

Lawn, M., & Grek, S. (2012). *Europeanizing Education: Governing a New Policy Space*. Oxford: Symposium Books.

Nesbit, T. (2005). Social Class and Adult Education. *New Directions for Adult and Continuing Education*, 2005(106), 5–14.

OECD. (2013). *OECD Skills Outlook 2013 First Results from the Survey of Adult Skills*. Paris: OECD.

OECD. (2018). *OECD Reviews of Vocational Education and Training: Apprenticeship in England, United Kingdom*. Paris: OECD.

Phillips, D., & Ochs, K. (2003). Processes of Policy Borrowing in Education: Some Explanatory and Analytical Devices. *Comparative Education*, 39(4), 451–461.

Raey, D. (2010). Sociology, Social Class and Education. In M. Apple, S. Ball, & L. A. Gandin (Eds.), *The Routledge Handbook of the Sociology of Education* (pp. 396–404). London: Routledge.

Reid, G. (2018). The Government Has Promised More R and D. Where Will the Money Come From? *The Guardian.*
Saltkjel, T. (2017). Welfare Resources and Social Risks in Times of Social and Economic Change: A Multilevel Study of Material Deprivation in European Countries. *European Journal of Social Work, 17*(1), 118–134.
Schneider, S. L. (2010). Nominal Comparability Is Not Enough: (In-) Equivalence of Construct Validity of Cross-National Measures of Educational Attainment in the European Social Survey. *Research in Social Stratification and Mobility, 28*(3), 342–357.
Schuller, T., Preston, J., Hammond, C., Brassett-Grundy, A., & Bynner, J. (2004). *The Benefits of Learning: The Impact of Education on Health, Family Life and Social Capital.* London: Routledge.
Spellman, R. (2017). *It's Time for a National Adult Learning Strategy.* https://feweek.co.uk/2017/02/06/its-time-for-a-national-adult-learning-strategy/.
UNESCO. (1979). *Terminology of Adult Education.* Paris: UNESCO.
UNESCO UIS. (2011). *International Standard Classification of Education (ISCED) 2011.* Paris: UNESCO.
Virkkunen, H. (2018). Towards an EU Leadership Role in Shaping Globalisation. *European View, 17*(1), 13–20.

3

The Message or the Bottle? Community, Associationism and Adult Learning as "Part of the Process of Social Change"

Sharon Clancy

Raymond Williams argued that "the impulse to adult education" was never solely focused on "remedying deficit, making up for inadequate educational resources in the wider society" (Williams 1983, in McIlroy and Westwood 1993, p. 257). Nor was it primarily a response to "meeting new needs of the society". This chapter argues, as Williams did, that adult education has to be more than "the bottle with the message in it, bobbing on the tides and waves of history" (ibid., p. 255), springing urgently, instead, from the "the desire to make learning part of the process of social change itself" (ibid., p. 257).

Williams' assertion suggests that adult education's political purpose comes through the lens of community and associationism and their contribution to an 'ethic of service' and to social justice. Concepts such as 'social mobility' and 'aspiration' are politically freighted ideas which mask real knowledge dispossession and social precarity. This chapter explores the important role adult education can play in 'left behind'

S. Clancy (✉)
University of Nottingham, Nottingham, UK
e-mail: Sharon.Clancy@nottingham.ac.uk

© The Author(s) 2019
E. Boeren and N. James (eds.), *Being an Adult Learner in Austere Times*,
https://doi.org/10.1007/978-3-319-97208-4_3

communities in the grip of decline, focusing on the role of residential colleges and also non-formal, family and community learning in engaging at community level with those who have no overt 'voice' in the political system. Finally, the chapter explores the role of adult education in consciousness raising and in the construction of 'resources for a journey of hope', examining how awareness of community history and labour struggles have provided continuity and resilience in times of escalating turbulence.

Historical Context

Class and education have been at the centre of political and intellectual struggles in Britain for at least the last century. In 1958, Stuart Hall called out the great inequities in British society, highlighting the difference between its tone and manner, the use of "the language of equality" and "popular democracy", whilst an elite controlled access to real knowledge and power:

> Surely there has never been a greater cleavage between the tone of our society, its manner and forms, and the gross realities. What happens to a society, rigidly class bound, which uses continually the language of equality? What happens to an oligarchy which conceals itself behind the rhetoric of the popular democracy? What happens when larger numbers are trained each year for responsibility and participation, but where the sources of power and decision grow everyday more remote? All our energies are expended in creating and consuming a culture whose sole purpose is to cover up the realities of our social life. (Hall 1958, p. 1)

Hall's commentary is remarkably prescient today, particularly his suggestion that control by the oligarchy masks the "gross realities" of our cultural and social life which become part of the natural order, seen through the distorting lens of a "debased political language" which uses democracy as a smoke screen (Hall 1958, p. 1). His use of the word "train" in relation to education is also significant and he emphasised the futility of such training when the sources of power retreat, chimera-like, further away from the world of the majority of us who are "creating and consuming" this same culture and are skewered by a rigid class structure. If the "realities of our social life" are so obscured, the prospect of a genuine knowledge democracy, as part of our shared associational life in which we collectively re-shape, re-think and re-frame what society should look like, becomes remote. In contemporary austerity Britain, in which class domination is achieved through a system of "accumulation by dispossession" (Sanchez 2018, p. 302), it is timely that we seek to reconnect with Hall's words.

Class, Knowledge Dispossession and Austerity

> Austerity is a class project that disproportionately targets and affects working-class households and communities and, in doing so, protects concentrations of elite wealth and power. (Cooper and Whyte 2017, p. 11)

The reality for many people in contemporary Britain is that we are living in increasingly precarious circumstances which are decoupled from an optimistic future, and do not provide spaces in which the complexity of modern economic life can be debated. Andrew Sanchez has argued that "conceptual models of the precariat fail to grasp class as a dynamic historical object that intersects with experiences of struggle, decline, hope, and fatalism" (Sanchez 2018, p. 303). For Sanchez, our concepts of ourselves as belonging to a particular class—not just a group of individuals living precariously—with a shared history, memories and instances of managing previous struggles, is all-important in countering a sense of despair and impotence, particularly in the communities hardest hit by the exigencies of the past three decades (and more), in the former coalfields and manufacturing bases.

Language is profoundly political. The British media has continued its steady and persistent drip feed of anti-immigration commentary, its rhetoric of 'the deserving and undeserving poor', 'chavs', 'scroungers and spongers', amplifying the demonization of those in precarious employment, living on the margins, and has led to deep rifts in British society, as exemplified by the Brexit vote. Statistics from the Joseph

Rowntree Foundation (Annual Report 2015) show that the proportion of people living in households with an income below the Minimum Income Standard (MIS) increased by nearly a third between 2008/2009 and 2012/2013. More recently, families have seen the greatest increase in poverty, with at least 8.1 million parents and children now living at an income level below that necessary to cover a minimum household budget, up by more than a third from 5.9 million in 2008/2009.

The Brexit Leave vote has been ascribed in large part to people from the traditional working class, from the old manufacturing bases, registering a vote of anger against the current order. This is an order in which social mobility has not improved but has worsened over the last 30 years. Precarious work and zero hours' contracts—the 'gig economy'—have dominated as modes of employment, with none of the hard-won rights and responsibilities of the labour movement in place. The Chartered Institute for Professional Development (CIPD) has estimated that "there are 1.3 million Britons employed in the gig economy, while the TUC says that one-in-ten British workers are in 'precarious work'" (*Wired* 2017). Many communities in the former coalfield areas have seen no resurgence of dignified work and some places act as little more than dormer towns supplying cheap labour to the bigger cities. The sense of being part of a settled community based on collectivised work, such as mining, has been eroded and transience is becoming routine due to market forces; as people have to move away for work, social networks are being eroded. Such communities are demonized, 'left behind', perceived as second class and as being in deficit—economically, culturally and intellectually.

Class, as an expression of our standing in the social hierarchy and, a perhaps more fluid concept, our social-economic status, has long been a central preoccupation in British life, though not always overtly. Its interconnection with conceptions of democracy, or a democratic society, are critical here, as are specific connections with education. Mass education was the result of the principle of education for all children expressed in the 1870 Elementary Education Act and the later 1944 Education Act, which created an education system which was free for all children and raised the school leaving age to 15. From the late nineteenth and early twentieth century, fear of the newly educated and recently enfranchised members of the working classes were writ large amongst a wide range of writers and public intellectuals. Virginia Woolf, for example, is illustrative of the not uncommon fear amongst her own class (upper-middle, educated) that mass education was endangering the role of the educated middle classes and the intelligentsia as the bastion of culture. Her anxiety was that democracy would distort, dilute and trivialise culture and that art, as common property, would cease to be sublime and would descend into banality. She felt that the working classes were both ill-equipped and too unstable emotionally, psychologically and intellectually for the challenge of preserving and promoting the best of culture, seeing this class as "A vast, featureless, almost shapeless jelly of human stuff - occasionally this way or that as some instinct of hate, revenge, or admiration bubbles up beneath it" (Woolf, quoted in McNeilie 1988, p. 3).

These issues were very much alive between the wars and in the post-Second World War period. In *The Road to Wigan Pier* (1937), George Orwell railed against the absurdity of the finer gradations of the social hierarchy, as "the shadowy caste-system of class; rather like a jerrybuilt modern bungalow haunted by medieval ghosts" (Orwell 1937, p. 113). He was also very precise in his description of his own family as "lower-upper-middle class" (Orwell 1937, ibid.), noting, sardonically, that this was the upper middle class without money. For him, class was not about money but, much more subtly, about conceptions of taste, culture and "decency". He argued that the "unthinking person of gentle birth" (as above, p. 123) needs only a spark to rouse his "dormant class-prejudice":

> In his eyes the workers are not a submerged race of slaves, they are a sinister flood creeping upwards to engulf himself and his friends and his family and to sweep all culture and all decency out of existence. Hence that queer watchful anxiety lest the working class shall grow too prosperous. (Orwell 1937, p. 123)

Richard Hoggart summarised the enduring power of the English preoccupation with class in his 1989 introduction to *The Road to Wigan Pier*. He stated that: "Class distinctions do not die; they merely learn new ways of expressing themselves. Orwell's stance in this matter is completely up to date. Each decade we shiftily declare we have buried class; each decade the coffin stays empty" (Hoggart 1989, p. vii).

Class fell out of fashion as a critical means of examining identity from the 1980s, replaced in large part by individual identity issues, with an emphasis on race, gender, sexuality and disability (Savage 2007). In 1997 the then new Prime Minister Tony Blair pledged that social class was no longer a relevant concept and that our collective aspiration should be towards a classless society in which no one social class should prevail over another. His means of achieving 'classlessness' was through education, conceived as a profoundly liberating force. Continuing with Margaret Thatcher's embrace of free market economics, Blair argued that we should all become entrepreneurs, self-made people living within a freelance culture in which the individual is paramount and in which education should support our capacity to work by offering us employability skills, making us flexible and responsive to constant change and uncertainty in an increasingly globalised economy. Like James Callaghan in the 1970s, the concept of education Blair outlined focused not just on academic pursuits and the massification of higher education but on creating a workforce equipped with the appropriate skills for the modern age. As Callaghan expressed it in his famous speech at Ruskin College in Oxford in 1976:

> There is no virtue in producing socially well-adjusted members of society who are unemployed because they do not have the skills. Nor at the other extreme must they be technically efficient robots. Both of the basic purposes of education require the same essential tools. These are basic literacy, basic numeracy, the understanding of how to live and work together, respect for others, respect for the individual. (Callaghan 1976)

Neoliberalism proposes that human advancement is best achieved by "liberating individual entrepreneurial freedoms and skills within an institutional framework characterized by strong private property rights, free markets, and free trade" (Harvey 2007, p. 2, quoted in Holford 2016, p. 544). Wider concepts of public education for the creation of "well-adjusted" human beings and citizens have tended to be reserved for the world of higher education. The primary pressure, and the funding impetus, over the last three decades and more has been to train people for roles and jobs. The emphasis on the trained individual is important here as the individual becomes the primary focus, rather than the community. 'Community' is many things to many people but it implies a sense of association—a commonality of purpose, interest or place; a network, a collective. The ideology of neoliberalism does not encourage debates about culture, community, class and history—it seeks to erase our collective memory, preferring a state of eternal present in which the "realities of our social life" are not subject to scrutiny. The self-made individual must run ever faster to stay in place, with the spectre of precarity looming at every turn. Tacit, community-based, knowledge, which is intuitive, sometimes hard to articulate and often acquired through lengthy practical experience, is outside of this frame of reference.

Recent research by the Institute for Voluntary Action Research (IVAR) into poor communities and how they are faring in the face of austerity shows fractures and rifts, increasing social isolation and mental ill health, greater dependence on food banks and a lack of community spaces in which to come together. It is what interview respondents have described as 'all-encompassing, post-industrial, deeply rooted social poverty' which consumes energy and time and militates against community engagement:

> The pressures of poverty militate against people's ability to engage with their communities – people's energies are consumed in the struggle to survive and they are frequently holding down several jobs and/or working in the insecure 'gig economy'. (IVAR 2018, p. 3)

Over the past two decades, Mike Savage has done much to revive the sociology of class and, in particular, an emphasis on class consciousness in the sense of shared understanding of lifestyles, cultural interests, social networks and political orientations, as Sanchez has also described it. Savage writes in the Introduction to *Social Class in the 21st Century*:

> We like to think of ourselves as living in a democratic society where individuals are supposed to have equal rights. Yet we also know that people's economic fortunes can be strikingly different. Symbolically, class is a

lightning conductor for the anxieties this discrepancy between economic realities and our beliefs provokes. (Savage 2016, p. 7)

He calls into question concepts of equality and the economic realities beneath them. The BBC's Great British Class Survey of 2011, with its on-line Class Calculator, prompted enormous public interest, creating the largest survey of social class ever undertaken in Britain. The Class Survey delineated several new groups and some existing, but the elite, and established middle class remained resolutely at the top and inter-generational changes remained small. Savage and his team took two years to analyse the data and, in 2016, published *Social Class in the 21st Century*. Savage argued that class has become newly important again in the first two decades of the twenty first century, due to rising social and economic inequality and particularly income disparity, which, despite Blair's focus on social mobility and meritocracy have worsened. In Savage's view "social class is now a very powerful force in the popular imagination" (Savage 2016, p. 6). There is every reason for this when educational statistics are considered in terms of class.

Class and Education—The Myth of Social Mobility?

The links between individual and parental income are still stronger in the UK than in any other Organisation for Economic Co-operation and Development (OECD) country and British schools are more socially segregated than in any other country. Added to this, the UK is one of the lowest performing countries for income mobility across the OECD. This issue came to the forefront of research and news in early 2018. Family poverty measures, such as eligibility for free school meals, remain a strong predictor of the kind of education young people access (or do not). Education is clearly not equally available or equally valued. This is particularly true for fee-paying independent schools and also for grammar schools, which remain the 'gold standard' for secondary schooling for many purveyors of the mantra of meritocracy. However, a recent study by Gorard and Siddiqui (2018) shows that grammar schools in England take only a very small proportion of pupils who are or have ever been eligible for free school meals (two per cent as opposed to 14 per cent nationally) and those they do take have been eligible for fewer years. Their concern is that this equates to a form of segregation on the grounds of class—"Segregation, whether racially or by religion or social class, may have alarming and dangerous consequences for the school system and for society more widely in the longer term" (Gorard and Siddiqui 2018, p. 4).

This inequity extends into higher education. Despite growing numbers of people participating in higher education, which reached 49% in 2015/2016 (Higher Education Initial Participation Rate [HEIPR]),[1] young people from lower socioeconomic backgrounds are not attending the elite Russell Group universities. According to a Sutton Trust report from 2017:

> there remain barriers to elite higher education….There has been no trend of improvement in the gap in Russell Group attendance by socioeconomic status. The gap is even starker for Oxbridge attendance; state school students eligible for free school meals (FSM) are 55 times less likely to attend Oxford or Cambridge. (Sutton Trust 2017)

According to a recent article in *The Times* (March 2018) Oxford University takes 2.8% of students from the "poorest households", which is similar to Cambridge.[2] On average people from lower socioeconomic backgrounds make up 11.1% of the overall student population, with a disproportionate number attending non-Russell group universities such as Sunderland University (which ranks 102nd in one UK university ranking) and Teesside University (which ranks 101st). The University of Hull tops the current equality of student intake poll by the Higher Education Policy Institute (HEPI), followed by the University of Derby. Students from lower socioeconomic backgrounds are far less likely

---

[1]The HEIPR continues to increase, reaching 49% in 2015/2016 up from 42% in 2006/2007, from Department for Education Participation Rates in Higher Education: Academic Years 2006/2007–2015/2016 (Provisional), SFR47/2017, 28 September 2017.
[2]University of Cambridge is first in the 2018 UK rankings and University of Oxford is second.

to attend university and students from the poorest households are 55 times less likely than independent school students to attend Oxford or Cambridge (Sutton Trust 2010). It would seem that the level of education completed, as well as the type of school and university attended, remain huge determinants of social mobility in Britain. Large educational gaps remain and entrenched privilege continues in higher education.

Social mobility, according to The Sutton Trust—an educational charity—is foregrounded in the ability to break the link between "an individual's parental background and their opportunities to reach their full potential in terms of income and occupation. It is about better opportunities for each generation and making access to these opportunities fairer, regardless of background" (Sutton Trust 2017). Diane Reay, by contrast, has argued that "social mobility is a red herring. Currently we don't have it—or very little of it….And the focus on social mobility neglects the fact that given the current high levels of inequality, social mobility is primarily about recycling inequality rather that tackling it" (Reay 2012, p. 5).

Reay's perspective would seem to be borne out by further research from The Sutton Trust which highlights that students from wealthier backgrounds are often advantaged in applying to Oxbridge by having greater access to information through their schools and family and social networks (Sutton Trust 2016). Pierre Bourdieu developed a sociology of culture to grapple with these very issues. His theory—largely focused on class issues—emphasised the concept of 'capital' (or power) and social reproduction, and sought to unpick how dominant groups in society claim a natural legitimacy for their readings of culture. He explodes the sanctity of "economic disinterestedness" postulating, instead, that the elite in society promulgate the notion that economic capital is not bound up with social capital, which Bourdieu describes as the "social obligations" (Bourdieu 1986, p. 241) which bind society. He argued that these very social connections or networks are "convertible, in certain conditions, into economic capital and may be institutionalized in the forms of a title of nobility" (ibid., p. 241). Bourdieu argued that cultural capital, like social capital, is convertible "into economic capital and may be institutionalized in the forms of educational qualifications" (Bourdieu 1986, p. 241). It can serve as a form of protection for the interests of those in power, ensuring that the educational system replicates "the reproduction of the social structure by sanctioning the hereditary transmission of cultural capital" (ibid., p. 241). This theorisation provides a very useful framework for understanding the structural aspects of learning and how they become encoded in human culture and within our internal mental and emotional frameworks, or habitus, by a set of acquired sensibilities, schemata, tastes and dispositions.

In 'A Winning Personality' (2016) De Vries and Renfrow draw a direct correlation between personality and background and how this impacts on future earnings and social mobility. Non-cognitive skills—such as confidence and personal presentation—play a critical role in standing out in the fiercely competitive world of work where "'essential life skills' are likely to be a key differentiator". They argue that "access to education and job opportunities is an ongoing issue with continued evidence of opportunity 'hoarding' through networks, information asymmetries, and social bias. Even when less well-off students attend the same university and study the same subject as their wealthier peers they earn over 10% less per year" (De Vries and Renfrow 2016). Choice in education is valorised but remains unequal in terms of access and distribution at both structural and psychological levels:

> It is not just the neoliberal rhetoric around diversity that has worked to bury social class as a crucial axis of educational inequality whilst sanctioning an increasingly divisive and segregated system, the current discursive and policy status quo is one that valorizes choice whilst rarely recognizing that choices come with resources that remain very unequally distributed. (Reay 2012, p. 6)

Raymond Williams identified the cultural hegemony implicit in elite education systems as leading to "a very restricted and privileged and stagnant view of the world" (Williams 1983, p. 255). We can add to this restricted picture a lack of professional representation of people from the working classes—in our cultural and political lives—and the impact this has on the education system and on notions of merit.

Oliver Heath has written powerfully about how "class has been pushed outside the political system....The working class have not become incorporated within the political system – they have become more marginalized from it" (Heath 2016, p. 21). This is evidenced by the lack of working class representation in parliament, particularly in the Labour party which historically drew many of its politicians from working class backgrounds. Heath's research shows that "in 1964, Labour was not just a party that saw itself as for the working class, but was in fact substantially comprised of working class politicians, with 37 per cent of its MPs coming from manual occupational backgrounds. By 2015 this figure had fallen to just 7 per cent" (Heath 2016). Many politicians are perceived as 'career politicians', with little experience outside 'the Westminster bubble' and higher education.

In the cultural and arts worlds, the critical absence of those from working class social origins is "a key characteristic of the British cultural and creative workforce" (Panic! Report 2018, p. 4). This is particularly true for the world of publishing but is also evident in the theatre, film and television. The report shows that "our cultural and creative workers have narrow social networks, suggesting a type of social closure within the sector" (ibid., p. 3).

The current education system is clearly only part of the issue. Whilst for many it is still out of reach, alienating, or restricted—real structural and cultural barriers persist and social networks prevail. Second chance learning, therefore, as an older adult outside the 18–21 age bracket, becomes a more urgent necessity in contemporary society, despite the uplift in education and qualifications overall. Added to this, we know that some people do not fare well in primary and secondary education and that the barriers to their learning are not primarily a failure of individual effort or agency but are connected with issues of social capital and with societal and familial issues which can disrupt compulsory schooling. These might include, for instance, growing up as a looked-after child where education is patchy or inconsistent, engaging in early drug use, family break up, having an undiagnosed mental health issue or learning disability. For many people in such situations, a flexible approach to higher education was vital and often gained through further and adult education courses. Supportive resources, however, such as the Education Maintenance Allowance (EMA), introduced by the last Labour government to increase the financial viability of continuation in study for young people aged 16–19 from less well-off backgrounds, was abolished by the Coalition government in 2013. Loans were made available for further education for those aged over 24 the same year, and this was extended to 19–23 year olds (studying at Level 3 and above) in November 2015. However, taking on a loan can be especially prohibitive for part-time and mature learners. Consequently there has been a dramatic decline in this group of learners over the past 7 years. The Office for Fair Access (OFFA) Report of 2017 noted that this trend 'shows no sign of levelling off' and regards the decline as 'deeply worrying', seeing this issue as 'hindering social mobility targets' (OFFA 2017, p. 3). The report refers to part-time and mature learners as an 'all-too invisible' disadvantaged group.

The student experience for those who do access higher education but who do not possess the right kinds of social and cultural capital can still be profoundly alienating. Such students can become lost in the higher education system, entering a "mapless journey" as Sarah Mann has described it (Mann 2001). This results in a dislocation with both the context of the educational experience, an uneasy relationship with the frame of discourse in which the education takes place—and particularly between student and teacher—and a feeling of being invisible and anonymous. Mann suggested that this situation is exaggerated for students from non-traditional learner backgrounds, including working class students, those from different countries and cultures, who struggle with an inexplicit and often 'hidden' cultural and academic hegemony. This can lead to a stifling of creativity or imagination and also to its distorted expression in other areas of activity, including in the areas of performance and academic conformity. The feeling of being a "stranger in a foreign land" results in a sense of alienation and powerlessness:

> the student's position is akin to the colonised or the migrant from the colonised land, where the potential for alienation arises from being in a place where those in power have the potential to impose their particular ways of perceiving and understanding the world – in other words, a kind of colonising process. (Mann 2001, p. 11)

As Reay has argued, the current elite representation of "the working classes as an unruly undisciplined mass has been transformed into a view of the working classes as made up of individuals who need to take more responsibility for their lives" (Reay 2012, p. 9). She argues that the prevailing view is that "class position and poverty are lifestyle choices: that anyone who wants to be, and tries hard enough, can be middle class. Changing such views is a vital precursor to a socially just educational system" (ibid.). Alienation from the sources of political and economic power is built into this rhetoric. Andrew Sanchez has suggested that employment security (and its lack in precarization) is itself "an act of elite class struggle" (Sanchez 2018, p. 302) and employment (and our earning potential) is critically connected with learning and social capital.

Raymond Williams was clear that education can be a "lottery" and cannot be merely "a matter of available intelligence and available learning interest", but is, instead, an "interlock between those and the kind of learning that is at any time available and the time of life at which it comes up. This is a point that adult educationalists have of course often made. It defeats the crude, ideological attempt to write the last chapter of adult education because all the bright boys and girls have gone through the system and up the ladder" (Williams 1983, p. 268).

Adult Education—A Space for Challenge and Resilience

Adult education—both current and historical—has provided an important space for communities, for part-time and mature learners, and for second chance education. It has enabled us to challenge the nature of learning and of what is deemed an appropriate subject to learn:

> …in a society in which learning is unequal certain distinctive kinds of ignorance accumulate in the very heartland of learning. This heartland defines itself; it defines what learning is; it deems what is a subject and what is not. (Williams 1983, p. 259)

Community

Social and economic inclusion has been reimagined in recent times in terms of social mobility and individual "success", resulting in an emphasis on using higher education to remove young people from their communities of origin. Raymond Williams described the democratising potential of education which escaped the elite-controlled schoolhouse and university and found its expression in the family, in churches, community centres, libraries and museums. Such an approach echoed earlier working class learning experience in the reading libraries, in pubs and kitchens. It also inhered in the potential for adult education classes, particularly residential, to act as spaces for discourse and dialogue, both formal and informal, both through the lecture and around the dining table. Adult education has taken numerous forms, including university extra-curricular education, colleges offering short- and long-term residential courses, co-operative education movements and informal discussion groups.

Throughout much of the twentieth century, and particularly in the inter-war and post-Second World War period, there was a drive to develop a "common centre" (British Institute for Adult Education (BIAE) 1924, p. 26) in each area, including the most rural, which would bring together all the bodies connected with the delivery of adult education under one roof. At this time, adult education was delivered through numerous agencies, including, in rural areas, the village club or institute, elementary and secondary schools and in urban areas public libraries, adult schools and working men's clubs. This was alongside evening classes offered by universities as part of their extra-mural activity and courses provided by the Workers' Educational Association. The "common centre" idea saw expression in the development of over 30 adult residential colleges, many offering short courses (a weekend to two weeks) and some—notably Ruskin College in Oxford, the oldest college established in 1899, and Fircroft College in Birmingham, established in 1909—offering much longer courses of one to two years. Whilst the short-term colleges were technically under local education authority control, they had considerable freedom and developed courses and programmes which responded to local area interest. Local area co-ordinators forged links with local communities at a grassroots level. As Michael Barratt Brown, former Principal of Northern College, established in 1978, described it, this was close to Raymond Williams' conception of a collaborative approach to adult education focused on the primacy of the 'lived experience' of the individual learner, a form of "action learning or engaged learning",[3] in which groups of learners came together to share ideas and issues based on personal experience. By this means learners could have a taste of learning on a short course which might spur them on to access longer courses. Barratt Brown described it as a "nursery slope", allowing individuals who had not previously had positive experiences to gain in confidence and to learn with other like-minded people in a focused and intense environment, away from the quotidian.

Links with trade unions and labour organisations at colleges like Northern, also created an opportunity for working class people to gain mature scholarships. In the late 1970s courses for coalminers took place at Northern College over 10 weeks, with the miners coming through evening classes and day release courses offered by the University of Sheffield in local communities, and funded by the National Union of Miners. Northern College, dubbed 'the Ruskin of the North', and Ruskin College in particular had strong links with the trade union and labour movements: until the 1980s at least their focus was on "the promotion in a residential setting of liberal education for working class students, recruited mainly from the trade unions" (Pollins 1984, p. 63). John Prescott, former Deputy Prime Minister to Tony Blair, went as a shop steward to Ruskin College in the 1960s and has stated that his attendance at Ruskin enabled him to gain a place at Hull University later that decade. Dennis Skinner also attended Ruskin College, in 1967, after completing a course run by the NUM at the University of Sheffield. Prescott wrote, in a letter to *The Guardian*, "Dennis Skinner and I went to the Labour trade union's Ruskin College in Oxford, where the entry qualifications were not O or A-levels but your

---

[3] I was privileged to interview Michael Barratt Brown on 15 December 2014 shortly before he died, aged 97 (7 May 2015). In 1978 he founded Northern College at Wentworth Castle, near Barnsley, as an adult and community education residential college, and was its first principal. He retired from the College in 1983.

involvement in strikes" (*The Guardian*, Letters, 7 July 2014). Both Prescott and Skinner are seen as genuinely representative of the working class backgrounds from which they came, in contradistinction to the 'career politicians' remarked upon in Heath's research.

Political and Social Consciousness

Research into residential adult education (Clancy and Holford 2017) examined the four remaining residential adult education colleges: Fircroft College, Birmingham; Hillcroft College, in Surbiton, Surrey; Ruskin College in Oxford; and Northern College, in, Barnsley, South Yorkshire. The residential colleges are unique in the contemporary sphere of further and adult education in two ways—they are now the only adult education institutions which are residential in nature and they are independently constituted charities, regulated by their own trust deeds, and are no longer under local authority control. At their best, what they appear to offer is a form of education which allows for a focus on criticality, a form of public pedagogy which is able to consider and scrutinise power differentials and fake authority, creating the space for the development of critical consciousness and political action. This could be described as education for social purpose, seeking a quantitative and then a qualitative change as its end point in real world applications. Seth Visvanathan has described this approach to education as "cognitive justice" which enables us to perceive that "diverse communities" have a stake in problem solving, based on conversation and reciprocity:

> What one offers then is a democratic imagination with a non-market, non-competitive view of the world, where conversation, reciprocity, translation create knowledge not as an expert, almost zero-sum view of the world but as a collaboration of memories, legacies, heritages, a manifold heuristics of problem solving, where a citizen takes both power and knowledge into his or her own hands. These forms of knowledge, especially the ideas of complexity, represent new forms of power sharing and problem-solving that go beyond the limits of voice and resistance. (Visvanathan 2009)

At the colleges a complex understanding of the social and economic world in which we live is achieved through small group discussion work. They are built on the traditions of adult education seen in the WEA and the university tutorial class movement. R. H. Tawney, the eminent adult educator, had argued that tutorial teaching should take place where students would be most comfortable, in the areas where they lived, and should be based on a small group format, of no more than thirty people, and not on formal lectures. The students agreed to read materials presented by their tutor; they agreed to undertake fortnightly essay writing and to meet once a week for a given period. The mutuality and respect emphasised by Thompson and Tawney was central. John Holford has described elements of Tawney's approach as "embryonically constructivist", in that "knowledge was created in the discussion", in a two-way exchange (Holford 2015, p. 103) which was not always comfortable but which challenged ideas of the teacher as 'guru' and fostered the notion of equality of status between the teacher and students. The residential colleges have followed this approach and, as the tutorial or seminar approach is closely associated with methods of teaching at Oxford and Cambridge, this led several of the students to refer to their own Oxbridge experience, with one person saying it was their taste of a privilege education—"a poor man's Eton" (Clancy and Holford 2017, p. 4). Critically, however, this style of teaching encourages genuine critical thinking. As Noam Chomsky expressed it, "the core principle and requirement of a fulfilled human being is the ability to inquire and create constructively, independently, without external controls" (quoted in Open Culture 2016). There remains a need for rebellious space and places of dissent where we can question, enquire and challenge without the dead hand of managerialism consuming democratic engagement.

Ethic of Service—"Social Purpose Education"

Because the majority of the students are from challenging backgrounds, they gain not just personal confidence through debate but also an understanding that they are not alone in their experience—the creation of networks and social capital. From this learning, they return to their own communities newly equipped with an understanding of the wider societal and economic context in which they live and with a passion to work with others to support this kind of consciousness. This is what we described in the residential report as an "ethic of service" (Clancy and Holford 2017, p. 4). This has been described as 'emotional labour', the 'emotion work' that the former students as social actors perform in the course of their daily lives when they return to their communities. This emotional labour, as Diane Reay has argued, is often part of affective and associational life—"emotional capital is generally confined within the bounds of affective relationships of family and friends and encompasses the emotional resources you hand on to those you care about" (Reay 2004, p. 60).

This 'handing on' is a source of resilience. As Sanchez identifies very poignantly in his paper, there is a complex interplay between precarity and hope. Knowing one's own history and that of the community in which one lives enables a deeper engagement with a possible future: "the degree to which persons and communities are able to construct hopeful visions of the future by drawing upon their experiences of the past is crucial to political consciousness and behaviour" (Sanchez 2018, p. 321).

Idealized perceptions of the past structure engagements with the political life of the future. Those who have known the power of collectivised labour movements and shared action, or know their history—what he calls the "labour aristocrats"—are more resilient to the onslaught of economic injustice and inequality than those who have never known anything other than precariousness. They have a different frame of reference; they know "what the 'good life' looks like and how one attains it" (Sanchez 2018, p. 302).

Resources for a Journey of Hope

"Resources for a Journey of Hope" was Raymond Williams' description of the communal means by which we seek emancipation in the last chapter of *Towards 2000* (1983). Linden West echoed Williams' cry for an enduring need for resources for hope in his 2016 book, *Distress in the City: Racism, Fundamentalism and a Democratic Education*. West suggested that these can be found in the best traditions of adult education and informal learning—education of an "informal, life-wide kind", which allows people to challenge the "taken-for-granted without experiencing paralysing anxiety", and in the cultivation of "relationships in which individuals feel legitimate" and can restore resilience (West 2016, p. 13).

So much of the legacy of adult education—and those aspects of it that endure (such as the residential colleges) is found in relationships, shared history and community. West refers to developments in informal education, such as Philosophy in Pubs (PiPs)—a growing movement close to the spirit of the old tutorial classes which supports grass-roots, community-based philosophy in public venues to debate important contemporary moral and philosophical issues. In a resurgence of interest in the power of adult education, these same smaller organisations continue to keep alive an alternative vision of radical, informal education which is about individual and cultural transformation. The Raymond Williams Foundation, a voluntary organisation with which I am personally involved, has espoused and promoted PiPs and utilises traditions of informal, often residential community-based discourse for democracy and social justice, in line with William's life-long social project, the creation of "an educated and participating democracy" (Williams 1961, reprinted 2001, p. 389). It does this through its support fund which was created to help adults—especially the financially and educationally disadvantaged—to attend residential education courses for lectures and discussions on big social, political, philosophical and cultural themes and through its emerging informal networks such as PiPs, pub/cafe lectures and discussion circles generally.

Social movements such as Momentum have emerged to promote new forms of political debate. In 2017, 'The World Transformed', a fringe event held during the Labour party conference, debated issues of education—and particularly challenges to elitism in higher education—and also hosted a series of powerful workshops on the lack of working class representation in arts and culture. The Cultural Manifesto, entitled *Movement for a Cultural Democracy*, produced as a result of these workshops states:

> A strong democracy is an inclusive democracy. It's a society where no-one is invisible and every voice is heard. Culture, as it has been, can be the preserve of the privileged few or instead, it can be the building block

that strengthens our democracy, celebrated as a basic human right, helping to create a world where all people are free to enjoy the benefits of self-expression, access to resources and community. Our goal is to ensure that in our time it is the latter that prevails and that this transformative value, of culture for all, by all, comes to permeate all corners of our social lives and political institutions. (Movement for a Cultural Democracy, 20 December 2017)

In November 2017, the Co-operative College hosted a conference entitled *Making the Co-operative University*. Its primary objective was to bring together thinkers and speakers from a range of alternative education sectors—including the Free University and Community University movements, the Social Science Centre, Lincoln—led by Professor Mike Neary—which is based on a mutual/co-operative model and leaders in Co-operative education. The conference challenged the hegemony of a marketised higher education and considered the nature of a socially just education.

To conclude, consciousness is all and change is coming. Raymond Williams argued that "this is a social order which really does not know in what crucial respects it is ignorant, in what crucial respects it is incompletely conscious and therefore in what crucial respects this collaborative process of Adult Education is still central" (Williams 1983, p. 264). The chapter has shown the important role adult education can play in 'left behind' communities in the grip of decline, focusing on the role of residential colleges and also non-formal, family and community learning in engaging at community level with those who have no overt 'voice' in the political system. The role of adult education in consciousness raising and in the construction of 'resources for hope' is critical, enabling us to examine how awareness of community history and labour struggles have provided continuity and resilience in times of escalating turbulence. To return to Williams' assertion that adult education has to be more than "the bottle with the message in it, bobbing on the tides and waves of history" (Williams 1983, p. 255) we must now reclaim adult and community education as a means of contributing to the change that is necessary "in a social order which has more need of it" (ibid.) than perhaps ever before.

References

Bourdieu, P. (1986). The Forms of Capital. In J. Richardson (Ed.), *Handbook of Theory and Research for the Sociology of Education* (pp. 241–258). New York: Greenwood.

British Institute of Adult Education. (1924). *The Guildhouse: A Co-operative Centre for Adult Education*. Being a Report Prepared by a Committee of Inquiry Appointed by the British Institute of Adult Education with a Foreword by Lord Eustace Percy. London: British Institute of Adult Education.

Callaghan, J. (1976). *Callaghan's Speech (18th October) Has Been Widely Reprinted*. The Text Is Available Online at: http://www.educationengland.org.uk/documents/speeches/1976ruskin.html.

Clancy, S., & Holford, J. (2017). *Life Changing Things Happen*. Adult Residential Report, University of Nottingham.

Cooper, V., & Whyte, D. (2017). *The Violence of Austerity*. London: Pluto Press.

De Vries, R., & Renfrow, J. (2016). *A Winning Personality: The Effects of Background on Personality and Earnings*. Sutton Trust/University of Cambridge/University of Kent.

Gorard, S., & Siddiqui, N. (2018). Grammar Schools in England: A New Analysis of Social Segregation and Academic Outcomes. *British Journal of Sociology of Education*. Published Online 26 March. https://doi.org/10.1080/01425692.2018.1443432.

Hall, S. (1958). In the No Man's Land. *Universities and Left Review* (3) (Winter), 86–87.

Heath, O. (2016). Policy Alienation, Social Alienation and Working-Class Abstention in Britain, 1964–2010. *British Journal of Political Science*, 1–21. Published Online 22 September.

Hoggart, R. (1989). Introduction. In G. Orwell, *The Road to Wigan Pier* (pp. vii–xi). London: Penguin Classics.

Holford, J. (2015). The Idea of the University in the Early Work of R.H. Tawney. In R. Stoilova, K. Petkova, & S. Koleva (Eds.), *Knowledge as a Value, Scientific Knowledge as a Vocation: Jubilee Collection in Honour of Professor Pepka Boyadjieva* (pp. 93–108). Iztok-zapad: Sofia.

Holford, J. (2016, October). The Misuses of Sustainability: Adult Education, Citizenship and the Dead Hand of Neoliberalism. *International Review of Education*, 62(5), 541–561.

Institute for Voluntary Action Research. (2018). Empowered Communities in the 2020s. *IVAR Research Briefing 2—Countries Dialogue January 2018: What Does the Future Hold for Communities in the Four Countries of the UK?*
Joseph Rowntree Foundation. (2015, November). *Annual Report.* MPSE.
Kobie, N. (2017, July 11). What Is the Gig Economy and Why Is It so Controversial? *Wired.* Accessed 1 October 2017.
Mann, S. (2001). Alternative Perspectives on the Student Experience: Alienation and Engagement. *Studies in Higher Education, 26*(1), 7–19.
McIlroy, J., & Westwood, S. (Eds.). (1993). Adult Education and Social Change. *Adult Education and Social Change: Lectures and Reminiscences in Honour of Tony McLean*, WEA Southern District, 1983 (pp. 9–24). *Border Country: Raymond Williams in Adult Education* (pp. 255–264). London: NIACE.
McNeilie, A. (Ed.). (1988). *The Essays of Virginia Woolf, Vol. III, 1919–24.* London: The Hogarth Press.
Office for Fair Access (OFFA). (2017). *Understanding the Impact of Outreach on Access to Higher Education for Adult Learners from Disadvantaged Backgrounds: An Institutional Response.* London: OFFA. Available at: https://www.offa.org.uk/wp-content/uploads/2017/07/Final-Report-Understanding-the-impact-of-outreach-on-access-to-higher-education-for-disadvantaged-adult-learners-docx.pdf. Accessed 31 July 2017.
Open Culture. (2016, April 28). Noam Chomsky Defines What It Means to Be a Truly Educated Person. *Education, Philosophy, Politics.*
Orwell, G. (1937). *The Road to Wigan Pier.* London: Penguin Classics.
Panic! Report: Social Class, Taste and Inequalities in the Creative Industries. (2018). Dr Orian Brook, Dr David O'Brien, and Dr Mark Taylor, Funded by the Arts and Humanities Research Council, Led by Create London and Arts Emergency.
Pollins, H. (1984). *The History of Ruskin College.* Oxford: Ruskin College Library Occasional Publication No. 3.
Reay, D. (2004). Gendering Bourdieu's Concepts of Capitals? Emotional Capital, Women and Social Class. *The Sociological Review, 52*(2), 57–74.
Reay, D. (2012, July). Think Piece—What Would a Socially Just Education System Look Like? *CLASS.*
Sanchez, A. (2018). Relative Precarity: Decline, Hope and the Politics of Work. In C. Hann & J. P. Parry (Eds.), *Industrial Labor on the Margins of Capitalism: Precarity, Class and the Neoliberal Subject* (pp. 297–331). New York: Berghahn.

Savage, M. (2007). Changing Social Class Identities in Post-War Britain: Perspectives from Mass-Observation. *Sociological Research Online, 12*(3), 6. http://www.socresonline.org.uk/12/3/6.html. Accessed 12 May 2016.

Savage, M. (2016). *Social Class in the 21st Century*. London: Pelican.

Sutton Trust. (2010). *Responding to the New Landscape for University Access*. Sutton Trust.

Sutton Trust. (2016). *Oxbridge Admissions*. Sutton Trust.

Sutton Trust. (2017, July). *The State of Social Mobility in the UK*. Boston Consulting Group, Sutton Trust.

The Complete University Guide. https://www.thecompleteuniversityguide.co.uk/league-tables/rankings.

The Guardian. (2014, July 7). Letters.

The Times. (2018, March 28). Rosemary Bennett, Oxford University Is Bottom of the Class for Accepting Poor Students.

Visvanathan, S. (2009). *The Search for Cognitive Justice*. http://www.india-seminar.com/2009/597/597_shiv_visvanathan.htm. Retrieved 3 October 2017.

West, L. (2016). *Distress in the City—Racism, Fundamentalism and a Democratic Education*. London: UCL, IOE Press.

Williams, R. (1961/2011). *The Long Revolution*. Swansea: Parthian Books.

Williams, in McIlroy and Westwood, 1993; p. 257. Article in *Adult Education and Social Change: Lectures and Reminiscences in Honour of Tony McLean*, WEA Southern District, 1983: pp. 9–24.

4

Keeping Going in Austere Times: The Declining Spaces for Adult Widening Participation in Higher Education in England

Lindsey Fraser and Kerry Harman

Introduction

A recent headline in the Guardian education section titled 'Part-time student numbers collapse by 56% in five years' (Fazackerley 2017) drew attention, yet again, to what some consider to be a crisis in English higher education. The article is the latest in a trail of higher education statistics and associated newspaper reports (e.g. Horrocks 2017; Pheonix 2017) which point to the drastic decline in part-time and mature student enrolments in higher education in England since the increase in the part-time fees cap in 2012 to £6750 per year. The increase in fees was the result of recommendations made in the Browne Report (2010) to lift the cap on universities fees and to shift the

L. Fraser (✉)
University of Leeds, Leeds, UK
e-mail: L.Fraser@leeds.ac.uk

K. Harman
Birkbeck, London, UK
e-mail: K.Harman@bbk.ac.uk

© The Author(s) 2019
E. Boeren and N. James (eds.), *Being an Adult Learner in Austere Times*,
https://doi.org/10.1007/978-3-319-97208-4_4

financial burden of funding higher education from the government to individual students. While the change in funding did not affect enrolments on full time degrees to the same extent, part-time numbers have plummeted over the past five years. According to Fazackerley (2017), there were 136,130 less part-time students in 2016 than in 2010. While it would be considered a catastrophe if fulltime, 18 year olds dropped out of the higher education system at these rates, the haemorrhage in part-time enrolments appears to have been largely ignored in the higher education policy arena.

We argue in this chapter that part-time and mature learners have become largely invisible in higher education policy, both at the national and institutional level, and we explore this using a widening participation lens. While the Higher Education Funding Council for England (HEFCE) stated in 2015 that widening participation was a key priority and that 'all those with the potential to benefit from successful participation in higher education (HE) should have the opportunity to do so' (HEFCE 2015), we contend there is now a default position in policy discourse whereby Widening participation equates to young people, unless otherwise stated. Current policy around widening participation in English universities is focussed on standard age applications and this is replicated in the research arena where there is a growing body of macro research concentrating on young people from backgrounds under-represented in higher education in relation to recruitment, retention and achievement. It appears that higher education is a right for some rather than **all** who might benefit.

We develop the argument in five parts. The first section of the chapter examines the higher education policy context in England with a focus on widening participation discourse in current policy documents. Next, we draw on Higher Education Statistics Agency (HESA) data in an effort to gain a better understanding of which groups are no longer accessing higher education at English universities. This is followed by a close-up analysis of a widening access programme at Birkbeck, which is part of the University of London, to examine enrolment trends over the past decade. Birkbeck has a long history of providing access to mature and part-time learners without traditional academic qualifications. As well as considering the effects of higher education policy on adult learners, we then extend the analysis to explore how cuts in public expenditure have had a detrimental effect on progression to higher education. This is illustrated by research undertaken at the University of Leeds in relation to their lifelong learning provision. Finally we explore developing practices at Leeds and Birkbeck which aim to support adult widening participation in these austere times and provide suggestions in terms of ongoing research and practice in widening participation.

The Higher Education Policy Context in England

A widening participation discourse sits at the centre of the recent White Paper on Higher Education (BIS 2016), with the Minister of State for Universities and Science announcing in the foreword that the proposals in the paper will:

> help to ensure that everyone with the potential to succeed in higher education, irrespective of their background, can choose from a wide-range of high quality universities, access relevant information to make the right choices, and benefit from excellent teaching that helps prepare them for the future. (p. 6, our emphasis)

However, on close reading of the White Paper, we suggest that by 'everyone', the Minister is not necessarily referring to adults. For example, the widening participation data provided in the White Paper only provides statistics for 'young students' entering higher education (under 21 years in fulltime study), which enables a more favourable picture to be presented in terms of increased access to higher education for under-represented groups since the introduction of increased fees for students in 2012. Moreover, a further analysis of the White Paper reveals that only 'young people' are referred to when discussing the ambition for widening participation in higher education. For example:

> 30. As a One Nation Government, we want to ensure that all **young people** with the potential to benefit have an opportunity to go to university. (p. 13, our emphasis)

While some goals outlined in the White Paper might suggest greater inclusion, as noted below,

> 31. The Prime Minister has set two specific, clear goals on widening participation in higher education: to double the proportion of people from disadvantaged backgrounds entering university in 2020 compared to 2009, and to increase the number of black and minority ethnic (BME) students going to university by 20% by 2020… (p. 14);

a later emphasis in the same point on 'young white males from lower socio-economic groups' (p. 14) returns the policy focus to 'young students'.

Furthermore, all the indications from government and the Office for Fair Access (OFFA) in relation to widening participation are that the monitoring age profile is that of 18 year olds. For example, the allocation of widening participation funding has followed this policy narrative, with a tranche of funding (30 million in 2016/2017, increasing to 60 million per annum from 2017/2018) distributed through the National Collaborative Outreach Programme (NCOP). This programme aims to: 'support the most disadvantaged **young** people in England to progress into higher education (HE)' (HEFCE 2017, our emphasis). Moreover, while OFFA has outlined concerns about inclusion, equality and diversity in relation to declining numbers of part-time students, the key benchmarks of interest to policy makers are associated with standard age students. For example, in the 2014–2015 English institutional Access Agreements, statutory for Higher Education institutions (HEIs) charging £6000 plus fees, only 12% of HEIs had any target relating to part-time student recruitment (OFFA 2015). As widening participation programmes and strategies within higher education institutions (HEIs) tend to follow the funding, this has reinforced the absence of mature learners in English higher education, both in policy and in enrolments.

Paradoxically, current policy and funding streams overlook evidence previously cited by OFFA, which points to a clear correlation between mature, part-time students and under-represented groups. OFFA states that mature students, aged 21 and over, as well as people studying part-time (over 90% of part-time students are mature) are more likely than younger learners to have characteristics associated with disadvantage and under-representation in higher education (OFFA 2015). OFFA also points out that mature learners are more likely to have non-traditional qualifications, to be located in lower socio-economic backgrounds and have family or caring responsibilities. Mature students are also more likely to have a disability, be from black and minority ethnic groups and leave higher education within a year of entering. The relationship between mature learners and disadvantage suggests this group should be a focus in widening participation policy rather than neglected.

This general absence of interest around mature learners in the policy context is replicated in the research arena. While there is a growing body of macro research concentrating on standard-age widening participation recruitment and different aspects of the student cycle and equality issues (e.g. Callender and Mason 2017; Harrison et al. 2015; Torgerson et al. 2014), there is a deficit in the literature in terms of examining these themes in relation to mature, disadvantaged learners. This is supported by research commissioned by OFFA examining the impact of financial support on access and student success in higher education which recommended more nuanced research which examines 'how specific groups of students respond to financial support' including students from 'part time, mature, specific minority ethnic communities and those from families whose household income is less than £15,000' (Nursaw Associates 2015, p. 38).

One notable exception is a collection of research on declining enrolments of part-time students, which can be found in a publication titled: 'It's the finance stupid!' (Hillman 2015). The edited book points to the impact of fee changes and loan systems introduced in 2012 following recommendations made in the Browne Review (Browne 2010). For example, Callender (2015) argues that the increase in fees has been a major deterrent to enrolling in higher education for mature and part-time students. More worryingly she identifies that:

> The falls have been greatest among older students, especially those aged 55 and over, those with low-level entry qualifications or none at all, and those studying less than 25 per cent of a full-time course who choose bite-size courses. These changes affecting the composition of the part-time student population, undermine part-time study's role in widening participation. (p. 18)

This point is reinforced by Butcher (2015), who concludes from an online survey of 1567 part-time students from across the UK as well as a sample of interviews with- that 'part-time higher education was not perceived as offering value for money and was considered barely affordable' (p. 50). Furthermore, in his forward to the book, Hillman asserts that the collapse in part-time study is 'arguably the single biggest problem facing higher education at the moment' (p. 4) and although there has been a great deal of concern expressed 'next-to-nothing' has been done about it.

More recently, however, there appears to have been some interest in the issue by policy makers, with the authors of this chapter engaged in an OFFA-commissioned study, which provides recommendations for evaluating outreach to mature, disadvantaged learners (Butcher et al. 2017). Indeed, the institutional case studies in this chapter were informed by quantitative and qualitative research arising from this project.

Data Which Points to the Decline in Enrolments of Mature Learners in Higher Education in England

While the absence of mature students might be overlooked in current policy and macro research on widening participation, an analysis of enrolment figures for mature learners in higher education in England, indicate that for those interested in social justice and the right for **all** groups who might benefit from accessing higher education, something has gone terribly wrong. Between 2010/2011 and 2014/2015, there was a 55% decrease (143,000 fewer entrants) in part-time enrolments in higher education in England, with a 10% drop (13,000 fewer enrolments) between 2013/2014 and 2014/2015 (Higher Education in England 2015). The table below, from a recent OFFA monitoring report (OFFA 2016), clearly demonstrates the disturbing trend in both mature and part-time numbers in English universities (Fig. 4.1).

A more fine grained analysis of the intersection between disadvantage, age and enrolment in higher education in England can be undertaken by examining the Higher Education Statistics Agency (HESA) data. The data reveal that in the 2010/2011 academic year 95,720

4 Keeping Going in Austere Times: The Declining Spaces... 77

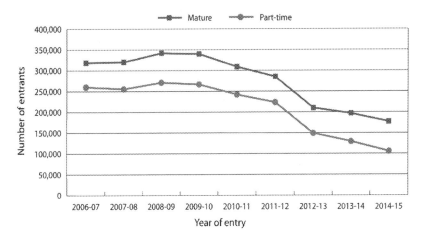

Fig. 4.1 Number of UK domiciled mature and part-time entrants in English institutions (*Source* Higher Education Statistics Agency: Widening participation performance indicators, Tables T2a and T2b)

mature students who had never been to university entered part-time study in higher education, and 16,965 were from low participation neighbourhoods. In 2013/2014 this had decreased to 49,775 entrants with no previous higher education, with 8890 from low participation neighbourhoods (HESA 2014). More recent figures point to ongoing decline. In 2015/2016, 36,735 mature students with no previous higher education experience enrolled in part-time study in England, with 7220 from low participation neighbourhoods.

A similar decline can be seen in the decrease in numbers of mature students with no previous university enrolled on other undergraduate programmes (i.e. programmes other than degrees). In 2010/2011 there were 26,295 students on other undergraduate programmes (with 3070 of these being from low participation neighbourhoods (LPNs) with no previous higher education) and this decreased to 10,455 students in 2015/2016 (with 1115 of these being LPN students with no previous higher education). In 2017, there was a dramatic fall with applications to full-time undergraduate programmes waning by 18% (a reduction of 10,200). These recent figures have led Les Ebdon, the Director of OFFA to remind the sector that:

> It is important that universities and colleges do all they can to support mature students. Not everybody wants to, or is able to, enter higher education straight after school, and it is crucial that a university's doors remain open for older students. Higher education is a life-changing opportunity and should be available to all with the talent to benefit from it, at whatever stage of their life they come to it. (THE 2017)

An Access Programme for Widening Participation Students at Birkbeck

But how are the national statistics playing out at the institutional and programme level? The Birkbeck case study examines the impact of increased student fees on the recruitment patterns and demographics of students enrolling on an access style programme at Birkbeck called Higher Education Introductory Studies (HEIS). The research on HEIS was conducted using institutional data on enrolment, retention and progression for students on HEIS between 2008/2009 and 2015/2016. This data is supplemented by interview data with nine students progressing from HEIS onto the BSc Social Sciences at Birkbeck. All students progressing to the degree were invited to participate in the interviews however only a small number of students took up the offer. Of the nine students interviewed, eight were either close to completing their degree programme or had already obtained their degree. One interviewee had discontinued their degree study. The interviews were approximately one hour in duration and students were asked about their experience of studying on HEIS and their degree programme. All the interviews were transcribed and analysed with a focus on identifying factors that contributed to their successful transition to degree study as well as the ways the programme could be enhanced.

Students successfully completing HEIS are awarded a Certificate in Higher Education and this nationally recognised level 4 qualification provides a pathway to degree programmes in business, arts and humanities, social sciences, nursing midwifery and health and social work. Various pedagogic techniques have been incorporated in the programme with the aim of supporting the successful 'transition' of students without university entrance qualifications to degree level study. These techniques could be loosely described as 'pedagogies for diversity and difference' (see David 2010).

The most significant trend in the institutional data on HEIS was the decline in enrolment on the programme after the introduction of increased fees following changes in government funding from 2012. Fees increased incrementally from £1000 in 2011/2012 to £6000 in 2014/2015 and they currently remain at this rate. Enrolments on HEIS peaked at 401 students in 2009/2010 and then declined significantly to 171 students in 2013/2014. Since then enrolments have been erratic. In 2014/2015 enrolments increased to 207, in 2015/2016 they decreased to 176 and in 2016/2017 enrolments increased again. They were still, however, less than 50% of the pre 2012/2013 enrolment figures, reflecting the decline in enrolments of part-time students across the UK. Institutional data on the percentage of students on HEIS broken down by age, ethnicity, gender and disability indicate little change between 2008/2009 and 2015/2016 suggesting the programme stills serves an important function in terms of providing access to students with widening participation characteristics. For example, in 2011/2012 approximately 70% of students were from BME groups with the same percentage of BME students enrolled in 2015/2016. Furthermore, when demographic data for HEIS students is compared with students enrolled on fulltime undergraduate degrees at Birkbeck, two key differences are revealed. First, HEIS students are older, with 60% HEIS students over 25 compared with 64% students enrolled on fulltime undergraduate degrees at Birkbeck now under 25. Second, HEIS students usually do not have formal qualifications in contrast to 61% Birkbeck full-time degree students having A levels.

Worryingly, the number of students in receipt of the Birkbeck bursary, which is an indicator of financial hardship and only available to low income students, reveals a lower percentage of low income students enrolling on HEIS post 2012. While institutional data on students in receipt of bursaries was not available between 2008/2009 and 2011/2012, we know that the majority of students enrolled on the programme were receiving a government subsidy available to low income students for part-time study (PTG1). Unfortunately, the government removed this subsidy in 2012. By 2015/2016, only 21% of HEIS students were in receipt of the Birkbeck bursary (a cash bursary available to low income students). This suggests that increased fees may be discouraging those on low income from applying.

Further evidence of the detrimental impact of fees on enrolments for mature learners has become available more recently. The announcement in the 2015 Government Spending Review (HM Treasury 2015) to discontinue bursaries for students on nursing degrees has resulted in a significant decline in enrolments on the Nursing pathway of study on HEIS. This is extremely problematic as this was one of the few part-time pathways available to students without formal qualifications and wanting to move into nursing degrees. Many of the students on this pathway work in (poorly paid) health care related roles and use the pathway as a way to develop their career.

As part of the research on successful transition to degree study, former HEIS students who had progressed to the BSc Social Sciences degree study at Birkbeck were interviewed. The focus of the interviews was not on fees, however this issue often arose when students were speaking about their study. Most of the students were philosophical about the increase in fees and going into debt. For example, one student said:

> I've put it to one side and not really let it affect [me]… cos there's nothing, there's no way of bypassing it….

However, students were far from pleased with the increase in fees:

> We live in a capitalist society. They don't want everyone with a degree, it's simple as that…I've spoken to people, they've done a degree, their fees were three thousand pounds or two thousand pounds, it's amazing but what can we do? I believe that one day there'll be a reform or something like that but I couldn't let it stop me. I had to go for it, you know.

This student was also sceptical about the introduction of the maintenance loan for part-time study:

> Hold on, they want to give maintenance loans so you end up in more debt?

An important finding was that the students interviewed felt that the institutional bursary had made an important difference to them being able to complete their studies:

> It eased, literally, the bursary…Like books cost money man, and literally, you've got to print pages now, five p, like it's five p, do that twenty-five times, it's a lot of money…So, it all adds up and the bursary… they'll probably get rid of that eventually, you know, that's the saddest.

The bursary had enabled another student to purchase a laptop, which provided her with more flexibility, particularly in terms of accessing digital learning resources. This was crucial as she was a sole parent and was also working part time:

> …How can somebody say it [the bursary] doesn't make difference? … Maybe they've never experienced being on a very low income and not having the money?

This provides a very different perspective to research findings, which question the importance of bursaries in encouraging widening participation at university (Ebdon 2016). For mature students on low income, the findings suggest that bursaries do make a difference in terms of easing the financial burden associated with studying in higher education.

In summary, the HEIS case study provides a close-up view of a more general phenomenon occurring across the UK, that is, the significant reduction in enrolment in higher education by mature learners from under-represented groups. Unfortunately, the case study reveals a similar pattern of declining enrolments of adult learners without formal qualifications, to the level where the future of this programme is uncertain. While demographics of students enrolling on the programme has remained relatively constant in the areas of age, gender, disability and ethnicity, it appears that low income students are much less likely to study on HEIS than previously. This is a disturbing trend. The HEIS case study echoes other research (e.g. Butcher 2015; Callender and Thompson 2018) indicating that the increase in fees has contributed to the decline in enrolments for this cohort of students. Furthermore, although a more systematic analysis is required, the case study suggests that financial support in the form of student bursaries for this particular cohort of learners is extremely helpful in enabling students to continue with their study, thus challenging a common view that financial support does not impact on ability to study in higher education.

The Broader Context—The Decline of Adult Education Provision

The Birkbeck case study illustrates the broader trend of the plummeting number of mature students without traditional qualifications accessing higher education. Whilst financial considerations are clearly a major factor as outlined by the independent Student Funding Panel (Universities UK 2015), and this has been further exacerbated by the demise of bursaries for nursing (UCAS 2017) and a decline in employer support for employees who are studying part-time (Mason 2014), one area that has not had attention is the impact of adult education cuts on mature student recruitment. Whether austerity measures, particularly those in the area of adult learning, which are essential in providing second chance pathways are likely to affect the number of low income mature learners accessing university education?

Whilst requiring further research, we propose that the closure of libraries, early years centres, voluntary and community sector organisations, the spaces where adult education activity has traditionally been offered, has had a detrimental impact on adults and parents accessing learning (OFSTED 2015, p. 69). For example in relation to higher education progression, the HEIS programme at Birkbeck had a flourishing partnership with community Sure Start Centres and had been running outreach at these centres for a number of years (Callender et al. 2014). Unfortunately, this innovative way of providing access to higher education to single parents is no longer available, in part due to reduced SureStart funding.

Furthermore, there is substantial evidence indicating public service cuts have a greater impact on those from social and economically deprived communities (Hastings et al. 2015). Since 2010, the adult skills budget, which funds vocational provision and community learning for those 19 or over, has been cut by 40%. Adult participation in further education post 2007 has reduced from 50 to 15%, with a drop of over 500,000 students aged 24 or more (National Institute for Adult and Continuing Education (NIACE) 2014b). The Association of Colleges has warned that adult education may not access any public funding by 2020. It is clear that this area has not been a priority for successive governments. The NIACE annual adult learning surveys reveal a pattern of declining participation and, worryingly, the greatest decrease are those with the least qualifications (2014b):

> Engagement in learning is not evenly distributed across society. In 2014, as in all previous years, the survey clearly shows that participation in learning is determined by social class, employment status, age and prior learning. Socio-economic class remains a key predictor of participation in learning. Around one-half of those in the higher classes [professional and managerial] have taken part in learning during the previous three years, compared with 34% of skilled manual workers and 25% of unskilled workers and people on limited incomes.

Moreover, a research report for the All Party Parliamentary Group for Adult Education (Hughes et al. 2016) provides evidence of the decline in adult participation in skills training as well as broader credit and non-credit bearing provision. It cites the reduced role by local authorities and the demise of University adult education departments or centres, giving the example of the Vaughan Centre for Lifelong Learning, University of Leicester, which has been disestablished.

Of particular interest to the widening participation in higher education agenda is community-based learning which provides accessible and inclusive educational opportunities in a familiar local environment, for example, early years centres and community centres where people with few or no qualifications are likely to feel more confident about engaging According to the Association of Colleges (AoC), there has been an increased allocation of funding for adult apprenticeships which has meant that the general adult education budget has been reduced and as a result, less community education available in England (AoC 2017).

Nationally, adult education providers indicate there is a government policy 'lopsided fixation' on both young people and apprenticeships, at the expense of other forms of adult education. Yet, the evidence base shows adult education often plays a significant role in reaching out and engaging people in learning through often outstanding partnerships with community groups, local authority departments and public services. (Hughes et al. 2016, p. 18)

Case Study 2: Outreach at Leeds

The adult education environment in Leeds mirrors the national picture. During the past ten years, the adult learning budget cuts have had a significant impact on community-based provision with the number of centres offering substantial adult programmes which actively support educational and training progression being decimated. In the further education sector, there has been a reduction from fourteen to three community-based centres. This has happened incrementally throughout the years, for example in 2015,

> In recent years, Leeds City College has had to look at reducing the number of community venues it operates out of as a result of continuing funding cuts to its adult budget. (College Spokesperson)

Many of the small providers involved in delivering community learning do not have the infrastructure or resource to expand curriculum which could enhance pathways and progression. Moreover, adult skills and community learning funding does not include community outreach and therefore is less likely to engage with non-participants (NIACE 2014a).

This is the context in which the University of Leeds Lifelong Learning Centre (LLC) has a remit of encouraging adults from low participation neighbourhoods to progress to higher education. This University has a long history of adult education in working class communities. For over thirty years there have been sustained partnerships with the local authority, Workers Education Association (WEA) and the voluntary sector. Prior to the 2012 fee changes in England, short course provision was a key mechanism for encouraging progression for adults from low participation communities. An example being the Islamic Studies programme, developed in 1996, which culminated in around 200 students per annum undertaking bite-sized credits in community centres throughout West Yorkshire. The remaining part-time provision targets adults in low paid employment or unemployed.

This case study utilises research data from the OFFA study, introduced previously. The methodology consisted of tracking data analysis as well as interviewing a sample of 14 mature students, who had arrived at the University via outreach activity. Residing in local neighbourhoods under-represented in higher education, this cohort did not possess traditional entry qualifications. Interviews indicated that attending community adult education had been a key driver in raising aspirations to progress further and commence higher education study. The provision delivered by providers such as at the local further education college community centres and the WEA was viewed as crucial in increasing potential choices and opportunities. According to those interviewed, community-based staff were extremely influential in raising confidence, self-esteem and providing encouragement:

> I know that I would have never ever have come if it hadn't of been for the tutor in the WEA class. I think she was the one that like planted the seed that it could even be possible.
>
> The teacher that actually taught us (community course) … is the only person that ever suggested that any of us could even think about a university. And we didn't believe her for ages either, I don't think. I mean, she just mentioned it and then we went to the study day and it just made it seem possible cos it never had before.

To many, the courses being situated in familiar locations, had been an essential factor. The offer of crèche provision was a catalyst for some returning to education—this support no longer being available. For others, the chance to socialise or to help their children with homework. Adult learning was also viewed as a second chance to gain their intermediate/level 2 qualifications to increase employment opportunities. The importance of community-based staff acting as support and signposters was a common theme, highlighting the role of a precariously-funded voluntary sector in providing guidance and support.

> I volunteered for a project in the Leeds City Centre, the lady there was amazing. She definitely believed in me and encouraged for me to pursue. But she definitely were like "Oh you could go to university" you know "I believe you could". And I'd just laugh it off.

The total randomness of people returning to adult education is a striking aspect of these interviews. Personal interactions were fundamental to participation. This included: family/friends, community-based workers, support workers or chance meetings.

> I got on the bus one day and I overheard a lady talking about a local centre that they had a crèche available and that finance was available for the crèche so people could do there GCSEs so I like, I interrupted her conversation and started asking her a whole bunch of questions.
>
> A couple of influences were the teaching assistants that worked in the school where I was a lunchtime supervisor, 'how did you get this job?' I found out I needed maths and English but then it weren't a big deal as they were doing a brush up your maths course at the local centre.

The arbitrary nature of opportunity is not surprising given the reported lack of advice or guidance. Careers advice at school was perceived as poor. Teachers were perceived as having low expectations families and carers, little knowledge of educational progression and interviewees generally felt they left school with limited opportunities. This brings into mind Helena Kennedy's maxim, 'if at first you don't succeed…you don't succeed' (Kennedy 1997, p. 21). There were mixed responses to whether families would have supported staying on in education, however, however a greater emphasis was put on earning and for some women, getting married. People were also influenced by friends and the wider community, *in the community that I lived in, not a lot of people pursued education.*

The lack of information, advice and guidance input continued for interviewees after leaving school. None had received careers or educational guidance…and there was a total lack of awareness about how these services could be accessed, *I definitely was confused with what education was available to me.* This point is cited by Hughes et al.

regarding their adult learner research which indicated a lack of knowledge about local provision and the fact that adults were not aware of services that may be available to them, leading Vine-Morris (cited in Hughes et al. 2016, p. 57) to conclude:

> More adults are in need of good quality information and guidance to help them make the right choices about the study options available to them, particularly those wanting to progress in work or looking for a career change. Adult education is vital on a lifelong basis and individuals need support to continue to learn and to acquire new skills in order to escape low pay jobs and to help businesses grow.

The research findings reinforce the impact of perennial structural economic, social and educational issues enhancing the probability of limiting people's potential. Even though the widening participation agenda has been in existence for over twenty years, for these interviewees, the notion of going to university had been a completely alien concept. Higher education was for people who '*were born into money*', for those who were '*well educated*' or '*absolutely brilliant*' and '*that would be from a different class from me*'.

Keeping Going, Finding Spaces

We have outlined existing hurdles to mature, low income students accessing higher education, including the lack of commitment in the policy arena to support part-time and mature students. However at an institutional level at Birkbeck and Leeds, there are initiatives to address these issues and to identify spaces in which we can continue to work with under-represented adults. For example, four-year integrated degrees, which incorporate a supported foundation year, have recently been introduced at Birkbeck in an effort to keep alternative pathways to degree study available to mature students without traditional academic qualifications. The additional cost of studying an extra year on the four year degrees may discourage low income mature students but this is being monitored by the college. Ideally, rather than the burden of the additional cost falling with the student, it would be preferable if the extra year could be written off the loan on successful completion of the degree, similarly to the +19 loans available in further education (GOV.UK 2017). Similar extended degrees in Leeds have bursaries attached to support both the recruitment and retention of students from widening participation backgrounds.

In terms of outreach work within the community, space for working with disadvantaged adult learners was recently established at Tottenham. Members from the widening participation team and academics at Birkbeck have been working in partnership with Haringey Council on the delivery of a range of outreach services at Tottenham, under the banner of 'Bridges to Birkbeck'. In 2016, 18 students enrolled on the HEIS programme at Tottenham and many of these students plan to progress to degree study at Birkbeck. Haringey Council made a generous contribution to the cost of programme fees as well as funding a community engagement officer who was based at Tottenham. The role of the community engagement officer has been vital to the success of the project as they were a key point of contact for those seeking to progress to higher education study.

There are also promising developments in collaborating with community groups working with asylum seekers via the Compass Programme. This programme provides scholarships to asylum seekers to commence study at Birkbeck. Asylum seekers are in an extremely difficult position in terms of accessing higher education in the UK as they are not eligible for the student loan and they are also not usually able to work until they gain refugee status. In an effort to overcome that obstacle, 20 fully funded scholarships have been made available to asylum seekers to commence study on Certificate programmes at Birkbeck.

There is a continuing commitment by the University of Leeds to supporting and resourcing the recruitment of mature students from under-represented backgrounds. This has been clearly evidenced by the Lifelong Learning Centre (LLC) being a key element in the University's widening participation strategy. A suite of targets that are reviewed on an annual basis pertaining to adult widening participation has been set by the University. These include outreach interventions, recruitment and retention. Funding for outreach activity is allocated from the institutional widening participation budget.

Local community adult engagement has been a key factor in the LLC maintaining its part-time degree recruitment numbers since changes in student fees in 2012, a contrast with part-time trends nationally. The LLC has worked hard with its partners to help alleviate the impact of budget cuts. An adult outreach framework, entitled 'Transforming Horizons', has been developed to articulate the work undertaken with adults from under-represented communities. The framework comprises three stages:

- initial links with non-formal learning and community groups
- engagement with adult GCSE groups (intermediate qualifications)
- preparation for progression to University foundation years and degree provision

As a means of countering adult education cuts, the LLC's outreach interventions include a range of non-accredited learning opportunities both in the community but also utilising campus as a space to bring together diverse groups of adults from all over the region. Research participants progressing to university had taken part in one or more outreach interventions. They talked about a '*drip, drip*' effect and the need to take '*tiny steps*' in raising confidence, self-esteem and self-belief. In other words, that going to university is a possibility:

> Yeah I think that contact is important because things can get in the way. Life gets in the way, you know, we have problems and stuff. But the fact that I was invited to this and then invited to that and then I'm going to progress to having a meeting, a one to one, it's given me like a pathway.
> I think Jumpstart (a 10 week non accredited course delivered by the LLC) were the key point where I actually thought, 'Yea, I could do this. It could be for me'. I think if I hadn't done a course like this I would have still been something that would have just been a discussion rather than actually coming to University.

As the case studies suggest, this type of work is resource intensive. Outreach activity is much more complex with adults than it is with young people where schools are the obvious connection point. However, at present, school-university collaboration seems to be the focus of government policy and funding in the area of widening participation in higher education in England. So how might outreach with adults be encouraged? In our view there is a requirement for a more directive approach by the decision-makers. In England, Access Participation Plans which monitor institutional annual resource allocation for widening participation activity and related targets, could be more prescriptive in demanding mature student recruitment targets, apportioning some widening participation budget to adult outreach and community engagement. As part of the widening participation agenda, there is a drive for universities to sponsor secondary schools, this concept could be extended to community-based adult education programmes.

Conclusion

The chapter provides further evidence that the fall in part-time and mature student numbers is clearly associated with the changes to student finance in 2012/2013. We also propose that the ongoing decline in enrolments in higher education of mature students without formal qualifications, who are often in poorly paid employment or unable to find employment, demonstrates the failure to engage with this issue in the policy arena. Our analysis of the absence of this agenda in key widening participation policy documents supports this view. Furthermore, there is an absence of widening participation research which examines access to and successful retention and progression of disadvantaged mature learners in higher education.

We have also introduced an argument that increased fees are not the sole cause for declining enrolments. We propose that budget cuts in other sectors have contributed to declining enrolments of widening participation mature and part-time learners in higher education. And this is where it starts to become more complex in terms of policy. While further empirical research is needed to validate the relationship between declining numbers of mature students without formal qualifications in higher education and public sector cuts, the initial findings from the research at Leeds point in that direction. The broader infrastructure that provided routes into higher education for these students is no longer in place. If those developing policy genuinely want to encourage mature learners to enrol in higher education, particularly those on low income, then these intersecting policy domains need to be examined in terms of the way they overlap.

Furthermore, rather than only identifying problems, we have also explored potential spaces and possibilities in terms of ensuring pathways to higher education remain open to mature learners from low income backgrounds in austere times. The areas discussed in the case studies above provide examples of how this type work can be organised. Further case studies are available in the recent report to OFFA (Butcher et al. 2017). There is also a wealth of adult education research, which provides a useful resource for widening participation practitioners in university planning to work with adult learners in the community (Crowther et al. 2005; McGivney 2000; Tett 2005).

Should policy makers be worried about the decline in enrolments of mature learners without formal qualifications? The decline in numbers of second chance learners and the connection with social mobility has been raised (Major 2018). Pragmatically, the fact that there are fewer younger people in the UK, coupled with growing skills shortages, which are likely to be further exacerbated by Brexit, policy makers should give credence to the importance of increasing the recruitment of mature students to higher education. Furthermore, following popular discourse espoused by the government that higher education is a means of enhancing social mobility for those from low income and disadvantaged backgrounds, then this would seem advantageous in terms of economics. And finally, pathways into degree study should remain available to **all** who might benefit from attending university.

References

Association of Colleges. (2017, January 13). *Briefing for MPs, Night Schools and Adult Education*. Retrieved from: https://www.aoc.co.uk/media-andparliament/our-work-mps/briefings-mps.
Browne, J. (2010). *Securing a Sustainable Future for Higher Education: An Independent Review of Higher Education Funding and Student Finance.*

Retrieved from: http://webarchive.nationalarchives.gov.uk/+/hereview.independent.gov.uk/hereview/.

Butcher, J. (2015a). Listen to Part-Time Learners and Smart Policy Will Follow. In N. Hillman (Ed.), *It's the Finance, Stupid! The Decline of Part-Time Higher Education and What to Do About It* (pp. 48–56). Oxford: Higher Education Policy Institute.

Butcher, J. (2015b). *'Shoe-Horned And Sidelined'? Challenges for Part-Time Learners in the New HE Landscape*. York: Higher Education Academy.

Butcher, J., Fraser, L., Harman, K., & Sperlinger, T. (2017). *Understanding the Impact of Outreach on Access to Higher Education for Adult Learners from Disadvantaged Backgrounds: An Institutional Response*. Retrieved from: https://www.offa.org.uk/wp-content/uploads/2017/07/Final-Report-Understanding-the-impact-of-outreach-on-access-to-higher-education-for-disadvantaged-adult-learners-docx.pdf.

Callender, C. (2015). Putting Part-Time Students at the Heart of the System? In N. Hillman (Ed.), *It's the Finance, Stupid! The Decline of Part-Time Higher Education and What to Do About It* (pp. 16–24). Oxford: Higher Education Policy Institute.

Callender, C., Hawkins, E., Jackson, S., Jamieson, A., Land, H., & Smith, H. (2014). *'Walking Tall': A Critical Assessment of New Ways of Involving Student Mothers in Higher Education*. Retrieved from: http://www.bbk.ac.uk/cscthe/projects/Nuffield%20Report%2019%20March%202014.pdf.

Callender, C., & Mason, G. (2017, May). Does Student Loan Debt Deter Higher Education Participation? New Evidence from England. *The ANNALS of the American Academy of Political and Social Science, 671*, 20–48. https://doi.org/10.1177/0002716217696041.

Callender, C., & Thompson, J. (2018, March). *The Lost Part-Timers: The Decline of Part-Time Undergraduate Higher Education in England*. The Sutton Trust.

College Spokesperson. (2015). *Leeds City College Centres at Armley, Meanwood and Morley Could Be Axed*. Retrieved from: https://www.yorkshireeveningpost.co.uk/news/leeds-city-college-centres-at-armley-meanwood-and-morley-could-be-axed-1-7321838.

Crowther, J., Galloway, V., & Martin, I. (Eds.). (2005). *Popular Education: Engaging the Academy: International Perspectives*. Leicester: National Institute of Adult Continuing Education.

David, M. E. (2010). *Improving Learning By Widening Participation in Higher Education*. London: Routledge.

Department for Business Innovation and Skills. (2016). *Success as a Knowledge Economy: Teaching Excellence, Social Mobility and Student Choice* (BIS/16/265). London. Retrieved from: https://www.gov.uk/government/uploads/system/uploads/attachment_data/file/523396/bis-16-265-success-as-a-knowledge-economy.pdf.

Ebdon, L. (2016). It's Time for Bursaries to Demonstrate Their Impact. Retrieved from: http://wonkhe.com/blogs/its-time-for-bursaries-to-demonstrate-real-impact/. Accessed 17 April 2017.

Fazackerley, A. (2017, 2 May). Part-Time Student Numbers Collapse by 56% in Five Years. *The Guardian*. Retrieved from: https://www.theguardian.com/education/2017/may/02/part-time-student-numbers-collapse-universities.

GOV.UK. (2017). *Advanced Learner Loan*. Retrieved from: https://www.gov.uk/advanced-learner-loan.

Harrison, N., Chudry, F., Waller, R., & Hatt, S. (2015). Towards a Typology of Debt Attitudes Among Contemporary Young UK Undergraduates. *Journal of Further and Higher Education, 39*(1), 85–107.

Hastings, A., Bailey, G., Bramley, G., & Gannon, M. (2015). *The Costs of the Cuts: Their Impact on Local Government and Poorer Communities*. York: Joseph Rowntree Foundation. http://www.jrf.org.uk/publications/cost-cutsimpact-local-government-and-poorercommunities.

HEFCE (Higher Education Funding Council). (2015). *Higher Education in England 2015: Key Facts*. Retrieved from: http://www.hefce.ac.uk/media/HEFCE,2014/Content/Analysis/HE,in,England/HE_in_England_2015.pdf. Accessed 10 June 2016.

HEFCE. (2017). *National Collaborative Outreach Programme (NCOP)*. Retrieved from: http://www.hefce.ac.uk/sas/ncop/.

HESA (Higher Education Statistics Agency). (2014). Higher Education Student Enrolments and Qualifications Obtained at Higher Education Providers in the United Kingdom 2013/14 (Press Release). Retrieved from: https://www.hesa.ac.uk/sfr210. Accessed 10 June 2016.

Hillman, N. (Ed.). (2015). *It's the Finance, Stupid! The Decline of Part-Time Higher Education and What to Do About It*. Oxford: Higher Education Policy Institute.

HM Treasury. (2015). *Spending Review and Autumn Statement*. Retrieved from: https://www.gov.uk/government/topical-events/autumn-statement-and-spending-review-2015.

Horrocks, P. (2017, October 12). Mature and Part-Time Students: The Real Crisis of the High Fees Era. *Times Higher Education*. Retrieved from: https://www.timeshighereducation.com/blog/mature-and-part-time-students-real-crisis-high-fees-era.

Hughes, D., Adriaanse, K., & Barnes, S.-A. (2016). *Adult Education: Too Important to Be Left to Chance*. Retrieved from: https://www2.warwick.ac.uk/fac/soc/ier/research/adult_education/dh_adult_education_full_report.pdf.

Kennedy, H. (1997). *Learning Works: Widening Participation in Further Education*. Coventry: Further Education Funding Council.

Major, L. (2018). *18,000 Fewer Mature Students Apply to University Sine Fees Increase*. Retrieved from: https://www.suttontrust.com/newsarchive/18000-fewer-mature-students-apply-university-since-fees-increase/.

Mason, G. (2014). Part-Time Higher Education: Employer Engagement Under Threat? *Higher Education Quarterly, 68*, 305–307.

McGivney, V. (2000). *Recovering Outreach: Concepts: Issues and Practices*. Leicester: NIACE.

NIACE. (2014a). *Reaching and Engaging Disadvantaged Groups in and Through Community Learning*. Retrieved from: http://www.learningandwork.org.uk/wp-content/uploads/2017/01/Reaching-and-engaging-guide-FINAL.pdf.

NIACE. (2014b). *Adult Participation in Learning Survey*. Retrieved from: http://shop.niace.org.uk/media/catalog/product/2/0/2014_headline_findings_final_web_2.pdf.

Nursaw Associates. (2015). *What Do We Know About the Impact of Financial Support on Access and Student Success?* Retrieved from: https://www.offa.org.uk/wp-content/uploads/2015/03/Literature-review-PDF.pdf.

OFFA (Office for Fair Access). (2015). *Topic Briefing: Mature Students*. Retrieved from: https://www.offa.org.uk/universities-and-colleges/guidance-and-useful-information/topic-briefings/offa-topic-briefing-mature-learners/. Accessed 10 June 2016.

OFFA (Office for Fair Access). (2016). *Outcomes of Access Agreement Monitoring for 2014–2015*. Bristol: OFFA. Retrieved from: https://www.offa.org.uk/wp-content/uploads/2016/05/2016.04-Outcomes-of-access-agreements-monitoring-1.pdf. Accessed 10 June 2016.

OFSTED. (2015). *The Annual Report of Her Majesty's Chief Inspector of Education, Children's Services and Skills 2014/15*. London: OFSTED.

Pheonix, D. (2017, June 6). How to Stop the Continuing Decline of Mature Students. *Huffington Post*. Retrieved from: http://www.huffingtonpost.co.uk/dave-pheonix/how-to-stop-the-continuin_b_16956218.html.

Tett, L. (2005). Partnerships, Community Groups and Social Inclusion. *Studies in Continuing Education, 27*(1), 1–15.

THE. (2017). Reaction: UK Higher Education Sector Responds to UCAS Application Figures. *Times Higher Education*. Retrieved from: https://www.

timeshighereducation.com/blog/reaction-uk-higher-education-sector-responds-ucas-application-figures. Accessed 7 March 2017.
Torgerson, C., Gascoine, L., Heaps, C., Menzies, V., & Younger, K. (2014). *Higher Education Access: Evidence of Effectiveness of University Access Strategies and Approaches.* Retrieved from: https://www.suttontrust.com/wp-content/uploads/2015/12/Higher-Education-Access-Report.pdf.
Universities UK. (2015). *Patterns and Trends in UK Higher Education 2015.* Retrieved from: http://www.universitiesuk.ac.uk/policy-and-analysis/reports/Documents/2015/patterns-and-trends-2015.pdf.

Kerry Harman is Programme Director for Higher Education Introductory Studies (HEIS) at Birkbeck, an access programme for mature students without A level, or equivalent, qualifications. She is interested in social change and transformation in Higher Education.

5

Mature Students and Social Isolation: Being Excluded or Choosing to Be Alone?

Charlie E. Sutton

Introduction: Age in an Undergraduate Context

Researcher: "Have you changed?"
Rebecca, aged 40+: "I haven't changed enough. I think my expectations were off. It hasn't been what I thought it would be. It is actually a lot more isolating than I thought it was going to be … I mean I didn't expect to be everyone's buddy, everyone's friend, you know there is a massive age difference. I knew that, but nobody will talk to you".

Most students have fears about fitting in when starting university. For many this subsides as they adapt to their learning environment and become familiar with their peers and the wider student community.

C. E. Sutton (✉)
University of Leicester, Leicester, UK
e-mail: Ces47@le.ac.uk

© The Author(s) 2019
E. Boeren and N. James (eds.), *Being an Adult Learner in Austere Times*,
https://doi.org/10.1007/978-3-319-97208-4_5

However, with a gap in their educational career, and often with different layers of responsibilities, mature students can feel this fear more acutely than their younger peers, as demonstrated in the above account. Their ability to adapt can be complicated by personal responsibilities, but also by the risks they have taken in returning to education. A dominance of traditional-aged students on a course, or within an institution, can also mean that mature students feel unable to integrate socially. Both attitudes and the design of university life can have an impact on students who become isolated.

This chapter explores social isolation amongst a group of students, of varied ages, during the first semester of their undergraduate degree. The views and experiences are drawn from the preliminary findings from a longitudinal mixed methods study on student experience, which focusses on one pre-1992 university, in England. The main discussion relates to this difference in experiences of social isolation and how experiences appeared to be directly influenced by a student's age. This issue may be particularly important in understanding why mature students drop-out of university. The Higher Education Statistics Agency (HESA) reports that mature students, on average, drop out of UK universities at around twice the rate of traditional-aged students (2009/2010, 2012/2013, 2014/2015). The persistence of this level of drop-out is concerning. Therefore, it is important to gain an understanding of the factors that influence students to leave university, before completing their studies.

Firstly, the policy context of mature students in higher education will be explored. Then the discussion will turn to the mature student population and patterns of participation by age. The next section will consider what is already known about mature students' decisions to drop-out and the factors that influence these decisions. Finally, the experiences of the students involved in this research will be explored to understand how experiences of social isolation can impact on students' ability to complete their degree.

The Policy Context: Mature Students and Higher Education

Mature students appear to have slipped from UK widening participation agendas in recent years. Since the late 1990s policy changes to widening participation funding have detracted attention from mature students towards younger students from lower socio-economic groups (Smith 2009). The coalition government underlined this shift in their comments when they launched their social mobility strategy 'Opening Doors, Breaking Barriers' (2011). The focus of this strategy was intergenerational social mobility: *'ensuring that everyone has a fair chance to get a better job than their parents'* (Deputy Prime Minister's Office 2011), which seems to suggest that young people were the focus of widening participation. However, a year later, the Department for Business Innovation and Skills (2012) claimed that they were committed to widen participation to everyone able to study in higher education, which prompted some scepticism about the Government's perception of the value of adult learning (Smith 2009).

The most recent white paper on higher education, 'Success as a knowledge economy: Teaching Excellence, Social Mobility and Student Choice' (2016), encourages higher education institutions (HEIs) towards internationalisation (Knight 2013), but also maintains a commitment to widen participation for home students. However, whether mature students are actually included within this discussion of widening participation is questionable, reinforcing a worrying pattern. As in the 'Opening Doors' strategy, mature students appear to be missing in the new white paper's (2016) discussion of higher education provision. Instruction is vague, with the paper seeming to suggest that institutions carry on supporting widening participation groups in the same way as they had previously. A worrying development here is that whilst the word 'young' is used fairly frequently in student descriptions in this white paper and the word 'mature' is notably absent. So, whilst pressure remains on institutions to control student drop-out, with no visible proviso for mature students in place, how institutions will respond to the white paper's (2016) vague widening participation guidance, is an issue for concern.

Whilst recruiting mature students presents retention risks, particularly in the current higher education climate, in the past it was hoped that their increased involvement could help sustain the expansion of higher education (Richardson 1994). This proved to be a fruitful plan. For example, in 1979/1980 full-time UK students over 21 only comprised 13% of new undergraduates (Squires 1981). Gorard et al. (2007) noted that a 55% increase in the participation of older learners was visible between 1981 and 1989. But the withdrawal of the older students' allowance (Gorard et al. 2007) and the introduction of variable fees in 2004, presented a rather bleak picture for the recruitment of mature students, due to their financial vulnerabilities (McGivney 1996). Further difficulties were feared by the tripling of the upper limit fee cap to £9000 per year in England in 2012, which threatened to price many students out of higher education participation (Burns 2012) and unravel widening participation gains in equalising access into higher education (Hinton-Smith 2012).

However, as will be discussed in the next section, full time mature students have shown themselves to be a resilient group in terms of enrolment in higher education, maintaining their proportion of the student population. This is in direct contrast to part-time mature students, whose numbers have declined considerably (HEFCE 2016). It is also evident that much has changed in terms of age-related policy in the UK, with age becoming a protected characteristic in the Equality Act (Her Majesty's Government 2010). The demands of the economy have been directly affected by the increasing amount of people living into very old age (Thane 2005). So with people living longer, healthier lives, the structure of employment needed to be more age-neutral, so that people could prolong their working lives (Equality Act 2010). Raising the age of retirement, from age 60 for women and 65 for men, up to 67 by 2044 (Her Majesty's Government 2007), was necessary to ensure that there would be state pensions for future generations. Education may benefit from these changes, providing opportunities for people to improve their skills, or change their career completely, because they now have to work for longer.

Aside from funding the national pension scheme, it is evident that people approaching retirement and those beyond retirement age, are eager to actively engage in employment (Department for Work and Pensions 2017) and education (University of the Third Age 2014). The changes in the Equality Act (2010) meant, that a person was protected from discrimination because of their age, both in employment and in the provision of services. It seems appropriate, therefore, that this legislation should have also had an impact on higher education provision, creating an environment where age has less of an influence on students' experiences. Whilst mature students are not specifically mentioned in the scope of widening participation in the recent white paper on higher education, there is a commitment to equal access and support for all, as seen in Jo Johnson's opening statement (Her Majesty's Government 2016, p. 6):

> everyone with the potential to succeed in higher education, irrespective of their background, can choose from a wide range of high quality universities, access relevant information to make the right choices, and benefit from excellent teaching that helps prepare them for the future.

In the next section, we will look at how mature students fit into the university population. Firstly, it is important to understand if age discrimination legislation has changed the way that institutions approach the delivery of higher education, to make it more age neutral to attract and improve the retention of mature students. Secondly, if this is not the case and age-related barriers remain, it might be possible that this might result in increasing rates of drop-out, as these barriers may be coupled with reduced widening participation support for mature students. Finally, with part-time entrants dropping and full-time study becoming the mainstay for mature students accessing higher education, there is also the potential for increased drop-out. This is because students who would have usually chosen part-time routes, face the increased pressure of full time study, often alongside paid employment or other responsibilities.

The Higher Education Population: Patterns of Mature Student Participation

As mentioned in the last section, despite the odds, full-time mature students have continued to apply to university, seemingly unperturbed by fees. The Higher Education Funding Council for England (HEFCE) show the overall increase in the numbers of full time mature students since 2002/2003 in Fig. 5.1. Although the hike in fees, from around £3000 per year to around £9000 per year (National Institute for Adult and Continuing Education (NIACE) 2014), had some effect on full time mature student enrolment, this was somewhat hidden by the overall drop in student applications. The numbers of full-time mature student applications in England, fell between 2010–2014, by 14% (NIACE 2014), but as applications for traditional-aged students also fell, mature students maintained their general proportion of the student population at around 20% (HESA 2012, 2013, 2014, 2015).

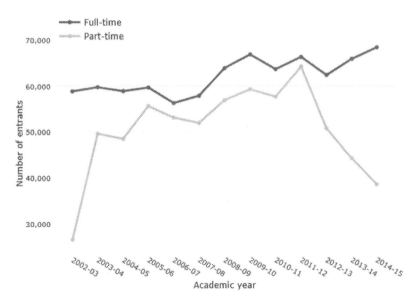

Fig. 5.1 Mature first degree entrants (*Source* HEFCE, 2016. *Note* UK-dominated students at Hefce-funded HEIs only)

The hardest hit were part-time applications where there was a dramatic drop in the number of mature students (40%) following this hike in fees. Dips in the number of full-time mature students are evident in 2006–2007, 2010–2011, and 2012–2013, but overall there was a fairly steady rise in the numbers of mature full-time first degree entrants.

HESA data (HESA 2013, 2014, 2015) confirms that the proportion of UK full-time mature students in the student population, nationally, has remained fairly static at around 20% of all students (2011–2012 20%, 2012–2013 21%, 2013–2014 21%). With recent figures highlighting a drop in total enrolment across higher education in the UK (HESA 2016a, b), a returned focus on mature students may help to make up the shortfall in numbers, in the same way as their involvement helped to sustain the expansion of higher education in the past (Richardson 1994).

However, it could be argued that mature students experience differential access into higher education. For example, higher education may become more inaccessible the longer people are out of education. Information from the Access to HE Diploma course, which is a primary route into higher education for many mature students, helps us to consider patterns of participation according to different age groups. Enrolment details from Access to HE annual reports (QAA 2011–2016), presented in Table 5.1, show that enrolment according to age groups has remained fairly static across the five years reported. There has been a slow but

Table 5.1 Age of Access to HE students, on enrolment

Access to HE diploma: Key statistics 2010–2014					
Age group	2010–2011 (%)	2011–2012 (%)	2012–2013 (%)	2013–2014 (%)	2014–2015 (%)
19 and under	11.8	12	13	13	14
20–24	35.1	37	38	37	36
25–29	19.5	19	19	20	20
30–34	13.5	13	13	13	13
35–39	9.6	9	8	8	8
40–44	6.1	6	5	5	5
45–49	2.9	3	3	3	3
50+	1.5	1	1	1	1

Adapted from Access to HE key statistics 2010–2016

steady increase in the number of younger students in the age 19 and under group, since 2010. This rise is set against a very gradual drop (1%) in the proportions of students in the 35–39 age group and 40–44 group. There is also fluctuation in the number of students in the most common age group (age 20–24) for Access to HE students (3% variation).

So whilst it is evident here that older mature students continue to be much less likely to engage in an Access to HE course than younger mature students, this appears to be a well-established pattern, seemingly unaffected by the introduction of the age discrimination legislation.

Policy reports such as the Leitch Review (HM Treasury 2006), suggest that adults should be skilled to graduate level or above, to ensure a strong economy. The long-term consequences of policies, such as these, raise concerns about the direction adult education has to take in order to meet these requirements. For example, Wolf (2002) argues that requirements for all adults to be skilled to certain educational levels tends to focus on secondary education rather than the post-compulsory system. This means that educational strategies can ignore those adults who need to reskill and focus largely on young people, who are still in education, as they approach adulthood. Field (2006) also highlights that not only do the unskilled face diminishing opportunities but, in effect, they hold back the pace of change, affecting the scope of success in a knowledge society. By failing to focus opportunities towards unskilled adults, beyond compulsory education, this neglects the contribution that they could make to the economy and wider society. It could be argued that many unskilled adults are simply written off, because they appear much harder to reskill. This is certainly echoed by the high drop-out levels for mature students, which may be put down to the difficulties they face when re-entering education.

For those that do go to university, as a mature student, it is important to consider both their initial engagement and what happens whilst they negotiate their studies at university. This might explain why the numbers of mature students who enter higher education and drop-out, is at around twice the rate of younger learners (HESA 2012). In 2012/2013, only 6% of traditional aged students dropped out, whilst mature students dropped out at a rate of 12%. Whilst comparisons are difficult from a policy perspective, filling up a predicted student short-fall with students who appear to be more likely to fail presents a risky strategy. Uncovering the reasons behind drop out, may help to highlight strategies to reduce the likelihood of failure for mature students in higher education.

Reviewing the Literature: Factors that Lead to Failure

There is a well-established body of literature which provides a range of explanations as to why mature students continue to drop out in such proportions. For example, well recognised barriers which can cause mature students to drop out are financial responsibilities (Burton et al. 2011; Gonzáles-Arnal & Kilkey 2009), caring responsibilities (Mannay and Morgan 2013) and problems adapting to study in higher education (Foster 2009). The proximity of HEIs is also underlined as important for many mature students (Elliot and Brna 2009), often because of the complexity of personal and financial responsibilities (James et al. 2013).

Despite the wealth of literature which highlights these issues, the consistency of non-continuation patterns from HESA suggests that little progress has been made to help to reduce the impact these barriers have on mature students. The body of research on strategies which tackles these barriers is often from small scale, case study research, which limits their generalisability. It is suggested that recognised barriers for mature students can be counter-acted or may change over time. For example Burton et al. (2011) found that financial barriers were not significant when bursaries and grants were available and students appeared well prepared and organised in gaining childcare support from extended family. Although this case study used a small sample of students from higher education courses in care, within one further education setting, it demonstrates that some of the significant barriers that influence mature students to drop-out, can be reduced or eliminated.

There are some successful strategies illustrated in the literature that appear to help mature students adapt. The results of a university e-mentoring scheme, was seen to help Access to HE students' transition more confidently into higher education (Edirisingha 2009). It is acknowledged that adaptation remains a difficult hurdle for mature students to overcome, but one that might be overcome by informal institutional support (Foster 2009; Burton et al. 2011) both before and during study. However, the scarcity of research on successful strategies to tackle adaption issues, suggests that more could be done in this area.

Many students have fears about adapting and fitting into university life, regardless of their age, as many of the factors associated with starting university are seen to cause loneliness and isolation (Rokach 1988, cited in Doman and Roux 2010): leaving home, starting a new career, being separated from loved ones, moving house, poor academic performance, a lack of feelings of belonging, intimacy and support. However, Doman and Roux (2010) maintain that young people aged 18–25 appear to be more prone to loneliness, suggesting that adaptation problems should be more evident for traditional-aged and young mature students.

So whilst isolation is not just a mature student problem, the time it takes to adapt, and for isolation to diminish, might be significant here. For many students, feelings of isolation subside as they quickly adapt to their learning environment and become familiar with peers and the wider student community. With a gap in their educational career, and often with different layers of responsibilities, mature students may often feel this fear more acutely than their younger peers. This might place more importance on their need to feel that they belong (Reay 2004; Read et al. 2003).

Adaptation can also be affected by factors relating to background (Bourdieu 1986), the practicalities of attending (Elliot and Brna 2009) and the risks students have taken in returning to education. The dominance of traditional-aged students can also mean that mature students may feel unable to integrate socially, due to the design of university life, the attitudes of their peers (Foster 2009) and as well as their own deep-seated concerns about being different. Difficulties in adapting and being isolated as a learner are largely viewed in the literature as having a negative impact (Ryan and Glenn 2004; Doman and Roux 2010), though research detailing this issue is limited. A more in-depth understanding of student adaptation, particularly in relation to different-aged students, may help to determine why isolation occurs, how it can persist and what impact it may have on decisions to drop-out. As much of the literature pre-dates the age discrimination legislation, it is difficult to see what impact it has had on students in higher education. The barriers that effect mature students may still seem to be significant, however, because drop-out rates remain high.

Methods

The observations in this chapter are drawn from an active piece of longitudinal research on the experiences of different-aged undergraduate students. The research focuses on a single cohort of full-time undergraduates who started their degree at one, pre-1992, English university in the 2015/2016 academic year. The main aim of the research was to explore whether age matters in higher education, specifically looking at whether motivation, barriers and adaptation differed according to the age of students. Mixed methods were chosen so that experience could be viewed across the breadth of this student cohort as well as at the level of individual experience. A pragmatic approach was taken in the design of the research, as the practical focus aligned well with the use of a range of methods (Morgan 2014; Baert 2005). Whilst this research will eventually cover the full three years of these undergraduate students degree, this chapter reports on one of the most notable preliminary findings from the students first year and focuses on a set of in-depth interviews undertaken with them.

Sampling was done through a large-scale questionnaire survey, conducted in the first two weeks of the academic year with 828 students. Twelve departments were invited to participate, selected according to the age profile of their new students. Courses were selected where there was a good cross section of ages and other courses where there were very few mature students in the cohort. Subjects with different sized cohorts were also targeted, to understand whether the size of the peer group had an effect on students' experiences. A diverse range of academic subjects was selected, from both science and arts disciplines, so that these differences could also be considered.

Eight departments agreed to take part in the survey phase of the study: Biology, Computing, Criminology, History, Law, Natural Science, Psychology, and Sociology. For seven of these departments, a first impressions questionnaire was handed to students when they entered introductory lectures and completed before their lecture started. All students in attendance completed these questionnaires (n. 795). An online version of the questionnaire was made available to the other department at their request. This generated another 33 responses from a potential 200 first year students enrolled in this department. As this chapter deals with the experiences of being an adult learner, and there were limited numbers of mature students completing the questionnaire survey, statistics based on the larger groups will not be presented here. The findings section focuses on the qualitative phase of the project only.

Students completing the questionnaires were invited to take part in the qualitative phase of research, which looked at individual students' experiences, using semi-structured interviews and diary entries. As this phase used quota to control for age, students who declared an interest in taking part were selected according to their age, but also controlled according to discipline, to see if this had any effect on experience.

There were 228 expressions of interest received for this phase, which were declared on the survey questionnaires. Only home students were included in the second phase sample and participants were recruited as detailed in Table 5.2. As only a few of the mature students who expressed an interest in taking part, responded to the recruitment email, it was only possible to recruit both mature students and traditional-aged students within three disciplines: Biology, Psychology and History.

Table 5.2 Participation in the interview and diary phase

Age group	Interest	Contacted	Agreed to participate
18–20 years	150	19	4
21–24 years	13	13	1
25–29 years	4	4	1
30–39 years	2	2	1
40+ years	5	5	3

Participants were all interviewed midway through their first semester and most were interviewed again, towards the end of the second semester. These semi structured interviews were based on questions relating to students' motivations, barriers and adaptions. For example, they were always asked about the 'highlights' of that term, which generally resulted in students explaining their achievements, modules they had found interesting, or activities they had enjoyed in university societies or sports teams. Often these highlights helped them to stay motivated or aided their adaptation to the demands of study. They were also asked about the 'lowlights', which, in general, revealed the barriers they had faced that term or the difficulties they had experienced in adapting. They were also asked to use an on-line diary form on a regular basis. The fields in the diary form were updated on a monthly basis to ensure that it was sensitive to the time period. Question fields were made relevant to starting a new term or experiences during exam periods, for example. Once collected, interview and diary data were coded, according to the themes found in the literature. Additional codes were added as other themes became apparent.

Findings

Isolation emerged as a significant finding from data collected in the first semester. Interviews and diary entries revealed that mature students were more likely to experience continued social isolation during their first semester, than their traditional-aged counterparts. In addition, whilst all mature students gave accounts of feeling like an isolated learner, for some mature students this was expressed as a choice made in order to successfully adapt to the academic demands of university: a coping strategy to help them manage their time effectively. For others this was expressed as a barrier: a result of their social exclusion by their younger peers, alongside other factors relating to the social environment and attitudes within the institution.

Age appeared to be a key factor in whether social isolation dissipated, continued or became magnified during the course of their first year. The traditional-aged (18–20) students in the sample reported feeling isolated in their first few days, but most explained that once they had attended their lectures, classes and fresher's events, they found they quite quickly developed a new social network. These networks were seen to be supportive, both academically and personally. They also seemed to be an integral part of their enjoyment at university.

Conversely, the mature students in the sample, who also felt isolated in the first few days, were more likely to continue feeling like an isolated learner and less likely to assimilate into social networks at university. Their search for someone 'like them' is a feature of all the mature students in this study. However, as will be outlined in the next section, the discussion of isolation was varied. For some mature students, particularly the younger ones, social isolation was actively chosen, initially, as a coping strategy. For others this was expressed as a result of how their younger peers made them feel, alongside other institutional factors.

Isolation as a Coping Strategy

All of the mature students aged 21–39 suggested that they actively chose to isolate themselves from other students. For one student, who had caring responsibilities for young children, isolating herself from social activities with other students was seen as necessary for her to cope with competing demands. This comment from her interview is reminiscent of the experiences of many mature students with caring responsibilities (Reay et al. 2009; Mannay and Morgan 2013):

> I am here primarily to learn and not to socialise…my focus is, once I have finished my lectures, getting back home to my family really. It is difficult enough trying to schedule enough reading time and revision without anything else, like going out and being able to do the workload anyway. (Sally, aged 30–39)

However, even those without caring responsibilities felt that they needed to isolate themselves from peers on their course and traditional-aged flatmates, so that they could make the best use of their time at university. This was also apparent from comments in interviews:

I just want to focus. I need more time to process things. That just means I have to sacrifice going out and stuff a little bit more. (Adam, aged 25–29)

because I know am a lot older as well… I just wanna get on and study and I thought maybe first years who are living together maybe probably wouldn't have been like that they would be hanging around together all the time and I thought I would probably feel isolated living like that. (Amy, aged 21–24)

Unlike the other traditional-aged students in the sample, this was also acknowledged by a Black traditional-aged student in her diary entry, below:

I haven't been as social due to university work, but also an ounce of laziness. But I have promised myself to change this attitude in 2nd semester because sometimes it's easy to feel lonely, and I don't need to be lonely because there are people I could spend time with, but I choose not to most of the time. (Hannah, aged 18–21)

However, unlike the mature students, for Hannah this was seen very much as a temporary coping strategy and one which she did not intend to continue. In comparison, all the mature students discussed continued isolation, particularly in their first year. This differs to Doman and Roux's (2010) view as people over 21 in this research appeared more prone to prolonged loneliness than the traditional-aged students in the research, who adapted quickly. As will be discussed in the next section isolation formed part of many older mature students' disappointments about university. In contrast, for those who had chosen isolation it appeared to be something that they felt positive about as they had no regrets about making this choice.

The university lifestyle seemed to be a major factor in this decision, with a number of younger mature students discussing the pressures to go out drinking in order to socialise at university. For example, Adam highlights here why he only socialised a few times with his university peers, because of feelings of 'déjà vu' and a lack of fit due to his age:

Only at the beginning I felt a bit lonely, and just like going out, after a few times, going the [students union] stood there feeling old. Not because people were saying "you look old", just like you are sat in a cinema watching your life again. I've done [partying] a lot. Just feeling out of place, almost, and ending up going home early. (Adam, aged 25–29)

Amy also discusses how she felt she had already lived that lifestyle before and didn't want to repeat it, similar to the miss-matched age feelings expressed above by Adam. Her comments also express her frustration at the dominant drinking culture at this university:

I didn't do freshers week, because I was 18 once and I've done that and I just didn't want to do it again … I don't really drink, it is just really not my thing and a lot of the events are drinking, which I struggled with, I did want to get involved, but I didn't want to go out every night, so I found that a bit bad…it is a drink culture which I don't think they should be advertising when you first come to uni. I think they should give you more opportunities to like speak to your tutors and just get to know people. Maybe do day trips…so I would have preferred it if it was a bit more like that. (Amy, aged 21–24)

This suggests that, whilst fitting in is a concern to younger mature students, this is not because they fear rejection by their peers. These students seem to actively reject the university lifestyle of their younger peers, because they feel they do not need, or want to participate in things they have already done. Some of the frustration with younger students, loosely discussed here, is also echoed in the accounts of the older mature students in the next section.

Isolation as a Result of Feeling Excluded Socially

In comparison to those who actively chose isolation, mature students in the 40 yr+ group did not describe choosing isolation, but felt that they were forced to accept isolation as a result of feeling socially excluded by their peers.

In contrast to all the other mature students, Rob took part in a range of fresher's activities, joining a number of societies. Like many mature students Rob's financial responsibilities (James et al. 2013) meant he had little time to socialise between his paid employment, to support himself and pay off debt, alongside a very demanding course. His initial commitment to these societies was driven by the desire to find common ground with other students on his course like many of the other older mature students. As Reay (2004) and Read et al. (2003) have highlighted, his comments here echo the importance some mature students place on feeling that they belong:

> They have had events which I've gone to cos I think it kind of provides a peer group based on shared interest, kindred spirits… based on kind of common ground, which I have got a lot of with people on my course, but I think because of my age they don't really see it that much. … I suppose these guys are a few weeks away from living with their parents and they think of someone like me as their parents, their parents' friends… they ask if they can sit with me, I don't know whether they do that with people of their own age in lectures. It is harder in the lecture, I suppose people are living in halls together and getting to know each other. I kind of feel like an outsider. (Rob, aged 40+)

What is interesting about Rob's account here is that when he talks about the rejection he experiences, he introduces many reasons that he is to blame for this rejection: his age; for being like their parents. He also suggested, later in this interview, that it might just be down to his own social anxiety.

This feeling was a common theme for all 3 of the students in the 40+ group. Rebecca explains that she felt consistently rejected in lectures and seminars whenever she tried to interact with her traditional-aged peers:

> if you open the conversation, I don't know if they think you are invading their privacy, or they don't want…In my heart I know I could sit here and not speak to anyone for three years, get my head down and get my degree, but that is not the point… I think it must be an age thing, it has got to be an age thing. I don't know if they don't want to or don't feel the need to. (Rebecca, aged 40+)

On one occasion, after a prolonged period of absence, Rebecca discusses a rare and unexpected occasion when one of her traditional-aged peers approached her in the library to ask how she was. Unfortunately, by this point her continued rejection was so engrained, that she begins to debate why they would ask how she was, and say that they missed her in classes, when they had never spoken to her before. Rebecca's feelings appear similar to Rob's in that they blamed themselves for being rejected. It appears that these mature students continued to be affected by their isolation and keen to understand why they were being socially excluded.

Indeed, all three of the students in the 40 yr+ group experienced this. Rebecca's comments above, are largely echoed here in John's discussion of trying to engage with his peers:

> I am not going to be an active member of my cohort… they are all aged 19, they all do their own thing together. I've tried to make inroads in terms of setting up a study group in our free time and they turned up once for a chat, and have not really engaged since. So I have really set my mind not that I come in just attend my seminars, extract what I need from the library. (John, aged 40+)

In this respect, isolation was seen as having a negative impact on their experiences at university; particularly the rejection they often felt following interactions with their younger peers. In addition, this rejection was not only experienced early in their first year, but continued throughout this first year despite their consistent attempts to engage. For both Rebecca and John, this resulted in them experiencing mental health difficulties at the end of the first year. Although John's attendance was effected both by his feelings of isolation and subsequent mental health problems he was able to continue to negotiate his study to continue on to the second year of his course. For Rebecca the strain of depression proved too much, impacting on both her attendance and her ability to study. She dropped out at the end of the second term, having only completed 40% of the required assessments.

The design of university activities, student spaces and attitudes of teaching staff within this institution also appeared to make most of these mature students feel excluded. Adam, Amy and Sally all expressed frustration with the activities that had been organised for Fresher's week, mainly because it revolved around the consumption of alcohol. The attitudes of academic staff also appeared to have a similar effect, making some of the mature students feel as if they were invisible or markedly different to the rest of their peers, which links in well to the findings in Ryan and Glenn's research (2004). They found that that seminar design can have an influential impact on first year students' performance and retention rates and it was evident that the exclusion, felt by all these mature students, came not only directly from peers but also indirectly from institutional sources. Sally gave a number of examples of this, such as lecturers using examples from the media to illlustrate concepts in lectures, which were only understood by traditional-aged students which had the effect of excluding mature students from discussions. Sally also maintained that when lecturers did use examples she understood, this would be followed by them saying that these were 'things that (students) wouldn't remember because they were too young' (Sally, aged 30–39). As Sally did remember these examples this again reminded her that she was different. These age-related reminders made them feel invisible; like they did not belong in the body of students. Ryan and Glenn's research is in keeping with these findings, as they highlighted that academic integration and the institutional commitment of students could be cultivated by redesigning seminars to reinforce the students' academic confidences as well as to develop learning skills. Reay et al.'s (2009) two year research study also shows that belonging can have a powerful impact on students' development as learners.

Another, less direct influence on the mature students' feelings of social exclusion was their frustration with their peers. In keeping with Foster's findings (2009) almost all of these mature students expressed annoyance at the way in which their younger peers behaved both whilst in university and outside of it. The frustration expressed about the attitudes and behaviour of their younger peers could be seen as mature students' rejecting the social networks and activities within university, although rejection from their traditional-aged peers might also have fed into this frustration. As discussed earlier, when asked about going to fresher's week activities, younger mature students implied that they didn't want to go out drinking with young students, because they had 'done it all before' when they were younger. Whilst the students aged over 40 years said they wanted to be included in social activities, with their traditional-aged peers, two of them also expressed annoyance with the way they behaved. The following examples show the consistency of this feeling from both older and younger mature students:

> I do feel that sometimes I am a bit of a fish out of water. Sometimes you are there and there is a mentality of giggling and talking over the lecturer, which annoyed me a little bit. (Sally, aged 30–39)
>
> the content of the chatter, [ ] initially it was asking the same things over and over again, and I was like 'oh for goodness sake', ... at 12 at night they go mental, and I have my phone charging next to my bed and I can hear my phone just going 'bing,bing,bing' and my husband is like "can you f'king turn that thing off!" and then I miss something important ... maybe it is just me being an adult and them being teenagers. (Rebecca, aged 40+)
>
> In the canteen we were talking about this guy, he was a bit introverted. I said "well he is young he has probably never left home before and is feeling vulnerable. Just give him time". And then one of them goes, "I remember one time when my mum and dad went out and left me for over a week once". I didn't get what he meant and then the others were like "Oh yeah they once left me alone for 9 days" and then I realised: yeah it has been 9 years since I have lived with my parents! (Adam, aged 25–29)

So it was apparent that, at least part of the mature students feeling of social exclusion was actually down to their rejection of younger peers, not necessarily because their younger peers had rejected them.

Discussion

The findings discussed in this chapter give a more detailed picture of the role of isolation in mature students' learning experiences at university. Whilst difficulties adapting to the university setting are often viewed negatively (Foster 2009; Ryan and Glenn 2004), it is evident that for some mature students, isolation can be positive in terms of success and retention.

The negative effects of isolation were certainly evident in all of the accounts of students in the over 40 age group. It also appears that when these experiences were combined with personal responsibilities or health barriers, as illustrated in Rebecca's case, they formed part of the decision to drop out. John and Rob seemed to be able to negotiate this, despite the challenges to their mental health, and continue their studies. However, the reasons for this difference are not clear cut. Arguably, Rebecca was juggling more responsibilities than Rob and John. Whilst Rob had to engage in a significant amount of paid employment, and John had caring responsibilities that occasionally took his attention away from study, Rebecca's priorities were more complex due to the combination of paid employment and caring responsibilities. With social exclusion added to this, it could explain why she felt unable to continue, feeling somewhat disconnected to both her course and the university. Comparing her experiences with those in the literature, it could also be argued that her gender may also have played a part in this (Mannay and Morgan 2013). As this was such a small sample, it is unclear why Rebecca felt she couldn't cope, yet Rob and John were able to battle through these challenges. Rebecca also appeared to be less motivated and less committed to her choice of course once she started to feel isolated, which perhaps reflects the vulnerabilities associated with mature students and the importance of belonging (Reay 2004). In comparison, Rob and John seemed to use the passion for their chosen subject to drive them through the challenges of isolation and negotiating their responsibilities. To understand this in more detail, research on a larger sample may help to reveal more concrete explanations. A better understanding may also be gained when this research has the full three years of experience to reflect upon.

Whilst they are somewhat limited in explanatory terms, these findings do confirm that isolation that results from social exclusion can be very harmful in terms of developing learner identities (Doman and Roux 2010; Reay et al. 2009), which in this case contributed to a mature student dropping out. Strategies for combating this, such as those detailed by Burton et al. (2011), Edirisingha (2009), and Ryan and Glenn (2004), might help universities in promoting successful adaptation and in helping older mature students to develop a sense of belonging. In particular, acknowledging that mature students are not a homogenous group is essential in designing appropriate support to help mature students effectively complete their degree. It also remains to be seen whether experiences like Rebecca's may be symptomatic of the decline of part-time degrees. If her degree had been available as a part-time route she may have been able to juggle her competing demands and have been less affected by her isolation at university. Further research would be useful in understanding the full impact of these experiences of isolation both during full-time and part-time study.

In direct contrast to Rebecca's experience, when isolation is the result of choice it appears to have had an emancipatory effect which helped these younger mature students cope with the demands of university. Unlike the students in the 40+ age group, they did not seem to need to feel a sense of social belonging, seeing it as an unneccessary distraction. However, it is important to also acknowledge that these are early findings from a long-term journey. Whilst, initially, this seems to have had a positive effect on these students ability to remain and perform successfully on their degree, it is essential to monitor how this affects them when moving into their second and third year. It may be possible that, in future years when academic challenges increase, they may regret isolating themselves from their peers. Also it may be possible that this initial frustration felt towards traditional age students may decline as the mature students become more comfortable in the university environment, and also as the traditional-aged students mature. It is hoped that the full findings of this research will give a clearer reflection of the consequences of chosen isolation.

References

Age UK. 2014. *Changes to State Pension Age*. Available at: http://www.ageuk.org.uk/money-matters/pensions/changes-to-state-pension-age/. Accessed 14 July 2014.

Baert, P. (2005). *Philosophy of the Social Sciences: Towards Pragmatism*. Cambridge: Polity Press.

Bourdieu, P. (1986). Forms of Capital. In J. Richardson (Ed.), *Handbook of Theory and Research for the Sociology of Education*. New York: Greenwood Press.

Burns, J. (2012). *Higher Fees May Deter Mature Students, a Study Warns*. Available at: http://www.bbc.co.uk/news/education-18162063. Accessed 31 March 2014.

Burton, K., Lloyd, M. G., & Griffiths, C. (2011). Barriers to Learning for Mature Students Studing HE in an FE College. *Journal of Further and Higher Education, 35*(1), 25–36.

Denscombe, M. (2009). *Ground Rules for Good Research: Guidelines for Good Practice.* Berkshire: McGraw Hill.

Department for Work and Pensions. (2017). *Older Workers and the Workplace: Evidence from the Workplace Employment Relations Survey.* Available at: https://www.gov.uk/government/uploads/system/uploads/attachment_data/file/584727/older-workers-and-the-workplace.pdf. Accessed 18 May 2017.

Deputy Prime Minister's Office. (2011). *Social Mobility Strategy Launched.* Available at: https://www.gov.uk/government/news/social-mobility-strategy-launched. Accessed 20 May 2016.

Doman, L., & Roux, A. (2010). The Causes of Loneliness and the Factors That Contribute Towards It—A Literature Review. *Tydskrif Vir Geesteswetenskappe, 50*(2), 216–228.

Edirisingha, P. (2009). Swimming in the Deep-End: An E-Mentoring Approach to Help Mature Students' Transition to Higher Education. *European Journal of Open, Distance and E-Learning, 1,* 1–12.

Elliot, D., & Brna, P. (2009). 'I Cannot Study Far from Home': Non-traditional Learners' Participation in Degree Education. *Journal of Further and Higher Education, 33*(2), 105–117.

Field, J. (2006). *Lifelong Learning and the New Educational Order* (2nd ed.). Stoke-on-Trent: Trentham Books.

Foster, T. (2009). *Alternative Routes into and Pathways Through Higher Education* (Research Paper no. 4). London: BIS.

Gonzáles-Arnal, S. (2009). Contextualizing Rationality: Mature Student Carers and Higher Education in England. *Feminist Economics, 15*(1), 85–111.

Gorard, S., Adnett, N., May, H., Slack, K., Smith, E., & Thomas, L. (2007). *Overcoming the Barriers to Higher Education.* Stoke-on-Trent: Trentham Books.

HEFCE. (2016). *Student Characteristics.* Available at: http://www.hefce.ac.uk/analysis/HEinEngland/students/age/. Accessed 11 July 2016.

Her Majesty's Government. (2011). *Opening Doors, Breaking Barriers: A Strategy for Social Mobility.* Available at: https://www.gov.uk/government/publications/opening-doors-breaking-barriers-a-strategy-for-social-mobility. Accessed 9 December 2014.

Her Majesty's Government. (2007). *Pensions Act 2007.* Available at: http://www.legislation.gov.uk/ukpga/2007/22/pdfs/ukpga_20070022_en.pdf. Accessed 2 May 2017.

Her Majesty's Government. (2010). *Equality Act 2010*. Available at: http://www.legislation.gov.uk/ukpga/2010/15/section/5. Accessed 21 July 2015.

Her Majesty's Government. (2016). *Success-as-a-Knowledge-Economy: Teaching Excellence, Social Mobility and Student Choice*. Available at: https://www.gov.uk/government/uploads/system/uploads/attachment_data/file/523546/bis-16-265-success-as-a-knowledge-economy-web.pdf. Accessed 21 November 2016.

HESA. (2012). *Non-continuation Following Year of Entry: Full-Time First Degree Entrants 2010/11*. Available at: http://www.hesa.ac.uk/index.php?option=com_content&task=view&id=2064&Itemid=141. Accessed 17 March 2014.

HESA. (2013). *UK Performance Indicators 2011/12: Widening Participation*. Available at: https://www.hesa.ac.uk/data-and-analysis/performance-indicators/. Accessed 2 May 2016.

HESA (2014). *UK Performance Indicators 2012/13: Widening Participation*. Available at: https://www.hesa.ac.uk/data-and-analysis/performance-indicators/. Accessed 2 May 2016.

HESA. (2015). *UK Performance Indicators 2013/14: Widening Participation*. Available at: https://www.hesa.ac.uk/data-and-analysis/performance-indicators/. Accessed 2 May 2016.

HESA. (2016a). *Higher Education Student Enrolments and Qualifications Obtained at Higher Education Providers in the United Kingdom 2014/15 (SFR224)*. Available at: https://www.hesa.ac.uk/sfr224. Accessed 22 May 2016.

HESA. (2016b). *UK Performance Indicators 2014/15: Widening Participation*. Available at: https://www.hesa.ac.uk/data-and-analysis/performance-indicators/receipt-of-dsa. Accessed 29 March 2017.

Hinton-Smith, T. (2012). *Widening Participation in Higher Education: Casting the Net Wide?* Available at: https://www.myilibrary.com?ID=418024. Accessed 22 July 2015.

James, N., Busher, H., Piela, A., & Palmer, A.-M. (2013). *Opening Doors to Higher Education Phase 2: Access Students' Learning Transitions: Final Project Report*. Leicester: University of Leicester.

Knight, J. (2013). The Changing Landscape of Higher Education: Internationalisation-for Better or for Worse. *Perspectives: Policy and Practice in Higher Education, 17*(3), 84–90.

Mannay, D., & Morgan, M. (2013). Anatomies of Inequality: Considering the Emotional Cost of Aiming Higher for Marginalised Mature Mothers Re-entering Education. *Journal of Adult and Continuing Education, 19*(1), 55–75.

McGivney, V. (1996). *Staying on or Leaving the Course: Non-completion and Retention of Mature Students in Further and Higher Education*. Leicester: NIACE.

Morgan, D. L. (2014). Pragmatism as a Paradigm for Social Research. *Qualitative Inquiry, 20*(8), 1045–1053.

NIACE. (2014). *Improving HE Access and Opportunities for Mature Students*. Available at: http://www.niace.org.uk/content/improving-he-access-and-opportunities-mature-students. Accessed 4 August 2015.

Office for National Statistics. (2013). *Full Report—Graduates in the UK Labour Market 2013*. Available at: http://www.ons.gov.uk/ons/dcp171776_337841.pdf. Accessed 9 May 2014.

QAA. (2010). *Access to HE: Key Statistics 2010*. Available at: http://www.accesstohe.ac.uk/AboutUs/Publications/Documents/Key-Statistics-10.pdf. Accessed 5 May 2017.

QAA. (2011). *Access to HE: Key Statistics 2011*. Available at: http://www.accesstohe.ac.uk/AboutUs/Publications/Documents/Key-Statistics-11.pdf. Accessed 5 May 2017.

QAA. (2014). *Access to HE: Key Statistics 2012–13*. Available at: http://www.accesstohe.ac.uk/AboutUs/Publications/Documents/AHE-Key-Statistics-14.pdf. Accessed 26 September 2014.

QAA. (2015). *Access to HE: Key Statistics 2013–14*. Available at: http://www.accesstohe.ac.uk/AboutUs/Publications/Documents/Access-to-HE-Key-statistics-2013-14.pdf. Accessed 5 May 2017.

QAA. (2016). *Access to HE: Key Statistics 2014–15*. Available at: http://www.accesstohe.ac.uk/AboutUs/Publications/Documents//AHE-Key-Statistics-2014-15.pdf. Accessed 5 May 2017.

Read, B., Archer, L., & Leathwood, C. (2003). Challenging Cultures? Student Conceptions of 'Belonging' and 'Isolation' at a Post-1992 University. *Studies in Higher Education, 28*(3), 261–277.

Reay, D. (2004). Finding or Losing Yourself: Working Class Relationships to Education. In S. J. Ball (Ed.), *The Routledge Falmer Reader in Sociology of Education* (Chapter 2, pp. 30–44). Abingdon: Routledge Falmer.

Reay, D., Crozier, G., & Clayton, J. (2009). 'Fitting in' or 'Standing Out': Working-Class Students in UK Higher Education. *British Educational Research Journal, 32*(1), 1–19.

Richardson, J. T. (1994). Mature Students in Higher Education: I. A Literature Survey on Approaches to Studying. *Studies in Higher Education, 19*(3), 309–325.

Ryan, M., & Glenn, P. (2004). What Do First-Year Students Need Most: Learning Strategies or Academic Socialization? *Journal of College Reading and Learning, 34,* 4–28.

Smith, J. (2009). *Mature Students in Higher Education and Issues for Widening Participation.* Available at: http://evidencenet.pbworks.com/w/page/19383511/Mature%20students%20in%20higher%20education%20and%20issues%20for%20widening%20participation. Accessed 13 March 2014.

Squires, G. (1981). Mature Entry. In O. Fulton (Ed.), *Access to Higher Education* (pp. 148–177). Guilford: Society for Research into Higher Education.

Thane, P. (2005). My Age Is a Lusty Winter: The Age of Old Age. In P. Thane (Ed.), *The Long History of Old Age* (pp. 9–30). London: Thames & Hudson.

Treasury, H. M. (2006). *Leitch Review of Skills: Prosperity for All in the Global Economy-World Class Skills.* Norwich: Her Majesty's Stationery Office.

University of the Third Age. (2014). *Learning Is for Life.* Available at: http://www.u3a.org.uk/. Accessed 26 May 2014.

Wolf, A. (2002). *Does Education Matter?: Myths About Education and Economic Growth.* London: Penguin Education.

6

Subjects in Formation: Women's Experiences of Access to Higher Education Courses and Entering Higher Education

Sherene Meir

Introduction and Context

Examining the experiences of 'non-traditional' students on Access to Higher Education (AHE) courses, designed for those without the qualifications needed to enter university (Busher et al. 2015, p. 3), is particularly important in the context of austerity. In England AHE courses have been affected practically, through funding changes that disadvantage mature students (Busher et al. 2015), and ideologically, through a shift towards a neoliberal politics of individualism that undermines the traditional AHE focus on social justice and equality (Thompson and Ryan, in Burke 2002, p. 8). The move towards a neoliberal model of education, which seeks to instrumentalise learning and students as forms of economic investment, predates the recent policy focus on austerity. The decreasing financial support for adults entering education under austerity, however, embeds returning to study for mature students

S. Meir (✉)
City of Bristol College, Bristol, UK
e-mail: Sherene.Meir@cityofbristol.ac.uk

© The Author(s) 2019
E. Boeren and N. James (eds.), *Being an Adult Learner in Austere Times*,
https://doi.org/10.1007/978-3-319-97208-4_6

deeper within a neoliberal logic that aligns 'responsibility' for participating in education with individual, as opposed to governmental, success or failure (Bowl 2017, p. 3). Within this system patterns of social inequality are reproduced for those from 'non-traditional' backgrounds who are less likely to participate in higher education (Jones 2016). Despite focusing on attracting 'non-traditional students' (mature students, ethnic minorities, working-class students, single parents etc.) into higher education since 1987 (Ball et al. 2002, p. 6), and being designated as an official alternative to A level routes (Busher et al. 2015, p. 2), AHE qualifications are still positioned as inferior to A levels—the 'preferred route' into higher education (Bekhradnia, in Burke 2006, p. 87). AHE has played a part in successive governments' strategies to reduce educational inequalities through 'redress[ing] educational exclusion amongst adult learners' and 'widen[ing] participation in higher education', though its role in providing alternative routes risks being undermined by recent funding changes that favour students under 24 (Busher et al. 2015, p. 2). This is in a broader context of rising tuition fees and the removal of maintenance grants (Shaw 2015).

In examining the experience of entering higher education through AHE I have chosen to focus on women as they may experience specific pressures related to parenting (Edwards and Ribbens 1998; Reay 2003) and be particularly marginalised within higher education cultures that can be seen to privilege masculine values (Burke and Jackson 2007). Discourses around participation in (A)HE are important in understanding which frameworks are available for women to understand themselves through when returning to study. As Stuart Hall notes, subjectivity is constituted in relation to discourse (in Burke 2008, p. 204); individuals develop their sense of self within (and perhaps against) the dominant social and political narratives that surround their experiences. Thompson and Ryan suggest that, from a focus on social justice, AHE courses have moved towards a 'neoliberal politics of…competition and individualism' (in Burke 2002, p. 8). The focus on 'non-traditional' students within higher education as 'under-exploited pools of talent' to increase 'economic productivity or competitiveness' (Mirza, in Archer 2007, p. 643) supports an 'instrumental' model of AHE (Barr, in Burke 2002, p. 20) which considers education in economic terms. Within this neoliberal model, Thomas (2015) argues that mature and part-time students are positioned as being 'in deficit'—lacking those qualities which are desirable in an higher education student. The widening participation (WP) agenda has also been critiqued for circulating deficit discourses about those (particularly working-class people) who do not choose to study at higher education level (Adnett 2015, p. 212), aligning aspiration and success with university participation and completion (Merrill 2015, p. 1860). Considered as potential higher education students, then, women on AHE courses are moving towards physical and discursive spaces that correlate higher education with individual success, aspiration and career progression, and in which mature undergraduates are positioned 'on higher education's periphery' (Thomas 2015, p. 38).

The research discussed within this chapter was conducted in 2016 as part of my MSc dissertation; a small-scale qualitative research project conducted with three women from different institutions who were in the process of completing, or who recently undertook, an AHE or equivalent course.[1] Two of the women were studying at further education institutions, whilst one woman's course took place within a higher education institution. All three women volunteered themselves for participation, having been informed about the research by their lecturers. The research aims to understand how women's subjectivities and personal narratives about their academic abilities are influenced by returning to education, using a 'biographical' (Merrill 2015, p. 1861) approach that considers the women's individual stories within their broader social contexts. Furthermore, it considers the potential for women from 'non-traditional' backgrounds to develop agency within the current AHE/HE model, contributing to debates around how higher education can better accommodate 'non-traditional' students. This is particularly pertinent in a context of austerity and funding changes wherein numbers of students over the age of 25 have been in decline since 2012 (HESA 2017). This chapter will begin with an overview of literature relating to female 'non-traditional' students, before outlining some theories of subjectivity and agency which are useful for understanding the

---

[1]One of the participants was enrolled in a Higher Education Introductory Studies course, equivalent to an AHE course.

experience of becoming a learner, and which form my theoretical framework. It will go on to summarise my methodology and then provide a comparative analysis of the interviews, structured in relation to three broad themes; 'returning to education as resistance', 'navigating changing identities' and 'relationships to academic cultures'. Finally, I will draw some conclusions and suggest directions for further research.

Literature Review and Theoretical Framework

Returning to education is typically conceived of as a process that shapes subjectivity (Burke 2002, 2008; Merrill 2015; Crowther et al. 2010; Busher et al. 2015; Skeggs 1997), defined here through a poststructuralist framework which recognises subjectivity as an individual's shifting relationship to, and understanding of, themselves, mediated by 'social, emotional [and] cultural…relations' (Burke 2008). The particular experiences of female mature students from working-class backgrounds are often marked by tensions between the identities that they are required to develop and perform within higher education, and those that they inhabit within other contexts (Merrill 2015; Reay 2003; Skeggs 1997; Edwards and Ribbens 1998). As Burke notes, the process of returning to study can intensify 'sensibilities of the self as fixed, against a subjectivity that is… multiple, complex and ever changing' (2002, p. 99). Burke's suggestion that adults returning to education often try to 'divide…different strands of self' that emerge through study to make them appear 'separate and compatible, rather than…overlapping, contradictory and discontinuous' (Burke 2002, p. 107) can be usefully theorised in relation to Deleuze and Guattari's theories of subject formation. The impetus for subjects (in this case women from non-traditional backgrounds entering higher education) to maintain different strands of self that appear 'separate and compatible', is understood by Deleuze and Guattari as a product of traditional Western forms of thought. Their work suggests that Western epistemologies depend on the idea of a 'stable' subject that is 'fixed and knowable', within a 'neutral system of representation' (Mansfield 2000, p. 143). They refer to this system of representation (and interpretation) that produces 'essential truth' (Mansfield 2000, p. 141) as 'arborescent', positing it as a structure that rigidly fixes subjects into categories—'aspirational', 'mother', 'successful'; these fixed categorisations serve to regulate human behaviour and limit agency (Deleuze and Guattari 2004b). In higher education, for example, practices around academic writing, which are falsely represented as neutral (Archer 2007; Burke and Jackson 2007), validate a particular form of 'correct' intelligence that can limit the inclusion of diverse 'intelligences, predilections … [and] cultural background[s]' (Parker 2007, p. 291). This can lead to institutional (and individual) rejection or disavowal of diverse identities and of ways of being and knowing that conflict with dominant, arborescent epistemologies. These (arborescent) notions of 'what counts as knowledge' and of 'who can be recognised as a legitimate 'knower'' (Burke 2008, p. 203) within higher education are central to shaping women's subjectivities if they return to education.

Deleuze and Guattari's analysis of subjectivity (Coleman and Ringrose 2013) raises questions around which narratives we recognise, and give authority to, that are central to both my theoretical framework and my methodological approach, alongside Lorraine Code's (1995) work on 'rhetorical spaces'. As Code suggests, '"truths" of the most compelling kind can…fail to compel assent when…rhetorical spaces are…closed against them' (1995, p. 61). Analysing how particular discourses come to be understood as 'descriptions of "reality"' (1995, p. x) and gain 'authorizing power[s]' (Butler 1992, p. 9) over subjectivity is central to my approach. Simultaneously, using Deleuze and Guattari's work, I attempt to examine those truths that may not ordinarily 'compel assent'. Whilst our lives are partially embedded within and lived along 'culturally sanctioned story lines' (Code 1995, p. 94), Deleuze and Guattari suggest that 'rhizomatic' modes of representation and interpretation make it possible to resist the categorisation into 'pre-allotted identities' that 'arborescent' modes demand (2004a, p. 10). Rather than locating individuals within 'fixed and knowable' categories, 'rhizomatic' interpretations remind us that a 'myriad of 'discourses… intermingle in a given text [subject]' (Beighton 2015, p. 119) and can help to recognise the 'multiple' and 'ever changing' (Burke 2002, p. 99) character of subjectivity. Through providing a means of recognising the contradictions and inconsistencies that emerge within a subject, rhizomatic analysis enables recognition of moments of agency and resistance to 'fixed' categories that may evade 'arborescent' readings. As Skeggs (1997, p. 11) notes, in examining how particular social categories shape the way women live and understand themselves, it is important to recognise how women 'challenge powerlessness'. This chapter considers the different 'rhetorical spaces' that determine the women's positions, using a 'rhizomatic' analysis that is attentive to subtle moments of refusal and resistance to 'pre-allotted identities' within each woman's narrative.

Methodological Approach

My research broadly fits with a grounded theory approach whereby 'theories, concepts [and] hypotheses' are derived from the data through inductive reasoning, rather than through a priori assumptions (Bogdan et al. 2016, p. 164), allowing me to explore the particular circumstances of my research participants. The design of my interview questions sought to encompass this approach and resist assumptions about women's experiences. Learning from Janet Parr's discussion of her own research, in which she notes that asking women about 'barriers' to education risked objectifying them (and restricting her own interpretations) (1992, p. 97), I aimed to use neutral language. Rather than asking 'has it been difficult to manage your time or balance your responsibilities?' for example, I asked 'has being on the course impacted on your life outside the course? If so, how?'. Hollway and Jefferson's adaptation of the 'biographical-interpretative' method (2013) also influenced my interview design. By constructing open-ended questions that establish interviewee's meaning frames and elicit stories (Hollway and Jefferson 2013, p. 32), they endeavour to invite 'free associations' that may reveal 'incoherences' and 'contradictions, ellisions, avoidance' (Hollway and Jefferson 2013, p. 34). Inviting these kinds of responses enabled me to be attentive to 'hesitation' (Roy 2008, p. 160), 'irrelevance' and 'self-contradiction' (Maclure 2013, p. 172) and offer tentative readings of what may be 'unstated' or 'unarticulated' explicitly (DeVault 1995, in Bogdan et al. 2016, p. 9). Following a pilot in which my questions elicited short, impersonal answers, I endeavoured to make participants more comfortable by emphasising that the conversation may be an opportunity to process their thoughts rather than provide definitive answers and I built an expectation that I was interested in stories, as recommended by Hollway and Jefferson (2013, p. 41). This approach to the three interviews, which permitted the women to make free associations and explore their thoughts and feelings relating to returning to education, resulted in transcripts of discussions which ranged from forty minutes to an hour and a half.

Maclure's 'ethical obligation to relieve research subjects… from the banality…of the…codes that hold them in place' (2013, pp. 172–173) is central to my methodological approach, which considers the risk of 'academic production' (Edwards and Ribbens 1998, p. 5) forcing people's experiences into predetermined frameworks that diminish the complexities of the social positions they inhabit (Richardson 1990; Edwards and Ribbens 1998; Parr 1998; Hoult 2012; Skeggs 1997). As Skeggs (1997, p. 2) notes in relation to her research on class and gender formation, research participants should be understood as 'active in producing the meaning of the positions they (refuse to, reluctantly, or willingly) inhabit' rather than as 'ciphers from which subject-positions can be read off'. Using a modified version of Natasha Mauthner and Andrea Doucet's voice centred methodology (1998) to analyse the interviews has enabled me to situate the women's narratives within the complex networks and relations in which they exist (Skeggs 1997), providing a means of analysing those 'culturally sanctioned story lines' (Code 1995, p. 94) that inform their narratives about themselves. Mauthner and Doucet advocate four readings of interview transcripts; an initial reflexive reading that seeks to understand how the speaker's narrative is shaped by the researcher's social positioning (1998, p. 127), a second reading for the way the speaker refers to themselves (1998, p. 128), a third for the language they use to speak about their interpersonal relationships (1998, p. 131) and a fourth reading to identify connections between speakers' narratives and broader political, social and cultural contexts (1998, p. 132). This 'relational ontology' (Mauthner and Doucet 1998, p. 125) begins to address issues around subjectivity and the notion of 'voice' raised in Deleuze and Guattari's work; as Beighton notes, for Deleuze and Guattari, 'the idea of a subject endowed with its own voice' can be problematic as often 'just at the moment when we believe we are most autonomous…we are most subject to the order words of the dominant culture' (2015, p. 123). The process of moving between multiple readings, which inherently deconstructs the idea that a subject speaks through a single voice, serves to challenge the idea that absolute narratives can be affixed to particular subjects' experiences.

Analysing the Interviews

The three interviews which make up this research took place in locations selected by participants. They were loosely based around a set of questions about the women's experiences of their course and changes to their lives outside the course, though I endeavoured to enable participants to feel comfortable to speak freely about whichever aspects of their return to studying felt pertinent to them, as discussed above. Oliwia,[2] whom I met in a café, is in her early twenties, the youngest of the three women, and has no caring responsibilities or work commitments outside her studying. She moved to England from Poland as a young teenager so undertook part of her schooling within the English system. Reema, who I met on a bench in her local town centre, accompanied by her two primary school aged children, is in her mid-thirties and moved to England as an adult from India, where she had been working in healthcare. I met Michelle, the oldest of the three, at her place of work; her children have now left home and she combines full-time work with evening study.

Whilst I integrated a reflexive reading of how my presence validated particular 'story-lines' throughout the process of data analysis, I examined each of the interview texts through Mauthner and Doucet's other three readings, which helped to develop themes around which to organise my analysis. Present in my reading of all the women's narratives through the 'I' voice were continuous comparisons between the 'I' of the past and the 'I' of the present; where in the past, Michelle's

---

[2]Pseudonyms have been used and identifying characteristics have been anonymised.

decision not to study was based on the idea 'I might as well get into work', for example, her return to study was guided by the question 'well what would I like to do now with my time?'. Recognising the increased sense of choice and agency that began to emerge through all of the women's present 'I' voices, I identified as my first theme the notion of education as resistance to previous positioning. Alongside contrasts between the past and present, tensions between the ways in which the women understood themselves in different contexts—with their families, at work, with fellow students—emerged through the three readings. I began to think about this within the wider context of women's relationships to their changing identities (and how different social contexts affect these relationships); navigating changing identities became the second theme through which my analysis is structured. Within this, the women had differing responses to academic cultures and practices; through examining this as my third theme, I began to explore the ways in which the women's circumstances outside their studies impacted on their relationships to education, and the role of these relationships in shaping their perceptions of themselves. This allowed me to analyse how different personal circumstances and socio-cultural contexts may impact on the extent to which education enables the development of agency.

Returning to Education as Resistance

Returning to education provided a space for all three women, to differing extents, to resist some of the ways in which they had been positioned previously and to begin to reject some of the 'categories of identification' (Skeggs 1997, p. 164) that were available to them in the past. Although none of the women refer to 'resistance' explicitly within their interviews, I use the term here to emphasise education's role in giving the women some control over the positions they inhabit, whether explicitly or implicitly. My discussion of 'resistance' takes into account Giroux's notion of the 'dynamics of resistance' (1983, p. 103) in education; acts of resistance may be overtly oppositional to particular oppressions on the basis of class, race or gender, but may also be inscribed within, and appear to express, the 'dominant culture'. Deleuze and Guattari (2004b, p. 16), similarly, suggest that the act of rejecting fixed categories of identification sometimes passes through 'signifying powers' from the dominant culture that act as 'footholds' for resistance. The potential for individual agency, within Deleuze and Guattari's (2004a, p. 238) work, is presented through the image of 'lines of flight' that escape from the 'overcoded' arborescent structures which constrain subjectivity. As Hickey-Moody and Malins (2007, p. 3, in Coleman and Ringrose 2013, p. 11) note, this attention towards subtle shifts or movements away from the 'dominant culture' permits an analytical approach that evaluates 'what [subjects] do, [and]…say, in relation to the ways of existing involved' ' and the 'potential and capacities that those ways of existing affirm'. By tracing the ways in which the women's experiences of returning to study constitute forms of resistance, I aim to consider education's potential to elicit agency and offers the women 'lines of flight' to 'refute that which is expected' of them (Skeggs 1997, p. 164).

At the time of the interview Reema had recently divorced her abusive husband; she describes how he controlled her life through isolating her socially and restricting her from studying and working. By narrowing the frames of reference through which she was able to identify herself, he effectively controlled how she perceived herself, leading her to lose confidence and struggle to '*face the world*'. She says: '*when I took the decision to divorce it you know gave me the strength that yes I am somebody, I'm not just…slave anymore so…that was a big change in myself that erm I've decided to do the course*'. Education constitutes a space within which Reema can refuse the label '*slave*' and begin to perceive herself differently. Enrolling in the AHE Nursing course provides Reema with a route to 'emancipation' (as for Jane in Hoult's study 2014, p. 108) that allows her to begin to control her own narrative where previously she felt she '*had no control*':

> One of the teachers said after the divorce all of the women jump into achieving something big, so you should not do that. But I thought, yes I am in the same shoes, but I don't see myself that that is the only option for me - I could work full time but I chose to go for the further education.

Reema refuses to be categorised as a typical divorced women, exerting some agency to challenge the 'powerlessness' (Skeggs 1997, p. 11) through which she was positioned during her marriage; she posits returning to education as a choice that she defines on her own terms. Her repetition of 'I' within this phrase differentiates her from other women, reinforcing her development of a distinct voice that resists domination by others. Although returning to education offers Reema a new context within and against which to define herself, disidentification with her ex-husband's image of her as 'useless' is not straightforward: *'I've developed my confidence more, I couldn't see that but people around me…say that they see me as a strong and brave woman [surprised tone] but I still feel scared inside'*. Education functions as a 'line of flight' through which Reema can refuse to be recognised as passive or weak, partly through her peers' readings of her, yet she is still negotiating past identifications and 'story lines' (Code 1995, p. 94) about herself.

Oliwia, too, perceives returning to education as a means of shifting her social positioning, particularly in relation to employment; whilst she initially studied a vocational course at college and begin working, after a couple of years she decided to enrol on an AHE course in humanities and social sciences. She describes her experiences of working as her main motivation to study;

> People didn't respect me…and I had the minimum wage…I got fired from one job because I wouldn't do what they told me to do…I had to do admin and then they asked me to clean…I was like, but I'm not a cleaner…they thought I had attitude and fired me…I wasn't special because I had literally no qualifications, I was easily replaced…you can easily replace people when you have no qualifications.

Oliwia's narrative around this experience of employment shifts from perceiving her employers as disrespectful and mistreating her, to attributing blame for the situation to herself—*'I had literally no qualifications'*. Although she critiques unstable or exploitative employment conditions, Oliwia sees herself as having done something 'wrong' and positions education as the 'right' route. As Reay (2003, p. 314) notes, in a (neoliberal) culture of 'individualisation', personal change and transformation are seen as the responsibility of the individual, masking social inequalities as individual problems. Oliwia's desire to enter education appears shaped by a desire to reject her positioning as '*easily replaceable*' and is accompanied by a sense that her negative experiences of employment signify 'personal failure' (Reay 2003, p. 314). She returns to the notion of being, or not being, '*special*', multiple times throughout the interview. Although aspiration is not directly mentioned, Oliwia's associations between doing what is 'right' and studying suggest that her personal desires are partly shaped by discourses aligning correct aspiration with higher education. Whilst her conception of education, and her judgement of herself in relation to it, is shaped through discourses created by the 'dominant culture', studying provides a 'foothold' that permits Oliwia a 'line of flight' to exert some agency over her material opportunities.

Whilst Reema and Oliwia's narratives consciously posit returning to study as a means of resisting the vulnerable positions they previously occupied, Michelle's narrative, on the surface, presents studying as something she wants to do to satisfy her own '*curios[ity] about the world*'. A single mother in her late fifties, Michelle made various attempts to enter higher education previously, however factors related to childcare and financial concerns have meant the only prior course she completed was a workplace accountancy qualification. Considered in the context of multiple attempts to study throughout her life, her decision to return to study becomes more complex; the pragmatic imperative to '*get into work*' and earn money rather than study, immediately after school and at other points in her life, as well as considerations about making things '*better*' for her children, emerge as dominant factors in determining Michelle's choices. She positions motherhood as a barrier to previous attempts to study and feels she must be fully attentive to, and responsible for, her children at all times (Lucey and Walkerdine 1989; Reay 2003), interacting with the school ('*if you [want to]help your child… make the time to go to…classes that the school provides*') and ensuring her children are involved in multiple activities ('*the Kumon for maths, erm, drama, music, a **lot** of the time was taken up, swimming, a lot of my time was taken up with doing those activities*'). Michelle's personal desires are partly inscribed within 'doing the right thing' for her children, a particular pressure for working-class women (Skeggs 1997, p. 88), and fulfilling her duties to her employers; *'I work in finance, it's month end, that takes priority at the moment...I wish I could say...I don't care about work...I can't do it, I get up in the morning and I come to work and that is a priority'*. Prioritising herself, then, and committing fully to pursuing her own *'curiosity'* through leaving her job and dedicating herself full time to studying when she begins higher education (at the time of the interview she has recently been accepted onto an higher education course), is perhaps an act of resistance against a culture wherein putting one's own desires at the centre is reserved for men and the middle classes (Reay 2003, p. 306). Where her choices were partly shaped by her children and finances, as well as her family's expectations that she prioritise work over education, studying enables her to begin to identify herself outside these demands and expectations. For Michelle, as for the other women, education provides an opportunity to 'take account of the possibilities that the [positions that have constituted her previously] systematically exclude' (Butler 1992, p. 9).

Returning to Study and Navigating Changing Identities

Whilst returning to education can enable the women to take account of new 'possibilities', it also forces them to negotiate the 'authorising power[s]' that have shaped (Butler 1992, p. 9), and continue to shape, their positionalities; the differing contexts within which they return to education, and their different motivations to study (discussed above), impact on the ways in which they experience and articulate their changing identities. Michelle, Reema and Oliwia relate differently to what is often characterised by working-class women entering formal education as a binaried experience that involves moving between 'two cultures' (Merrill 2015, p. 1865) or 'two worlds' (Edwards and Ribbens 1998, p. 7). Although Oliwia and Reema partially dissolve this binary by privileging education as a means of constructing a future that marks a separation from a difficult past, and Michelle seeks to draw a sharp distinction between studying and other areas of her life, the different 'ways of being and knowing' (Edwards and Ribbens 1998, p. 7) demanded by different spaces filter into the ways each of the women relate to the 'contradictory…multiple' (Burke 2002, p. 99) subjectivities that develop through returning to education.

Implicit within Michelle's text is the sense that studying entails a changing relationship to her working-class background and an accumulation of 'cultural capital', which can perhaps 'be traded' (Skeggs 1997, p. 82) in spaces outside those she currently inhabits; on the surface of the text, however, Michelle asserts her identity as unchanging—*'I'm still me'*. Michelle alludes to the social currency of knowledge about the arts, describing herself and her relationship to the arts before studying as lacking or naïve (she used to ask herself *'what is it about Shakespeare that people are so interested in?'*), a perspective perhaps filtered through 'deficit discourses' attributed to non-traditional students (Burke 2008; Adnett 2015) and working-class groups (Skeggs 1997). She also positions learning as a *'process of joining the dots'* and feeling *'at home'*, correlating studying with wholeness and a connection to the wider world that she previously felt excluded from. Education operates as a space that can perhaps facilitate Michelle's inclusion into middle-class spaces (Skeggs 1997, p. 82) but also evokes some uncertainty about her shifting positionality—a tension working class women returning to education often struggle to negotiate, as discussed above. At moments in the interview Michelle appears tentative about the impact of studying on her shifting identity. In response to my first question about her experience of being on the course she answers hesitantly; *'to find the right word…the first thing that's come into my head is, the first word that comes into my head is exhilarating but I'm not sure if that is the right word'*. She questions her use of language again later in the interview:

> Why have I chosen the course, arts and humanities? Because it covers those areas that I'm really passionate, passionate? Yes I am. I love music I love dancing, I love reading, I love, I enjoy all those things, music, reading, writing.

Shifting from using the word '*love*' to '*enjoy*' and instinctively questioning her use of the words '*passionate*' and '*exhilaration*', her responses suggest unease or discomfort around incorporating strong emotions about education and the arts into narratives about herself. Her language and the enthusiasm with which she speaks invokes a sense of liberation, yet her speech appears simultaneously constrained; although Michelle seeks to retain 'separate and compatible' identities, her narrative seems to recognise the 'discontinuous' or 'contradictory' (Burke 2002, p. 107) identities emerging through her studies, which could potentially distance her from family and friends. She perhaps partially seeks to defend herself from these contradictions by keeping her studies secret from everyone except for her sons and one friend, although she tells me in the interview that when she begins the higher education programme onto which she has been accepted she will inform family and friends.

Although Oliwia's motivation for returning to education more explicitly enacts a desire to move away from spaces that previously defined her, and she recognises that education is changing her, articulating the complexities of her shifting identity, as for Michelle, is difficult. Oliwia's changing ways of thinking associate her with other educated people and her narrative suggests a sense of inclusion within higher education (she uses '*when you go to uni*', aligning her with other university students, rather than '*when I went to uni*'), yet remnants of ways of thinking from social spaces she previously inhabited infiltrate descriptions of her own identity. Asked to describe herself, Oliwia's narrative slows down; '*I would say I'm really serious now…I'm a loner…I dunno….,I would probably, some people would probably call me boring*'. What she describes as a '*love*' of learning is refracted through the perspectives of the social networks that she inhabited before her studies, though she recognises '*if I met more people that are like me they would never call me boring…I don't think I'm boring*'. The 'culturally sanctioned story lines' (Code 1995, p. 94) of her past, in which she was always socialising and surrounded by friends, persist in her articulation and understanding of herself now— the language of '*seriousness*' and being a '*loner*' linger from her life before studying. Contrasted with the ease and pragmatism with which Oliwia discusses the value of her studies in tangible terms, correlating transferable skills such as being '*professional*' with developing a CV that '*looks good*' through her degree—discussing how studying has impacted on her personally is more difficult: '*I've really changed. I'm a completely different person since I went to uni, like in college I don't even, I'm so, I'm just, I can't…I love being alone now it's weird. I dunno…*'.

The prevalence of neoliberal discourses around education (Archer 2007; Burke 2002) seem to render it easy for Oliwia to insert herself into 'arborescent' narratives around AHE and higher education as progress towards a career, however the internal shifts that occur through her return to study, hinted at through the repetition of the word '*change*' that appears multiple times throughout the interview, do not have a familiar language. The hesitations and faltering rhythm through which these 'changes' enter into language indicate the rhizomatic forms of the experiences and emotions that constitute Oliwia's subjectivity as it moves beyond a 'pre-allotted identity' (Deleuze and Guattari 2004a, p. 10). Oliwia's narrative (like Michelle's) repeatedly reverts to the (significant) material changes that accompany her '*change*'—'*I enjoy being alone*', '*I love reading books and staying home*', '*I started walking a lot*'—leaving the less tangible implications of the word '*change*' to hover just beyond the text: '*everything changes basically, that's all I can say*'.

Reema is the only woman of the three for whom entering higher education does not necessitate confronting contradictions, perhaps because she explicitly understands returning to education as signalling a '*change*' in herself and perceives returning to study and 'reconstructing' (Merrill 2015) her identity as intrinsically connected. Although initially Reema found balancing work, childcare and her recent divorce '*intimidating*', after a month '*everything fell into routine*'. At first she brought in 'ways of being' from outside her studies, hoping she could get by in the same way as she did in other spaces—'*I was trying to keep my distance…I was good at avoiding people*'—however being approached by other students who nominated her as class representative allowed her to quickly feel included. Reema highlights the communal aspect of her studies, something non-traditional students frequently emphasise (Ball et al. 2002; Busher et al. 2015), suggesting that the supportive group enabled everyone to achieve together through a '*team effort*' (which counters neo-liberal discourses of educational success as individual achievement [Reay 2003]). She conceptualises education as a space that can positively alter her positioning in other spaces and allow her to:

> Set a role for my kids that just earning is not enough, you need to find your identity…give something back to the community, so that's why I chose this course to do the health access course so I can lead my career into nursing.

For Reema, the '*identity*' that she hopes to develop through education is multiple and corresponds with many mature female students' motivations to study; it allows her to be a role model for her children (Reay 2003; Crossan et al. 2003; Burke 2002), to contribute to society (Reay 2003) and to develop a career that reflects her ambition and opens up possibilities for the future. Education allows her and her family to access material changes—learning maths, for example, helps her to support her daughter to gain a scholarship place at a private school—but also enables her to perceive herself differently; she has learnt that '*being scared will not achieve anything…so don't just go outside the swimming pool and think that you will be drown if you go in there…you need to go in the water to see how you can survive*'. Although Reema begins AHE with clear ideas of the impact that education will have on her life, it also allows her to learn to inhabit new spaces with more confidence, understanding her identity as fluid and open to change.

Whilst Reema's narrative partially subverts discourses that align higher education with individualism and competition (Thompson and Ryan, in Burke 2002), Oliwia's account of her changing identity illustrates the dominance of 'instrumental' notions of higher education (Barr, in Burke 2002, p. 20), which relate to wider social attitudes towards unskilled workers that constitute part of how she understands herself. Both Michelle and Oliwia's narratives allude to the idea that education is differently valued in different social contexts (Skeggs 1997) which partially unsettles their sense of themselves as having a 'fixed', stable, familiar identity. Whilst Michelle attempts to retain the idea of 'separate' and 'compatible' selves, reflecting tensions between her working-class identity and that of being an higher education student (Hoult 2012; Merrill 2015), Oliwia begins to recognise her contradictory, rhizomatic identity, yet struggles to find a readily available discourse within which to slot her experience. Reema's metaphor of entering the water, too, suggests that her experience of education cannot straightforwardly be captured within her existing narrative about herself. Whilst not all experiences pass through language (Maclure 2013), understanding why particular experiences seem to evade language can help to consider the implications of particular discourses and the 'rhetorical spaces' they legitimate, as well as the 'ways of existing ' and the 'potential and capacities' enabled by those discourses (Hickey-Moody and Malins 2007, p. 3, in Coleman and Ringrose 2013, p. 11).

Returning to Study and Academic Cultures

Exposure to academic knowledge and practices, for all three women, provides a new framework through and against which to understand themselves and their position in the world. The ways in which they relate to academic study vary greatly, perhaps connected to the space that returning to study occupies within their broader life context. Where Reema is already familiar with parts of the content of the course in Health Studies through her work in India, Michelle was at school almost forty years ago and has less confidence in her academic ability: '*education has come on a long way…I need to go back to school*'. For Oliwia '*it hasn't been that long…out of education*', but her attitude to academic study is very different; where previously she '*didn't care*', she is now keen to get a First and progress onto an MA or perhaps to a PhD. These differing contexts and the women's differing motivations to study, discussed above, impact on the extent to which they position academic knowledge and practice as belonging to 'closed communit[ies] of expertise and expert knowledge' (Parker 2007, p. 290) to which they must conform, or as tools which they can actively engage with and utilise.

As discussed above, Michelle appears to position herself as 'lacking' or 'deficient' in relation to academic knowledge—this is expressed particularly in relation to 'linguistic capital' (Burke 2008); she returns to her difficulties with academic writing '*in the format required*' nine times within the interview. Academic writing is a source of anxiety,

> When I started I sort of wrote in my thing, 'right Michelle you're writing for your audience, who is your audience?' Right it's my lecturer and it could be the class, right 'what is it you want to say?' And it's like 'ahh [mimes having no words] what do you want to say?' 'I don't know' [comic scared voice] [laughs]... five hours later, 'why haven't you written anything?'.

She shifts from recounting events to reliving the embodied experience of writing, demonstrating the affective experience of negotiating academic work; the lecturer, her class, her own expectations of herself and perhaps the notion of the '*format required*', haunt her writing process. Michelle articulates academic writing as a '*skill that needs to be acquired*', stating that she will enrol on writing skills workshops for '*as long as it takes*' to 'understand academic writing styles'; correct academic performance is an objective '*skill*' that she lacks. Whilst Michelle does not question the values inscribed within academic practice (Burke and Jackson 2007), her judgement of her own academic capacity appears to be structured through them. Where an opportunity to '*just write*' and '*forget about structure*' in one course allows Michelle to feel '*in [her] element*', her capacity to confidently articulate her thoughts is stifled by academic writing practices. The importance Michelle attributes to gaining a degree, her desire to '*complete [her] education in its entirety*', and her feelings of exclusion from, or naivety about, cultural pursuits (discussed above) may contribute to her deference to 'expert knowledge'; achieving particular academic standards seem to contribute to her judgements of her own self-worth in an academic context within which she can exert little agency.

Although Michelle largely positions academic knowledge and practices as neutral (Burke 2008) and representative of ways of understanding the world which she previously could not access, she posits her understanding of the UK education system, and her experience of having two black boys within the education system, as different to that of her class; '*well my experience and your debate are different*'. Within the interview this moment uniquely represents Michelle questioning and challenging academic knowledge. Whilst in class Michelle says she just listened and felt she disagreed, the interview perhaps offered a space within which to rehearse 'new scripts' (Code 1995, p. 78) that allow her lived experience to intersect with and complicate academic knowledge (Merrill 1986; Hoult 2012), positioning her in a more active role in relation to her studies.

Reema's relative confidence in relation to the course content, along with social aspects of the course discussed above, allow her to more actively utilise knowledge that she gains through the course to develop her confidence. Analysing health related news in a weekly 'news diary' as part of the Social Policy component of Reema's AHE course enabled her to find out '*how the welfare system works here in this country*' and feel more '*able to ask for help*'. Where engaging with academic knowledge and practices can be experienced as painful for non-traditional students (Merrill 2015; Weil 1986), for Reema, knowledge gained through her course operates as a mechanism of inclusion and means of becoming more integrated into, and benefitting from, the '*system*'. Studying can be seen to function as a microcosm of the wider world that Reema is preparing to enter and a space in which she can perform what Braidotti, drawing on Deleuze and Guattari, terms 'nomadic shifts' that allow her to rehearse new ways of being, and to 'trace paths of transformation' (1994, p. 6). Her familiarity with some of the course's academic content lead her to become someone classmates come to for help; '*we used to sit in the library and I used to go through all this in simple language… the reproductive system, the respiratory system*'. Although Reema does not think of herself as a '*leader*', her classmates' perceptions of her in this role allow her to perform 'as if' (Braidotti 1994, 6) this is the case, creating space for her to explore a new, more confident subjectivity. Central to Reema's understanding of the relationship between education and gaining confidence is the notion of learning as an active process: '*you can only discover walking on that path, you can't just discover sitting or standing there*'. Engaging with academic knowledge allows Reema to perform new roles and to explore pathways of 'transformation' through which she is able to develop agency, saying she feels entitled to '*want more*', rather than just being '*content*' to '*settle down*'.

Whilst Oliwia, similarly, is able to instrumentalise academic knowledge in relation to politics and her newly gained feminist perspectives, her narrative wavers between deference to academic knowledge and recognition of her own 'potential and capacities'. In response to an intervention I hesitated to make, mentioning that other women sometimes experience relationships ending or *changing* when they begin to study, as Oliwia did, her questions seem to position me (someone further along in my academic career) as a 'legitimate knower' (Burke 2008); '*is that something common then?*', '*do you know why [relationships end when women study]?*'. Although initially Oliwia privileges academic knowledge as the motivation for her leaving her abusive boyfriend; '*I would say it was college mainly that helped me because we had sociology…that kind of touched on these subjects*', she later mentions conversations with peers from her course going through similar experiences and her realisation that she can '*depend on [herself]*'. The superior social status that Oliwia accords to higher education participation (discussed above) perhaps partially shapes her deference to academic knowledge, however the process of learning and discussion alongside peers also provides her with the confidence to begin to perceive herself as someone who knows and can have opinions.

For Reema, although 'positions of authority and expertise are unevenly distributed' (Code 1995, p. ix) in academic spaces, her prior education and experience enables her to occupy an 'authoritative' status that allows her greater agency in relation to academic knowledge, where Michelle, and to a lesser extent Oliwia, struggle to attribute themselves authority within an academic context. Despite this, however, engagement with academic knowledge begins to raise questions about how knowledge is formed for both Oliwia and Michelle—for Oliwia in relation to her changing ideas about gendered relationships and for Michelle in the context of her lived experience of race and the education system.

Although, as Deleuze and Guattari note, Western forms of knowledge (into which UK higher education practices generally fall) attempt to portray a 'neutral system of representation' in which reality is 'fixed and knowable' (Mansfield 2000, p. 143), engagement with higher education that questions how knowledge is formed can begin to disentangle fixed notions of reality and offer 'lines of flight' towards new positionalities and possibilities.

Conclusion

Education, for all three women, functions as a space to explore new perspectives. The extent to which returning to study plays a role in shifting all three women's understandings of themselves, however, varies in relation to their personal circumstances. For Reema, studying constitutes a means of determining a future trajectory for herself that rejects her ex-husband's positioning of her. Her capacity to develop agency and inhabit the new possibilities and identities offered by education appears largely unconstrained by her circumstances; prior to entering education she was socially isolated, thus the identity she is developing through education does not come into direct conflict with other positionalities. Although not the case for Reema, whose social exclusion prior to studying is perhaps starker than that of Michelle and Oliwia, AHE's purpose of redressing educational exclusion amongst adult learners can be seen to be restricted by widening participation narratives which rely on divisions between those with, and those without, aspiration. These divisions can filter into non-traditional students' readings of themselves; Oliwia's account of her return to education, for example, indicates the ways in which discourses that present those who do not study as 'deficient' can impact on individuals' understandings of themselves. The decreased funding available for adult learners under austerity, in a neoliberal context wherein choice about university participation is positioned as an individual responsibility, exacerbates divisions between those with and those without aspiration; this perhaps contributes to the tensions which non-traditional students can experience between the different social contexts they inhabit. Within Michelle's account of her return to education, for example, social class, and the hierarchical structures of academic knowledge, seem to partially limit the extent to which she is able to engage with her studies. The tensions between Michelle's social context and the extent to which she is able to develop agency and incorporate changing perspectives into her identity, demonstrate the means through which social class, and the hierarchical position that higher education occupies within the UK social context can inhibit some of education's transformative potential. Despite Michelle's narrative, and to a lesser extent Oliwia's, being partly determined within 'rhetorical spaces' that diminish their agency, by identifying moments in which their narratives strain away from available understandings of themselves, I have suggested that agency and resistance to fixed identities can emerge within the 'dominant culture' and against neoliberal educational discourses. Oliwia and Reema's narratives also indicate the ways in which social networks and communal aspects of studying can resist discourses that position education in terms of individual success; although austerity shapes the ways in which AHE and higher education are framed, female non-traditional students' experiences can counter some of these narratives.

Through this research I have explored how women's subjectivities and narratives about themselves are influenced by returning to education through AHE, within a framework that considers how people's lives are intimately connected to, and at times limited by, the 'rhetorical spaces' they inhabit. My methodology, although limited by the scope of this chapter, has attempted to reflect this conception of subjectivity by referring to dominant discourses surrounding higher education whilst simultaneously tracing moments of resistance or agency within the women's narratives, with the aim of shifting the 'rhetorical spaces' within which 'non-traditional' female students are constituted. I have attempted to write about the women in ways that resist damaging labels of 'non-traditional' students as 'deficient' and that demonstrate the ways in which their experiences of education partially resist neoliberal discourses that align higher education with individualism and 'productivity'. At the same time, I have indicated how the women's readings of themselves are partially 'closed' or constrained on the basis of the 'rhetorical spaces' created by dominant discourses. This mode of analysis has the potential both to critique inclusion practices for 'non-traditional' students within higher education, and to begin to consider alternative practices to render A(HE) accessible for a broader range of students.

Understanding the constraints and possibilities for female students (and 'non-traditional' students more broadly) within (A)HE could further be examined through a comparative analysis of the ways in which particular institutions, lecturers, curricula or pedagogies inhibit or enable students to develop agency. An analysis of different institutions' practices (in recruitment, support, assessment etc.), for example, could contribute to developing an understanding of the ways in which normative discourses around higher education students and hierarchical academic cultures are countered or perpetuated, helping to develop an understanding of the 'potentials and capacities' (Coleman and Ringrose 2013, p. 11) that are affirmed for 'non-traditional' students through diverse practices. Exploring the effects of courses that, for example, explicitly invite greater self-reflection, make connections between course content and individual's lives and use more diverse, creative forms of writing or assessment, could further inform practices and pedagogies that may render A(HE) more accessible for non-traditional students. (These kinds of pedagogies benefited Reema in writing her news diary and Michelle in being given the opportunity to 'just write'.) The 'rhetorical spaces' legitimated through neoliberal educational discourses limit the womens' abilities to identify and fully express the shifts in their subjectivity when they begin to study, so further research could examine the effects on learners' confidence, and sense of agency, of a short unit or forum for collective discussion around the process of returning to study alongside an AHE course. This could provide a space for students to recognise and articulate the 'myriad of discourses' that constitute their experience of studying, and perhaps challenge or critique some damaging discourses relating to 'non-traditional' students within A(HE). Whilst further research to improve practice is critical to supporting 'non-traditional' students to more fully inhabit the possibilities engendered through their learning, however, just as the women in this study are shifting and moving away from some of the rigidity and fixedness of their previous positionings through entering A(HE), higher education institutions, too, should be flexible and able to learn from 'non-traditional' students.

References

Adnett, N. (2015). The Economic and Social Benefits of Widening Participation: Rhetoric or Reality? In A. Benett, M. Shah, & E. Southgate (Eds.), *Widening Higher Education Participation: A Global Perspective* (pp. 211–222). Waltham: Chandos Publishing.

Archer, L. (2007). Diversity, Equality and Higher Education: A Critical Reflection on the Ab/uses of Equity Discourse Within Widening Participation. *Teaching in Higher Education, 12*(5–6), 635–653.

Ball, S., David, E. M., & Reay, D. (2002). 'It's Taking Me a Long Time but I'll Get There in the End': Mature Students on Access Courses and Higher Education Choice. *British Educational Research Journal, 28*(1), 5–19.

Beighton, C. (2015). *Deleuze and Lifelong Learning: Creativity, Events and Ethics*. Basingstoke: Palgrave Macmillan.

Bogdan, R., DeVault, M., & Taylor, S. J. (2016). *Introduction to Qualitative Research Methods: A Guidebook and Resource*. New Jersey: Wiley.

Bowl, M. (2017). University Continuing Education in a Neoliberal Landscape: Developments in England and Aotearoa New Zealand. *The International Journal of Lifelong Education, 29*(6), 723–738.

Braidotti, R. (1994). *Nomadic Subjects*. New York: Columbia University Press.

Burke, P. J. (2002). *Accessing Education: Effectively Widening Participation*. Stoke-on-Trent: Trentham Books.

Burke, P. J. (2006). Fair Access? Exploring Gender, Access and Participation Beyond Entry to Higher Education. In B. Francis & C. Leathwood (Eds.), *Gender and Lifelong Learning: Critical Feminist Engagements*. London: Routledge.

Burke, P. J. (2008). Writing, Power and Voice: Access to and Participation in Higher Education. *Changing English: Studies in Culture and Education, 15*(2), 199–210.

Burke, P. J., & Jackson, S. (2007). *Reconceptualising Lifelong Learning: Feminist Interventions*. London: Routledge.

Busher, H., James, N. & Suttill, B. (2015). 'We All Know Why We're Here': Learning as a Community of Practice on Access to HE Courses. *Journal of Further and Higher Education, 40*(6), 765–779.

Butler, J. (1992). Contingent Foundations: Feminism and the Question of 'Postmodernism'. In J. Butler & J. W. Scott (Eds.), *Feminists Theorize the Political*. New York: Routledge.

Code, L. (1995). *Rhetorical Spaces: Essays on Gendered Locations*. London: Routledge.

Coleman, R., & Ringrose, J. (2013). Introduction. *Deleuze and Research Methodologies* (pp. 1–22). Edinburgh: Edinburgh University Press.

Crossan, B., Gallacher, J., Field, J., & Merrill, B. (2003). Understanding Participation in Learning for Non-traditional Adult Learners: Learning Careers and the Construction of Learning Identities. *British Journal of Sociology of Education, 24*(1), 56–67.

Crowther, J., Maclachlan, K., & Tett, L. (2010). Adult Literacy, Learning Identities and Pedagogic Practice. *International Journal of Lifelong Education, 29*(6), 651–664.

Deleuze, G., & Guattari, F. (2004a [1972]). *Anti-oedipus*. London and New York: Continuum.

Deleuze, G., & Guattari, F. (2004b [1980]). *A Thousand Plateaus*. London and New York: Continuum.

Edwards, R., & Ribbens, J. (1998). Living on the Edges: Public Knowledge, Private Lives, Personal Experience. In R. Edwards & J. Ribbens (Eds.), *Feminist Dilemmas in Qualitative Research: Public Knowledge and Private Lives* (pp. 1–23). London: Sage.

Giroux, H. A. (1983). *Theory and Resistance in Education: A Pedagogy for the Opposition*. London: Heinemann Educational Books.

Higher Education Statistics Authority (HESA). (2017). Who's Studying in HE? Retrieved from: https://www.hesa.ac.uk/data-and-analysis/students/whos-in-he. Accessed 18 March 2018.

Hollway, W., & Jefferson, T. (2013). *Doing Qualitative Research Differently: A Psychosocial Approach*. London: SAGE.

Hoult, E. (2012). *Adult Learning and La Recherche Féminine: Reading Resilience and Hélène Cixous*. Basingstoke: Palgrave Macmillan.

Jones, S. (2016, May 2). It's Not Easy to Raise Prior Attainment, But Universities Could Better Contextualise Student's Grades, LSE Blog [Blog]. Retrieved from: http://blogs.lse.ac.uk/politicsandpolicy/its-not-easy-to-raise-prior-attainment-but-universities-could-be-less-picky-about-applicants-grades/. Accessed 26 August 2017.

Lucey, H., & Walkerdine, V. (1989). *Democracy in the Kitchen: Regulating Mothers and Socialising Daughters*. London: Virago Press.

Maclure, M. (2013). Classification or Wonder? Coding as an Analytic Practice in Qualitative Research. In R. Coleman & J. Ringrose (Eds.), *Deleuze and Research Methodologies* (pp. 164–183). Edinburgh: Edinburgh University Press.

Mansfield, N. (2000). *Subjectivity: Theories of the Self from Freud to Haraway*. Sydney: Allen & Unwin.
Mauthner, N., & Doucet, A. (1998). Reflections on a Voice-Centred Relational Method: Analysing Maternal and Domestic Voices. In R. Edwards & J. Ribbens (Eds.), *Feminist Dilemmas in Qualitative Research: Public Knowledge and Private Lives* (pp. 119–146). London: Sage.
Merrill, B. (2015). Determined to Stay or Determined to Leave? A Tale of Learner Identities, Biographies and Adult Students in Higher Education. *Studies in Higher Education, 40*(10), 1859–1871.
Parker, J. (2007). Diversity and the Academy. *Teaching in Higher Education, 12*(5–6), 787–792.
Parr, J. (1998). Theoretical Voices and Women's Own Voices: The Stories of Mature Women Students. In R. Edwards & J. Ribbens (Eds.), *Feminist Dilemmas in Qualitative Research: Public Knowledge and Private Lives*. London: SAGE.
Reay, D. (2003). A Risky Business? Mature Working-Class Women Students and Access to Higher Education. *Gender and Education, 15*(3), 301–317.
Richardson, R. (1990). Narrative and Sociology. *Journal of Contemporary Ethnography, 19*(1), 116–135.
Roy, K. (2008). Deleuzian Murmurs: Education and Communication. In I. Semetsky (Ed.), *Nomadic Education: Variations on a Theme by Deleuze and Guattari* (pp. 159–170). Rotterdam: Sense Publishers.
Shaw, B. (2015, July 8). Maintenance Grants Scrapped and Tuition Fees to Increase—Your Reaction. *The Guardian*. Retrieved from: https://www.theguardian.com/higher-education-network/2015/jul/08/maintenance-grants-scrapped-and-tuition-fees-to-increase-your-reaction-budget-2015. Accessed 30 August 2016.
Skeggs, B. (1997). *Formations of Class and Gender: Becoming Respectable*. London: SAGE.
Thomas, K. (2015). Rethinking Belonging Through Bordieu, Diaspora and the Spatial. *Widening Participation and Lifelong Learning, 17*(1), 37–49.
Weil, S. (1986). Non-traditional Learners Within Traditional Higher Education Institutions: Discovery and Disappointment. *Studies in Higher Education, 11*(3), 219–235.

7

Further Educations: Transformative Teaching and Learning for Adults in Times of Austerity

Vicky Duckworth and Rob Smith

Introduction

In this chapter, a decade on from the financial crisis that heralded the introduction of austerity measures in the UK, we will outline our perspective on the impact of cuts on adult participation in further education. Then, through reference to the *FE in England: Transforming Lives and Communities* research project—a study that set out to identify and celebrate examples of transformative teaching and learning (TTL) in further education—we will illustrate how further education still transcends its reductive and instrumentalist neoliberal purposing by

---

V. Duckworth (✉)
Edge Hill University, Ormskirk, UK
e-mail: Duckworv@edgehill.ac.uk

R. Smith
Birmingham City University, Birmingham, UK
e-mail: Rob.Smith@bcu.ac.uk

providing a counter-hegemonic and 'differential' space for adult learners. Evidence from the project shows how despite straitened finances and the constraints of a constantly-changing annual funding methodology that incentivises college self-interest and gaming, further education providers continue to empower people and their communities. In doing so, they challenge intergenerational inequality and enhance agency and hope.

Since Prime Minister Jim Callaghan's *Great Debate* speech of 1976, the policy agenda in the UK has placed an increasingly instrumentalist onus on compulsory education to connect with the needs of industry. The Further and Higher Education Act of 1992 incorporated further education colleges, thereby laying the ground for a transformation of their role away from being historically rooted, organic expressions of local and municipal industrial need and into agents of national economic and skills policy (Smith and O'Leary 2013). The Act restructured educational provision for adults and young people over the age of 16 and connected the new further education 'sector' through the umbilicus of a newly devised funding methodology to central government. Apart from the erosion of further education teachers' working conditions and a series of disruptive re-regulations of their professional status, the last quarter century has been characterised by a string of policy interventions (for example, General National Vocational Qualification [1994], Modern Apprenticeships [2001], Train to Gain [2006], Entry to Employment [2003], the 14–19 diploma [2008] and the launch of 'New' Apprenticeships [2017], see Smith and O'Leary 2015, p. 176) many of these having a significant impact on college teachers' work and students' learning experiences. While there was a policy commitment to lifelong learning during this period, since 2009 this has increasingly fallen by the wayside. The focus instead has been on 16–19 provision, the recent setting of a target for the recruitment of 3 million apprentices by 2020 being the latest example in a line of 'new' vocational qualifications.

Contextual Constraints: Notions of the Knowledge Economy

In the UK and internationally, democracy and notions of *community* are being (re)conceptualized in our public institutions through the lens of neoliberal ideology. Neoliberalisation is the dominant political force of our time, bringing with it a focus on de- and re-regulation, economic competitiveness (both national and institutional) all framed by discourses of globalisation (Davies 2014). This has resulted in so-called 'free market' competition displacing social democratic policy as a structuring force in many areas of public life. Under the premise of building a 'knowledge economy', the central duty of the nation's education system is assumed to be to provide a flexible, adaptable and skilled workforce to make the country competitive in the globalised economy. The knowledge economy is a hypostatised concept that positions education instrumentally as a conduit and a sorting house through which the population is processed in order to provide human capital (Becker 1993). Interestingly, the two tier (academic versus vocational) system that has long been entrenched in the English context consequently reifies a cleavage in the traditional bell curve of ability (Dorling 2011, pp. 46–49) resulting in a bi-sected bell curve. The notion of IQ that has long formed the underpinning measure for academic achievement across the ability ranges being added to by an amorphous notion (and even more suspect in terms of measurability) we might call *employability quotient* or EQ. Between the two, education institutions are structurally positioned as providers with a responsibility to supply human capital with an EQ sufficient to fulfil the 'skills needs' of employers.

While neoliberal educational policy often pays lip-service to social justice through the discursive vehicle of social inclusion (Hope 2002), behind this promise of social mobility through educational attainment is a 'skills discourse' (Smith and O'Leary 2015, p. 175) that depends upon the objectification of students and their stratification within an intractable structure that perpetuates divisions between 'academic' and 'vocational' pathways. With reduced funds to adult learning, it also appears that the age-staged tyranny of compulsory education presents the main or only opportunity for individuals to transcend their family's social background (if that is what we take social mobility to mean). If nothing else this reaffirms governmental complacency in the face of ongoing social divisions. What remains of the 'social mobility' dimension of the policy rests on a reliance on supply-side intervention in the labour market (Keep 2006) while largely ignoring measures to adjust employer demand. Underpinning the whole approach is an ever less convincing fable about economic growth and the classic neoliberal assumption about social benefits accruing from a 'trickle-down' as a result of 'wealth creation' activities on the part of employers (Harvey 2005, pp. 64–65).

From such evidence, a key effect of neoliberal policy appears to be the replication of social divisions and inequalities rather than any systematic or meaningful counteraction against them. For example, learners from socio-economically deprived areas are unlikely to have the same access to educational opportunities as those who live in more affluent areas who are more able to attend high achieving state schools or be privately educated (Duckworth 2013). The recent area reviews for colleges of further education appear to have contributed to the geographical embedding of privilege and stratification by closing college campuses in urban areas with high levels of social deprivation and/or allocating curriculum in relation to the socio-economic profile of particular areas.

Thus, for example, a college conglomerate formed from a number of merged colleges may locate its A level provision in an area with low levels of unemployment and a large proportion of high income households; meanwhile, for a campus situated in another area of the same city, with higher concentrations of working class households it might locate its vocational courses; on a third site, perhaps nearer to industrial districts, it might concentrate its apprenticeship courses. In terms of adult and community provision, the efficiency drive associated with the recent Area Reviews community 'outlets' and campuses were especially vulnerable (see Smith 2017). In that sense, the marketisation of further education, in this case through the imposition of 'efficiency' measures, can be seen to contribute to social inequality by allowing geographical concentrations of the cultural and economic capital that accrues to some classes to shape decision-making about the types of courses offered in different locations.

As Boeren (2016) has pointed out, there is evidence to show that students with high levels of achievement in compulsory education are more likely to engage in further education and lifelong learning. Participation statistics may well show that adult involvement is reducing (this is also occurring in Apprenticeships, see Tovey 2017) but this is a direct and predictable effect of the economisation of further education cultures. The manipulation of funding tariffs for adults in diverse circumstances since 2009 has created an uneven landscape. While Access to HE courses incur costs (often repaid by loans or through 'progression' arrangements) and costs for ESOL classes are similarly passed on to students, Apprenticeships are still, effectively subsidised by government. In a marketised system that is funding driven and policed to produce ever increasing efficiencies, the geography of available courses (or not) is as good an explanation as any for the so-called Matthew Effect. In this complex and commodified funding environment, the *FE transforms* project sought to identify parameters connected to TTL: the extent to which it is still occurring, the 'ingredients' that make it up and to gather narratives from teachers and learners and others about its impact.

It may not be surprising that the stratification that underpins the neoliberal purposing of education, with its entrenched academic/vocational divide and its newfound reliance on the mysterious capital of 'employability' alienates the students it brands as failures. We should remind ourselves that in 2016 just under a third (33.1%) of young people did not achieve the national benchmark of 5 GCSEs at A*-C (OFQUAL 2016). The impact of this is considerable. As Dorling points out:

> People and especially children crave recognition and respect. Telling children they have ranked low in a class is a way of telling them they have not earned respect. … almost everyone wants to fit in, to be praised, not to rank towards the bottom, not to be seen as a liability as those as the bottom are seen. (Dorling 2011, p. 54)

In the neoliberal imaginary of which the so-called knowledge economy forms a part, for adults there are new ground rules. These rules impact on people and their lives. Being successful in the knowledge economy requires the acquisition of particular skills and competencies and the ability to adapt to a wide variety of knowledge domains. This mythology insists that people must be able to apply these skills effectively to partake in the ever-changing knowledge economy. Lifelong learning is envisaged as a mechanism for ongoing up-skilling, whereby a person must expect and make ready for transitions in her/his life (Field 2000, 2008; Field et al. 2009; Ade-Ojo and Duckworth 2015, p. 16; Duckworth and Smith 2017). This upskilling includes developing literacy/language/numeracy skills as well as those associated with new and emerging technologies. As we noted above, the current funding landscape requires adults to be prepared to invest in their future. With further education courses for adults now requiring them to apply for a loan to cover tuition fees, financial considerations, particularly for those adults with families, are likely to impact strongly on the choices they make and it seems likely that the number of adults on courses will decline.

The Research

The *FE in England: Transforming Lives and Communities* research project,[1] sponsored by the University and Colleges Union, is a study that records and celebrates narratives about TTL in further education. Further education in England is comprised of colleges, training providers and work-based as well as community learning. In the current context of sustained budget cuts and Area Reviews, this chapter presents research findings that identify within further education a 'differential space' (Lefebvre 1991) in which learners, supported by critical pedagogy, are able to experience education as transformative—of themselves as learners but also as connecting them to new opportunities in life

---

[1] http://transforminglives.web.ucu.org.uk/.

and work (Mezirow 2000; Duckworth 2013). Through more than fifty interviews and narratives that explore participants' educational journeys, the study probes a wide range of issues and can help to make sense of the impact of economic change and emerging social trends and how these play out in further education settings. When exploring adult education, the research illuminates how it relates to other factors in people's lives such as health and well-being, work, and family and community life. The research explores how adult education can draw on notions of 'self-invention', 'transformation' (Walkerdine et al. 2001) and 'bettering oneself' to provide a catalyst for hope and choice (Duckworth and Smith 2018).

Connecting Critical Pedagogy to Critical Methodology

The research did not only focus on gathering evidence about the impact of adult learning on people and communities, but through a critical methodological approach, that conceptualised the research as a social practice (Herndl and Nahrwold 2000), it also affirmed participants' achievement and their positive learning identities. The methodological approach adopted for the study grew out of the critical literacy background of the researchers. Both researchers are experienced literacy educators and made the decision to deploy principles derived from critical pedagogy (Freire 1996; Breunig 2005) as an integral feature of the methodological approach. For that reason, care was taken to frame research conversations (we use this phrase in preference to the term 'interviews' to move away from the sense of an unequal and unidirectional relationship and distribution of power) to foster a sense of equality between the participants and the researchers. We met participants face to face, usually in the further education setting where they were studying. There, we attempted to generate an informal atmosphere by sharing stories and cups of tea in order to acknowledge that the research aspect of what we were doing was one part of a broader social encounter. Reciprocity was also important: we shared our own stories to establish openness and informality.

The research conversations provided participants with an opportunity to share their narratives, allowing for the sharing of obstacles and the solutions to overcome them. Through the medium of video, these narratives themselves then constitute capital which can be shared with and drawn on by others to inspire and offer strategies to move forward. Thirty five of the videos are individual narratives, fifteen are edited compilations centred on specific themes (e.g. Literacy, Women and further education). The research conversations were dialogical because stories were exchanged and opinions and feelings shared. The collective experience that the website enabled us to share challenges the neoliberal educational discourses which privilege individual over collective learning. The narratives are empowering and can take the form of a capital for resistance against the barriers faced by many learners, for example, struggling at school with reading and writing, being poor, labelled and stigmatised. Rather than the stories being hidden in shame the project participants took ownership of them and reclaimed them as stories of success while recognising the structural inequalities that they challenged and resisted to take agency in their lives and communities (Duckworth 2013; Duckworth and Smith 2019). Social capital (Field 2008) is not a homogenous resource equally available and accessible to all members of communities. For the project participants, who may have been constrained by factors such as class, gender or ethnicity, both they and their communities benefitted from the telling of their stories.

Other important features of the research conversations included the affirmative nature of the conversation. Once again, there is a connection here with critical pedagogy: the research positioned itself in such a way as to extend the *affirmative regard* that we see as underpinning transformative learning experiences. In other words, the conversations sought to affirm the positive learning identities that participants had re-discovered during their studies.

The research conversations also provided opportunities to document and build on what Tedder and Biesta refer to as 'narrative learning':

> By narrative learning we mean that learning can take place as a result of articulating stories from one's life, through the process of talking about and reflecting on life experiences, in other words from the very narration

of one's biography; and can take place as a result of presenting stories from one's life, by having stories with content and structure, by having a narrative that says something about what and how you have learned. (Tedder and Biesta 2009, p. 89)

In this way, the research conversations were positioned as an extension of the TTL experiences that were the central concern of the project. The learners described how they were able to be actively involved in decision making and dialogue with the positive outcome of a democratic environment and culture being co-constructed both inside and outside the classroom. For many of the learners and teachers, this inclusive approach to education and community action was the antithesis to what they had experienced previously.

The project utilised a digitally orientated research methodology to gather, explore and share project data. The data comprised a series of rich narratives from learners, teachers, employers and learners' family members. These were collected through video recorded interviews which were then shared via a project website. Pink (2007, pp. 96–97) discusses how using a video camera can disrupt the relationship between researcher and participant. The loss of eye contact when the researcher peers into the viewfinder can heighten the participant's awareness of 'being filmed'. In our project, the autofocusing equipment, with its large screen display, enabled us to set up the camera on a tripod, start recording and then to start the conversation, occasionally checking and refocusing. A Youtube channel[2] and twitter account[3] were further features of a multi-faceted digital platform that were used to create a project audience and an interactive critical space which garnered further contributions in the form of written accounts, photographs and artefacts. The use of these digital tools and the way they contribute to make the project data accessible can be seen as a way of "overcoming the 'silo-ing' of knowledge into discrete disciplines" that

---

[2]https://www.youtube.com/channel/UCkDeirtGCmeBs361BgibXnA.
[3]@FEtransforms.

Halford et al. (2012, p. 186) see as an aspect of a "disciplinary carve-up of knowledge… {that is} the outcome of social and political struggles for identity, power and resources…." The digital platform was the catalyst to what we describe as *virtually enhanced engagement* adding to the data in an organic way and extending the influence and meanings of the project in the public domain—for example by connecting the researchers directly with a key policy maker. The sharing of the narratives—with the consent of the participants—across the public domain facilitated the power of the collective over individual approaches. The website became a vehicle for the co-construction of a virtual community bringing together learners, teachers, academics, activists, policy makers. Project participants' voices in this way were able to reach out and cross different domains to challenge stereotypes and unsettle hegemony. The first year of the project culminated in a conference that brought together participants from across the country: students, teachers, researchers, employers and policy influencers.

Ethics

The use of a digital platform with a particular focus on video in the project brought up a number of ethical considerations. The project was scrutinised by the Ethics Committees of both researchers' HEIs. We offered all participants anonymisation at the recruitment stage, but as the focus was on the transformative qualities of their educational experiences, most wanted their real names to be used. Each video was edited and then shared with the participant prior to publication. Re-edits were undertaken at the participant's request. The emphasis throughout was on maintaining their dignity while presenting their stories in their own words. The stories of many were closely connected to particular colleges and even specific teachers. Where these were mentioned, we also sought permission to include these. The publication of videos on Youtube raised the issue of the need to remain aware of public comments and to respond, edit and delete these where appropriate. We adhered closely to the BERA ethical guidelines (2011) throughout.

Findings

In this next section we will share some of the participants' narratives. We analysed the data thematically by identifying recurrent themes and exploring these through a range of theoretical concepts. We have selected these particular participants as they are illustrative of key themes relating to the aspects of further education that we categorise as transformative. Adult learning can be transformative in the way it empowers individuals and communities. By empowering here we mean enabling students to rediscover their agency and themselves as learners in cooperative and egalitarian learning spaces. Empowerment can feel overused as a term and its meaning compromised. But we use it to describe how participants were able to reposition themselves not as free-floating individuals in the entrepreneurial individualistic sense but as beings rooted in communities and able also to move into new and different spaces and in effect to change their positionality in the social world—and move away from labels and identities that may have been imposed on them. The use of digital media contributed to the notion of transformation here in the sense that not only did the research practice affirm participants' new and emerging identities, but through the presentation of their narrative via a video posted on the project website, participants could see themselves as belonging to a "hybrid community" centred on TTL. James and Busher describe the crossover between physical and online communities in this way:

> Communities have always overlapped and been part of wider constellations, but the development of cultures that have become multifaceted through media development, telecommunications, computer-mediated communications, has created hybrid sites of social interactions for individuals and communities where practices, meanings and identities are constructed. (James and Busher 2013, p. 195)

This sense of belonging through a shared experience might be virtual to begin with, but the website offered the potential for online networking with others who shared experiences of TTL and face to face at the project conference that took place eighteen months into the research.

Transformative Teaching and Learning as a Lifeline of Hope

Schools are sites where identities and futures are formed and the *Transforming Lives* project traced the sometimes detrimental impact of that. Rather than being sites that offer an egalitarian model where everyone is on an equal footing, schools are often experienced as sites of inter-generational marginalisation, social exclusion, and labelling by teachers and peers, our research revealed. For some learners this is experienced as symbolic violence. Their bodies were sites for symbolic violence, which affected their experience of education and had a huge impact on their learning experience, how they define themselves and their subsequent trajectories. For adults in further education settings, TTL experiences often involve a revisiting and a revisioning of the spoilt learning identities created in primary and secondary education by the labelling process which targeted them for being poor and struggling with educational achievement.

Anita, a female participant from the North East of England, provides an example of someone who was regarded as a failure at school, in this case because of undiagnosed dyslexia:

> I've always been told I was thick. Always been told I was stupid.... The teachers at school assumed I was born to fail. Dyslexia... had (only) just been identified. So you were thick, you were stupid and if your parents didn't even have any faith in you, you're not going to have any faith in yourself.

Anita describes how her dyslexia was not addressed at school. In child and adulthood, she felt stigmatised and struggled with being dyslexic. However, she gradually accumulated a body of experience in her working life that signalled administrative, organisational and interpersonal abilities. Encouragement by her partner and a chance opportunity to stand in as a project manager led to her resuming her education. Anita's tutors were key in building on this.

In eighteen months, I'll be a qualified social worker. My tutors are the ones that got me here… They encouraged me. They never once doubted me. They made me grow… They are the first people, apart from my partner who ever had any faith in me.

Her story shows us how further education can offer opportunities that build confidence in learning environments with an affirmative culture. This in turn facilitates the development of new knowledge and new identities. We would not separate teaching and learning in any analysis of these transformative experiences. TTL environments offer a dialogical experience that involves students in learning interactions with teachers and other students. These commonly draw on students sharing understandings of their prior learning experiences as a basis for moving forward.

For Anita, TTL has meant:

I am actually going back, doing something and not just sitting in a cakey shop. And now I have my bits of paper, I have my confidence, I have my voice and I have a future. That's what education has given me: a life, a new life, a better life. It just opens up a whole new world and a whole new you. Suddenly, people are seeing you as you really are and not in the box that they have put you in.

The Foucauldian notion of the 'subject as an effect of power' (Foucault 1982) can help us understand the impact of TTL. Her transformative learning experience has impacted on her identity as a 'subject'. Here the subject is not just how we regard ourselves but maps across to how the person we are features within the different power networks that we connect to. This isn't just about self-esteem but involves her sense of social standing and status as she interacts with others in wider society. A corollary of this is that TTL also heralds changes within existing social networks and the connection to new and different social networks.

I can now talk to people that I've never felt I could talk to: the doctor, the clinician. But now I have my bits of paper…, I have can talk and I ha e valid points to make. And I have a voice. If it wasn't for college, I wouldn't have that voice.

Anita's account is important in the way it emphasises how her life experience, including suffering bereavements and moving away from abusive relationships fed into her choice of career, in this case social work. It seems appropriate to use the term 'vocation' to describe her enthusiasm and commitment to this career. In choosing it, she is drawing on her existing experiential capital and potentially, through her work, affirming her own journey as she interacts with people in her work.

> I now want to be that person where I can say: 'Come to me I can help. I can give you the tools and as much support as you need to get you to a better place.' Whether that's out of an abusive relationship, whether it's parenting skills, whether it's education so you can have the better job so you can have a better life for you, your kids, your family. I have moved, maybe not physically but mentally, emotionally and I've grown.

In addition to providing evidence about the impact of TTL on the self as subject, Anita also talks about how her learning journey brought about a change of expectations in her family:

> Through that, I've been able to inspire my kids. One's at Manchester University… he's in his final year. My daughter wants to go to Oxford to do Medicine. My oldest one has gone into the building trade and is doing fantastically well. He's gone into the management side. He would never have done that but he saw that I could do it. If mum can do it, I can do it. I like to think I have inspired them.

What we have called the ripple effect of TTL extends from the individual, to their families but also beyond that and into the communities in which they live. A concrete example of this comes from Anita as she talks about how, since returning to further education, she has actively persuaded others to do the same:

> I love people…. There isn't anyone that I have met who hasn't got some good in them, something you can bring out and something you can nurture. There's a girl that I met… she's just started her foundation degree in Health and Social Care. I persuaded her to do access…I met her in a pub, she was in bad place. She started coming in for a chat. I encouraged

her. Over a period of time she did the progression course…. Another one that I've recommend: a young lad in the village… I absolutely badgered him. He was good kid going to waste. He's a hard worker. He just needed direction. He saw the resources that they've got (in college) and he was in his element. He signed up there and then. He's settled… it's lovely to see.

In this passage, Anita illustrates how she became an advocate for returning to education in informal social spaces within her community. There are two points to make here: first it seems inconceivable that the two people she talks about would have returned to education without her intervention. Her intervention provides an illustration of how further education that is embedded in communities is less likely to have an issue with accessing 'hard to reach' students and communities. In this way, her interventions also reveal the hollowness of notions of marketing and public relations that underpin the commodification of further education in these neoliberal times and that may be governed by commercial interest rather than the care and concern informing Anita's actions.

David, a participant from a traveller background, began attending literacy classes in Rochdale and spoke about how being unable to read and write made it difficult to navigate through everyday social encounters:

> When you can't read and write out there, it's really hard. And it's scary. Now I can actually read and write and sign my own name. When I go to the doctor I can sign a note… You need education to learn about everything that's going on outside.

What's striking about the passage is David's use of the word 'fear'. This stemmed not just from an inability to decipher a given text but the uncertainty that comes from not knowing when you might next be called on to do so. David's reasons for not being able to read and write stemmed from his childhood:

> I had a bit of a bad childhood….. I didn't really have help while I was at school. I'm an English gypsy so I was raised in a travelling family. So it was quite hard. I never went to school, I went to work instead. There's a lot of people in the travelling community, mostly with the boys they don't

read and write, a lot of them don't. It's normally down to the women to do that kind of thing, the reading and writing of letters and things. Like the gas and the electric bills and all that: They normally sort all that out. The men normally go to work. (At) about eight I went to work. Started working with my dad, till I was about fifteen or sixteen…

In this example, David's motivation to improve his literacy skills is in effect a way of ensuring his children have more choices than he had. TTL in David's case is about breaking intergenerational patterns of poverty through education. David stressed how learning to read would enable him to get his driving licence. This clearly connected in his mind to being able to work. But the primary motivation David had for learning was connected to his role as a father: he wanted to be able to read bedtime stories to his four-year-old daughter:

> I've got a bit more confidence, I never had much confidence. I couldn't read at all. Now I've started picking up words. It feels great. My little girl, she used to read stories to me and I couldn't read stories back to her. But now I can actually read back. It feels brilliant. It's only from coming here that I've got that… You can do these things, you've just got to want to do it.

For David then, an effective way in tackling his literacy issue was to focus on habitual practices with a finite number of texts, so that these could be revisited in a safe environment. Bedtimes stories offered him the perfect opportunity. Children have favourite stories and enjoy hearing them repeatedly. Claiming literacy was also a catalyst for David to take part in our democratic processes.

> I never voted in my life ever. I sat down and read the thing that came through the letterbox and I thought yeah I'll give that a go. And I voted for the first time. I'd never ever voted before and you need to vote. Everyone needs to vote. Now I can actually read and write and sign my own name. When I go to the doctor, I can sign a note… You need education to know what's going on outside: the politics and all that. I'd never voted in my life, ever. I read the thing that came through the letterbox and I voted for the first time.

7 Further Educations: Transformative Teaching and Learning ...

While David had moved away from his traveller background, the impact of participation in adult learning has clearly had a multi-faceted impact on him in the community that he and his family are now a part of. Not only has his further education given him confidence in a range of everyday social situations, crucially, it has also given him entry into our democratic practices.

Nyomi was another project participant that we met in the north east of England. The narratives of participants in this area of the country all carried a historical subtext dating back to the Miners' Strike of the early 1980s. The mining villages surround Durham were severely affected by the pit closures that happened in the wake of the dispute. Many villages often depended on the mines as the main employer in the area. Consequently, pit closures resulted mass unemployment and on future job prospects. A mother with a young daughter, her story was one that involved completing a Diploma in Youth work but then finding, as a result of local authority cuts, that there were no jobs in that area of work either. This, coupled with her responsibility as a carer for her partner isolated her and had a negative impact on her mental health.

> I kind of spiralled into quite a bad depression. I got pregnant, had my daughter and luckily my daughter gave us a little bit of a boost, so I went and got help for my depression... It was the Health Visitor that spoke to us and tried to get us to get a little bit of motivation and to go back out into the world and try again.

In Nyomi's case, being on benefits carried a social stigma. She talked about the way she and her partner were 'looked down on' by neighbours while they were unemployed and on benefits. Nyomi's hopes for the future and plans were affected by the economic and employment conditions of the local area added to complex personal and family circumstances. Enrolling on an Access to HE course and having support for her dyslexia provided Nyomi with an opportunity to experience TTL. Nyomi talked about the ripple effects of her further education and the benefits for her family.

> I became a mam of somebody with a health condition. That was who I was. I wasn't who I had been. As soon as I got depression I went on a downward spiral. I found it very difficult going out… I had spent the last four years extremely depressed because of the way my life was panning out. I didn't think… I didn't see myself in education again. And it's hard when you come from living and not having a job and you know that you should be working… and nobody employing you… The only thing I could do to give my daughter some kind of life was to do the Access Course. It's been amazing… I came off anti-depressants which I'd been on for quite some time. I made friends with people. And I haven't really spoken to a lot of people in years. It really does change your life. It's allowed me to get back out… Within two months I was a completely different person.

Nyomi's narrative is important because it shows how adult education has a role in providing opportunities for people who are caught up in geographically specific socio-economic circumstances. While the impact of these circumstances are felt by individuals on a social and physical level, locally situated adult education opens doors that offer people hope. Nyomi's further education did not involve her signing up for a 'retraining package'—important as such initiatives might be—rather, it was accessed informally, almost as a form of social prescription. Nevertheless, its impact has clearly been massive and has resulted in renewed hope within the family unit.

> I went from being in the house all the time or going to hospital appointments with my daughter to having something to look forward to. It (also) changed my partner into a more confident person. We were both in quite a bad situation when we were depressed because he was depressed too – but his was more to do with his health. So giving him some extra responsibility… he changed completely. Two years ago, he would never have gone back to college because he just didn't have that confidence. So he hid away from a lot of things.

Nyomi's narrative illustrates how adult education offers a way out of despair and how this positive impact fed into her family situations. Clearly, the transformation of her aspirations is likely to impact on the dynamics of the family and on her daughter's well-being. Nyomi's empowerment as a student fed into her confidence and the value she felt in her role as a mother and partner.

Discussion

In this next section, we will reflect on the current state of adult education in the UK and comment on what we have learnt from the narratives we have gathered.

Class Matters in Times of Austerity

Since the 1980s research and debates surrounding class may be seen as being side-lined in political discourse. Indeed, notions of class loyalty and solidarity, in many ways, were torn apart under Thatcherism. In 1997 New Labour came into power. This heralded a re-invigoration of conservatism and the notion of a classless society was seen and heard in party rhetoric of meritocracy and equal opportunities. Individualism and self-improvement were driven under this premise as were ideas that 'talent' was based on ability rather than privilege (Lucey and Reay 2002; Reay and Lucey 2003; Reay 2004). These ideologies were deeply embedded in the neo-liberal rhetoric of 'choice for all'. However, there is overwhelming evidence that in economically unequal societies, those with enhanced resources/capitals are in the best position to make choices and those who are at a structural disadvantage who may be poor or who have grown up in economically depressed areas, have much more limited options (Ball et al. 2000; Ball 2010; Duckworth and Smith 2017).

The notion that class identities have diminished in significance over recent decades is also a key feature of some contemporary social theory. This may be seen as a result of the cultural shifts aligned with individualisation, de-traditionalisation and post-modernism (for examples, see Beck 1992; Giddens 1991; Bauman 1987, 1998). The idea of class going 'out of fashion' was a consequence of post-modern thought with its emphasis on multiple identities, an atomised social reality and its challenging of the 'grand narratives' that provided the underpinning for much Marxist thought at the time. The forces of globalisation including the demise of the USSR trumpeted by Fukuyama (1989) as signalling the 'triumph of the West, of the Western idea' and 'the total exhaustion of viable systematic alternatives to Western liberalism', appears however to have reconstituted society in ways which mean social class remains a powerful explanatory concept.

Our study argues that class still plays a key explanatory role in understanding educational trajectories today. This is reflected in the narratives of adult participants in the study. Many expressed feelings about having been written off as 'thick' at school (Anita) and having to battle with teachers' and others' low expectations. This data challenges the trend of political dismissal of class and instead places it as a key thematic strand that explains the way people are oppressed and communities are silenced. If sociologists and educationalists are to understand how social class and gender impact on adult education, it is vital to trace the links between people's experience of schooling and to recognise how further education is able to reconfigure the trajectories set by these negative experiences of schooling, enabling people to fulfil their real potential and giving them hope.

Social, Cultural and Educational Capitals Matter

Beck (1992) and Giddens (1992) discuss the move from traditional relational customs, to 'de-traditionalisation' and individualisation. They argue that the significance of class, gender, family and religion is fading and that tradition is being replaced by individualisation and personal fulfilment in relationships. We could argue this is a simplistic analysis and that structural inequalities such as class, gender and ethnicity continue to shape people's lives and trajectories. Social, cultural and educational capitals impact upon so-called 'freedom of choice'. Under these lenses, the notion of individualisation is problematic. Friends and family in our research provide important sources of social and emotional capital. Adult education offers spaces in which these capitals can be enhanced. Anita, David and Nyomi all spoke about the importance of the supportive relationships they experienced in the 'differential space' of the further education settings they accessed. These affirming relationships encompassed those with teachers but also with other students. The role of teachers was in nurturing and sustaining a learning environment founded on dialogical and collective learning and this was underpinned by an ethic of care (Feeley 2014).

According to the neoliberal model of rational economic 'man', social mobility is about the individual improving her/his economic prospects within existing social circumstances—perhaps with some positive spillover into the life chances of the individual's immediate family. But in our research social mobility meant more than this. It was more than individual, instead it connected strongly to changing family circumstances and cultures and orientating these towards education as a public good. It also entailed a raising of a broad critical consciousness that was retrospective in terms of helping adults to understand the background to their educational (non) attainment to date and involved a forward-looking orientation that often included the individual's wider community. In our research, TTL takes account of existing social cultural and education capital and uses these to springboard renewed agency and progression. TTL involves subverting deficit labels and the lack of confidence derived from negative prior educational experiences, re-building self-esteem and (re) constructing positive educational identities.

Communities Matter

Further education providers are embedded in communities in a way that no other educational institutions are. Not only do they have historical roots that connect them to industry and employment but, unlike schools, they have populations that draw on diverse communities beyond neighbourhood boundaries. Critical in this positioning is the history of each provider—many colleges have grown out of particular needs and economies which connects them strongly to their context and situations. The communities from which Anita, David and Nyomi come were important industrial locations. But with the demise of Rochdale's textile industry and the pit closures in the north east, local communities have been hit by unemployment and poverty has escalated. Now, both areas are a tapestry of cultures and ethnic groups. While old industries may have withered away and certainly can no longer offer the kind of long term stability that was once on offer, colleges are still connected to local employers and industries.

Many project participants made it clear that further education colleges were important because they provided spaces of social cohesion in which people from different ethnic backgrounds could mix and interact. The colleges we visited as part of the project had roots woven into the social/cultural and economic fabric and history of the landscapes they inhabited; landscapes that shaped the lives of the learners that came through their doors. For example, when talking to learners on Access to HE provision at a college in the north east, it became clear that while the college was drawing in students from outlying villages that, until the mid-1980s, had been economically dependent on coal. The communities in these villages had a legacy of unemployment and the associated impact of this in terms of poverty, health and well-being. In that sense, 30 years after pits had closed, the college was still addressing the impact of the closures, providing education and employment opportunities for young people and adults, offering them hope, real career choices and, as a corollary, a way out of cycles of mental ill-health. Nyomi's story powerful testimony of this.

Formulating Some Recommendations for Policy and Practice

Our research provides evidence that despite the instrumentalisation of the curriculum in further education colleges, TTL is still taking place. Transformative education through the enactment of a curriculum that challenges rather than reproduces social inequality, offers a frame for understanding learners' accounts of their educational and personal journey. What do these examples imply for policy and practice?

One remarkable aspect of the narratives is that the social benefits of each of the participants' journeys are far greater than the achievement of a single (funded) qualification. This is illustrative of the idea that the further education that colleges provide is about more than 'just' the achievement of funded qualification aims. For this to become a reality though, a change to the way further education for adults and young people needs be effected. While colleges and other providers are incentivised to organise their provision in order to garner maximum returns, rather than to focus on addressing individual and community needs, further education will continue to be dominated by performativity and gaming. Despite policy rhetoric trumpeting the need to put the student 'at the heart' of the process, current funding arrangements objectify students: their interests are subordinated to colleges' financial bottom-line—and this has been intensified under austerity. This has to change.

This first point also suggests that further education requires a particular kind of leadership, one that is ethically-grounded and driven by the voices and needs of local communities. What is needed is college leadership that sees value (unmeasured by funding metrics at present) in engaging with community organisations and in community outreach. Furthermore, it needs to fully appreciate and facilitate the powerful ripple effects of transformative learning, understanding how it deeply benefits not just individuals (like Anita, David and Nyomi) but their families and local communities too. Ultimately, this kind of conscious, ethical leadership connects with our country's democratic culture.

Finally, further education in England bears the marks of OECD knowledge production and policy-think—what Grek calls the 'new technology of the governance of the European education space through indicators and benchmarks' (Grek 2008, p. 215). It isn't hard to view the impact of PISA data and the influence of the OECD in general as 'deeply penetrating and consciousness-moulding' (ibid.). One consequence of this is the continued reification of the abstract space conjured into being by the term 'FE sector'. This abstract language not only disguises the hugely heterogeneous nature of the different contexts in which teaching and learning take place but is also a totalising strategy that enables policy interventions that impose neoliberal meanings on what is better thought of as local educational provision. To move away from the abstraction of 'FE' is to assert that there is no singular experience of further education; just as there are multiple compulsory educations that 'work' better for some individuals and social groups than others, in the same way, there are multiple further educations. Within a broad canvas in which the structures and cultures that shape further education have been decisively governed by an instrumentalist agenda, spaces still exist in which TTL takes place. But TTL depends on an ethos which does not seek to objectify students within a 'skills discourse'. While TTL may see a student's social class as a starting point, it doesn't use that background to label, impose restrictions and limit expectations. TTL by definition is about overthrowing the institutionalised symbolic violence which seems to be so much a part of the neoliberal conceptualisation of education/employment. TTL as experienced by adults is also strikingly individual, following distinctive and by definition not-standard pathways. In many ways it can be regarded as a necessary compensation for an overly normative compulsory education system.

Conclusion

The implementation of austerity measures has hit further education budgets particularly hard. We are now in a time and space where the gap between the richest and poorest has grown to its widest for several generations (Savage 2015) and policy reform, governed by the monetarist principles of austerity, is hitting the most vulnerable hardest. Education has a central role in the pursuit of social justice, and is pivotal to the sustained challenge to injustice. Educators are at the helm of this.

Interestingly, the current harsh funding environment has thrown the significance of TTL into sharp relief. Austerity has meant not just a reduction in funding but the consolidation of managerialist cultures (see Smith and O'Leary 2013) that undermine holistic pedagogies. Despite these hostile conditions, there is still evidence of students experiencing education as transformational. But a transformative approach to education that aligns with social justice means more than replacing the existing dominant frame with another that fails to attend to the structures of power underpinning the ways in which we position learners from marginalised backgrounds. The case studies of participants are based a dialogic engagement which emphasises listening and importantly sharing our experiences. This requires a conceptualisation of the theoretical and methodological issues involved in understanding and representing educational practice that includes the practices, knowledge and skills that learners bring into the classroom. The real-world experiences of our learners are a crucial component for thinking about how to incorporate transformational approaches in education; integrating discussion about society, representation, power, and ideology is a tool for consciousness raising, transformation and hope. Care and solidarity, driven by dialogue with learners, offers new imagined possibilities that flow to the learners, their families and their communities.

References

Ade-Ojo, G., & Duckworth, V. (2015). *Adult Literacy Policy and Practice: From Intrinsic Values to Instrumentalism*. London: Palgrave Macmillan Pivotal.

Ball, S. J. (2010). New Class Inequalities in Education: Why Education Policy May Be Looking in the Wrong Place! Education Policy, Civil Society and Social Class. *International Journal of Sociology and Social Policy, 30*(3/4), 155–166.

Ball, S., Maguire, M., & Macrae, S. (2000). *Choice, Pathways and Transitions Post-16: New Youth, New Economies in the Global City*. London: Falmer Press.

Bauman, Z. (1987). *Legislators and Interpreters: On Modernity, Postmodernity and Intellectuals*. Cambridge: Polity Press.

Bauman, Z. (1998). *Globalization: The Human Consequences*. Cambridge: Polity Press.

Beck, U. (1992). *Risk Society: Towards a New Modernity*. London: Sage.

Becker, G. S. (1993). *Human Capital: A Theoretical and Empirical Analysis with Special Reference to Education*. London: University of Chicago Press.

Boeren, E. (2016). *Adult Lifelong Learning Participation*. London: Springer.

Breunig, M. (2005). Turning Experiential Education and Critical Pedagogy Theory into Praxis. *Journal of Experiential Education, 28*(2), 106–122.

British Educational Research Association. (2011). *Ethical Guidelines for Educational Research*. https://www.bera.ac.uk/wp-content/uploads/2014/02/BERA-Ethical-Guidelines-2011.pdf?noredirect=1. 29 January 2018.

Davies, W. (2014). *The Limits of Neoliberalism*. London: Sage.

Dorling, D. (2011). *Injustice: Why Social Inequality Persists*. Bristol: Policy Press.

Duckworth, V. (2013). *Learning Trajectories, Violence and Empowerment Amongst Adult Basic Skills Learners*. London: Routledge Research in Education.

Duckworth, V., & Smith, R. (2017). *Further Education in England—Transforming Lives and Communities: Interim Report*. London: University and College Union.

Duckworth, V., & Smith, R. (2018). Transformative Learning in English Further Education. In C. Borg, P. Mayo, & R. Sultana (Eds.), *Skills for Sustainable Human Development of the International Handbook on Vocational Education and Training for Changing the World of Work*. London: Springer.

Duckworth, V., & Smith, R. (2019). Research, Criticality & Adult and Further Education: Catalysing Hope and Dialogic Caring. In M. Hamilton & L. Tett (Eds.), *Resisting the Neo-Liberal Discourse in Education: Local, National and Transnational Perspectives*. London: Policy Press.

Feeley, M. (2014). *Learning Care Lessons: Literacy, Love, Care and Solidarity*. London: Tufnell Press.

Field, J. (2000). *Lifelong Learning and the New Educational Order*. Stoke-on-Trent: Trentham Books.

Field, J. (2008). *Social Capital*. London: Routledge.

Field, J., Gallacher, A., & Ingram, R. (Eds.). (2009). *Researching Transitions in Lifelong Learning*. London: Routledge.

Foucault, M. (1982). The Subject & Power. *Critical Inquiry, 8*(4), 777–795.

Freire, P. (1996). *Pedagogy of the Oppressed*. London: Penguin.

Fukuyama, F. (1989). *The End of History*. https://ps321.community.uaf.edu/files/2012/10/Fukuyama-End-of-history-article.pdf. 15 November 2017.

Giddens, A. (1991). *Modernity and Self-Identity: Self and Society in the Late Modern Age*. Cambridge: Polity Press.

Giddens, A. (1992). *The Transformation of Intimacy: Sexuality, Love and Eroticism in Modern Societies*. Stanford, CA: Stanford University Press.

Grek, S. (2008). From Symbols to Numbers: The Shifting Technologies of Education Governance in Europe. *European Education Research Journal, 7*(2), 208–218.

Halford, S., Pope, C., & Weal, M. (2012). Digital Futures? *Sociological Challenges and Opportunities in the Emergent Semantic Web, 47*(1), 173–189.

Harvey, D. (2005). *A Brief History of Neoliberalism*. Oxford: Oxford University Press.

Herndl, C., & Nahrwold, C. (2000). Research as Social Practice. *Written Communication, 17*(2), 258–296.

Hope, M. (2002). New Labour's Policy on Inclusion: Will Practice Match Principles? *Forum: For Promoting 13–19 Comprehensive Education, 44*(3), 93–98.

James, N., & Busher, H. (2013). Researching Hybrid Learning Communities in the Digital Age Through Educational Ethnography. *Ethnography and Education, 8*(2), 194–209.

Keep, E. (2006). State Control of the English Education and Training System—Playing with the Biggest Train Set in the World. *Journal of Vocational Education & Training,* 58(1), 47–64.
Lefebvre, H. (1991). *The Production of Space.* Oxford: Blackwell.
Lucey, H., & Reay, D. (2002). A Market in Waste: Psychic and Structural Dimensions of School-Choice Policy in the UK and Children's Narratives on "Demonised" Schools. *Discourse,* 23(3), 253–266.
Mezirow, J. and associates. (2000). *Fostering Critical Reflection: A Guide to Transformative and Emancipatory Learning.* Mahwah: Jossey-Bass.
OFQUAL. (2016). *A Guide to GCSE Results, Summer 2016.* https://www.gov.uk/government/news/a-guide-to-gcse-results-summer-2016. 1 December 2017.
Pink, S. (2007). *Doing Visual Ethnography.* London: Sage.
Reay, D. (2004). "It's all a Habitus": Beyond the Habitual use of Habitus in Educational Research. *British Journal of Sociology of Education,* 25(4), 431–444.
Reay, D., & Lucey, H. (2003). The Limits of "Choice": Children and Inner City Schooling. *Sociology,* 37(1), 121–142.
Savage, M. (2015). Introduction to Elites: From the 'Problematic of the Proletariat' to a Class Analysis of 'Wealth Elites'. *The Sociological Review,* 63(2), 223–239.
Smith, R. (2017). Area Reviews and the End of Incorporation: A Machiavellian Moment. In M. Daley, K. Orr, & J. Petrie (Eds.), *The Principal.* London: UCL IOE Press.
Smith, R., & O'Leary, M. (2013). NPM in an Age of Austerity: Knowledge and Experience in Further Education. *Journal of Educational Administration and History,* 45(3), 244–266.
Smith, R., & O'Leary, M. (2015). Partnership as Cultural Practice in the Face of Neoliberal Reform. *Journal of Educational Administration and History,* 47(2), 174–192.
Tedder, M., & Biesta, G. (2009). …. In J. Field, J. Gallacher, & R. Ingram (Eds.), *Researching Transitions in Lifelong Learning.* London: Routledge.
Tovey, A. (2017, November 23). Apprenticeship Levy Behind 60pc Collapse in Number of People Starting Training Courses. *Daily Telegraph.* http://www.telegraph.co.uk/business/2017/11/23/apprenticeship-levy-behind-60pc-collapse-number-people-starting/. 27 November 2017.
Walkerdine, V., Lucey, H., & Melody, J. (2001). *Growing up Girl: Psychosocial Explorations of Gender and Class.* London: Palgrave.

8

Adult Education in Community Organisations Supporting Homeless Adults: Exploring the Impact of Austerity Politics

Katy Jones

Introduction

This chapter explores the education provision in third sector organisations which aim to support homeless adults. More specifically, it focuses on the impact of austerity politics on the adult education offered and facilitated in these community settings. The chapter begins by introducing the concept of homelessness, and its relationship with adult education in both policy and practice. It then presents data gathered from 27 semi-structured qualitative interviews with practitioners working across the Greater Manchester homelessness sector. It argues that 'austerity politics' has impacted upon education in these contexts in two key ways: first, through the reductions in the resources organisations are able to access to support such activities and second, through the impact austerity has had on the people they seek to support. However, whilst an impact can no doubt be observed, it is suggested that the 'politics of austerity' do not

K. Jones (✉)
University of Salford, Greater Manchester, UK
e-mail: K.E.Jones@salford.ac.uk

© The Author(s) 2019
E. Boeren and N. James (eds.), *Being an Adult Learner in Austere Times*, https://doi.org/10.1007/978-3-319-97208-4_8

represent a major shift in the provision of adult education in these contexts: it appears to have always occupied a precarious position, due both to poor resourcing and the multiple and complex needs of the people who homelessness agencies seek to support.

What Is Homelessness and Who Are Homeless People?

Homelessness is a complex and challenging social phenomenon which takes multiple forms and has multiple causes (Fitzpatrick 2005). There is no single agreed definition of, cause of, or solution to homelessness (Neale 1997; Wagner 2012). People living in a range of conditions can be described as homeless—including those who are 'roofless', 'houseless', and those living in insecure or inadequate housing (Amore et al. 2011). Homelessness is a dynamic phenomenon, affecting a large number of households at different points in time (Wagner 2012). It has been shown to have many 'causes' including a lack of resources to cover the costs of housing, substance and alcohol misuse, exclusion from the paid labour market, relationship breakdown and domestic abuse.

The focus of the research presented in this chapter was on organisations offering services designed to support those often referred to as 'single homeless people'. The current homelessness legislation in England enshrined in the 1977 Housing (Homeless Persons) Act denies most single homeless people a right to housing, as those in this group are not generally considered to be in 'priority need'. As such, they are often owed no legal duty of support from the state. Single homeless people (hereafter, homeless people) can be found in a range of housing situations. Some live in temporary accommodation, including hostels and supported housing projects, some sleep rough, reside in squats, or 'sofa surf' (Fitzpatrick et al. 2016). Whilst policymakers recognise single homeless people as a group with particular support needs,[1] local authorities in England currently have

---

[1]For example, through funding projects through the Help for Single Homeless Fund, http://bit.ly/2m3CkLr, accessed 20 February 2017.

no legal responsibility to assist them. As such, support for this group is often limited to that provided by third sector organisations.

Whilst all experience a lack of secure accommodation, homeless men and women are a diverse group of people with different backgrounds, experiences, capabilities, aspirations and constraints. A high proportion of homeless people have multiple and complex needs (for example, mental and physical ill-health, drug and alcohol misuse) which exist alongside their housing insecurity, and can make identifying solutions and developing appropriate support a challenging endeavour (Dwyer and Somerville 2011).

Homelessness and Education

The relationship between homelessness and education is a complex one which has received little attention in both the grey and academic literatures. Data limitations are a well-known problem in research concerning homeless people (due both to an absence of robust data collection activities and the transient and often 'hidden' nature of the homeless population) (Anderson 2010), and evidence on education and skill levels is restricted to that provided by ad hoc and infrequent surveys of homeless service users (within the context of the UK, these are also predominantly London-based). Despite its limitations, the available data suggest that homeless people generally have low formally defined skill and education levels (Fitzpatrick et al. 2000; Barton et al. 2006). According to a survey conducted by Crisis (Luby and Welch 2006), for example, '*homeless people are twice as likely as the general population to have no qualifications*'. In addition, a survey of Thames Reach service users found that only 13% have one or more qualifications, ranging from Entry 1 to Level 2 (Olisa et al. 2010), and only 18% of St Mungo's Broadway service users surveyed reported having any qualifications above Level 2 (Dumoulin and Jones 2014). A small but growing evidence base also suggests many homeless adults have weak literacy and numeracy or 'basic' skills (Dumoulin and Jones 2014; Luby and Welch 2006; Olisa et al. 2010). Recognising significant skills issues within the single homeless population is not to say that all homeless people have low skills and qualification levels. Indeed, reflecting the diverse pathways leading to homelessness, those who might be formally considered to be highly skilled and well educated may find themselves without a home (Hough et al. 2013). That being said, the majority of homeless people have faced poverty and social exclusion throughout their lives and as such those homeless people with high formally defined skill levels can perhaps be considered an exception rather than the rule.

Participating in learning has the potential to have a positive impact on multiple aspects of adult's lives. For those experiencing homelessness, studies have shown the benefits of learning engagement to range from increasing confidence and reducing social isolation to being better able to manage a tenancy and move into (or closer to) work (Castleton 2001; Dumoulin and Jones 2014; Luby and Welch 2006; DCLG 2007; Homeless Link 2012). Scholars have also emphasised the transformative potential of adult education, with community education in particular identified as a site for empowering learners, and through which social and economic inequalities can be identified and challenged (Tett 2010). However, previous studies have also highlighted significant challenges in engaging those facing social and economic disadvantage in adult education provision (Crowther et al. 2010). Barriers to adult participation in learning have been shown to exist at individual and institutional levels, alongside factors relating to the broader policy context in which adult education provision and adult learners are located (Boeren 2016). Similarly, the available evidence suggests that homeless people are often excluded from opportunities and support offered through adult education services (Barton et al. 2006; Luby and Welch 2006; Reisenberger et al. 2010; Olisa et al. 2010; Dumoulin and Jones 2014). Research has consistently found that homeless people are often reluctant to engage with, or do not benefit from, the provision of adult education with mainstream, or 'formal' education institutions (as is also the case with a range of other public services such as healthcare) (Barton et al. 2006; Luby and Welch 2006; Reisenberger et al. 2010; Olisa et al. 2010; Dumoulin and Jones 2014).

Adult Education for Homeless Adults: The Policy and Practice Context

Recognising both the barriers to accessing mainstream provision alongside the benefits that engagement in learning can bring, the homelessness sector provides a variety of both informal and formal learning opportunities for its service users (Homeless Link 2012; Pleace and Bretherton 2014). Across the sector, adult education is supported alongside other interventions to address the diverse range of complex and multiple needs that many homeless people have (including a lack of accommodation, isolation, drug and alcohol dependency issues, mental and physical health impairments) (Dwyer and Somerville 2011). Perhaps most well-known are Crisis' 'Skylight' centres which focus on providing education, employment and arts-based activities at a number of centres across the country (Pleace and Bretherton 2014). However, it is not just the largest, long-established organisations in which learning takes place: according to the umbrella body Homeless Link: *'the vast majority of homelessness services are supporting people to enter work, training or to engage in other activities'* (Homeless Link 2012). Although providing education and training opportunities is not typically a primary focus of the work of third sector homelessness agencies, these and other community organisations have long been identified as important sites for learning, especially for the most 'excluded' groups in society (Reisenberger et al. 2010; Tett 2010). Furthermore, exclusion from mainstream adult education provision and a preference to engage with non-governmental, charitable organisations can mean that the support homeless people are able to access depends on what these local services are able to offer outside of the mainstream adult education system.

Whilst not the only factor at play, government policy and funding at both the national and local level has an important impact on the work of many homelessness organisations, including the education and learning opportunities offered within them (Buckingham 2010; Dumoulin and Jones 2014). For many organisations, financial support from the government is integral to their operations and, given the diverse needs of the homeless population, several policy domains (for example, housing, health, education and skills and social security) can impact both directly and indirectly on the services available to those who find themselves within it.

Over the past couple of decades, a number of policy initiatives have been introduced which cut across both adult education and homelessness policy. The 'Places of Change Agenda', for example, which sought to encourage homelessness services to do more to '*move service users into appropriate training and sustainable employment*' (DCLG 2007, p. 6), saw a proliferation of "education, training and employment" (ETE) and "meaningful activities" in services supporting single homeless adults. Prior to this, the Skills for Life Strategy identified homeless people as a target group in need of support to improve their literacy and numeracy skills (DfEE 2001), thus stimulating the development of basic skills programmes in a range of community settings, including some services supporting homeless adults (Barton et al. 2006). More recently, additional government funding was provided, through STRIVE (Skills, Training, Innovation and Employment) pre-employment pilots, which took place in London in two national homelessness charities, jointly funded by the Department of Business Innovation and Skills and the Department of Communities and Local Government (DCLG/BIS 2014). STRIVE was a small scale 'pre-employment' programme, providing an opportunity for homeless people to build their confidence and develop their basic IT, maths and English skills. Commenting at the pilot's inception, the then Skills and enterprise minister, Matthew Hancock, said:

> It is wrong that until now excellent education projects led by St Mungo's Broadway and others have been denied government funding – today we are putting that right. There is no doubt that charities like St Mungo's Broadway and Crisis are the best placed to reach those in need of help, but we are backing them in this vital task.[2]

---

[2]http://www.localgov.co.uk/Employment-pilot-for-London-homeless-wins-government-support/36111, accessed 12 May 2017.

However, despite policy rhetoric around the value of engaging homeless adults in education, the amount of statutory funding for learning and skills flowing into homelessness agencies has been minimal. According to a recent survey of homelessness organisations in England, only one percent of accommodation projects had received any 'employment and education' funding, for day centres this was seven per cent (compared to five per cent for all homelessness services in 2010). Beyond STRIVE, it is unclear what the current government's commitment to this agenda involves. Three years after the pilot's inception, no further statements have been forthcoming. In addition, following broader policy shifts towards 'localism', policy decisions relating to adult education are increasingly taken at a local level. Whether local decision makers will share the then Ministers sentiments on adult education in homelessness services is yet to be seen. Moreover, under the politics of austerity, homelessness organisations have been under increasing strain, with cuts to government funding presenting considerable challenges for homeless agencies and the range of services they provide (Fitzpatrick et al. 2016). Within the current context of fiscal austerity, the range of potential funding streams available to homelessness agencies have experienced drastic funding reductions resulting in significant cuts to the public resources flowing into third sector homelessness agencies (Homeless Link 2015; Fitzpatrick et al. 2016). Despite this, it is striking that 50% of homelessness day centres reported directly providing 'employment, training and education' activities in-house in 2015. A further 70% provided 'meaningful activities' (Homeless Link 2015). Thus, whilst typically not in receipt of skills funding, the sector appears committed to supporting learning amongst its service users.

A Study of the Greater Manchester Homelessness Sector

The importance of engaging adults experiencing homelessness in education has at least in part been recognised by both policymakers and homelessness service providers, reflected in both publicly funded (albeit very small scale) initiatives and the prevalence of education and training provision across the homelessness sector. However, beyond the limited information that can be gleaned from sector surveys, little is known about what this education provision looks like in practice. In addition, whilst the adult education world has undoubtedly been squeezed by the politics of austerity (as demonstrated through the other contributions to this edited collection), it is unclear whether education provided in a sector where this is not typically the primary aim of the services included within it will be impacted by the 'politics of austerity' in the same way.

In order to address these knowledge gaps, this chapter presents a case study of the Greater Manchester homelessness sector. It draws on data from an empirical study investigating the ETE support offered by third sector organisations supporting homeless adults. The study was conducted in 2015 and involved 27 semi-structured qualitative interviews with staff working in different roles (including support/project workers, volunteer coordinators, chief executives) at a range of levels ('operational', 'managerial', 'strategic') across twelve third sector homelessness organisations operating in the Greater Manchester area. The sample comprises workers from organisations of different types and sizes, including accommodation projects, activity centres and social enterprises. Except in one instance, the provision of education and learning opportunities was not a key aim of the organisations from which the sample was drawn. Whilst the focus of the wider study was on the support offered by services which sought to help their service users to move into or closer to work, discussions were wide-ranging, providing an insight into the range of education activities facilitated within each of the organisations and the factors shaping them.

Adult Education Provision Across the Greater Manchester Homelessness Sector

Interviews with workers from homelessness agencies across the Greater Manchester area highlight a wide range of education and training opportunities currently (or recently) taking place within these settings. These included opportunities to:

- develop digital and budgeting skills,
- gain new vocational skills through work experience and volunteering,
- participate in reading and creative writing groups,
- access support to improve literacy and numeracy,
- learn about and manage changes in the benefit system,
- participate in gardening and arts classes; and
- attend cooking classes.

Reflecting community learning principles, these activities were reported to have been developed in response to their service users' needs and aspirations, building on their existing skills and achievements. Interviewees also emphasised the importance of improving confidence and self-esteem rather than focusing solely on improving a person's skill levels or employment prospects. Activities varied in formality and were supported by a mix of external education providers offering outreach work within these settings, and in-house by staff and volunteers.

Recognising the benefits associated with but also barriers to their service users attending college, several interviewees emphasised the value in hosting adult education provision within their services, and as such had in the past gladly welcomed and hosted external education agencies within their settings. So long as external providers understood and worked well with their client group, they were open and willing to engage with any agencies they felt could benefit or 'strengthen' their service users. To this end, many of the staff working in homelessness organisations also helped their service users to identify learning opportunities within the wider community—either because they were unable to offer them in-house, or as part of efforts to help people to expand their social networks and 're-integrate' into mainstream society.

Participants were asked to identify any factors shaping the education they provided or facilitated within the context of their organisation. Whilst primarily driven by the needs of their service users, whether or not activities were in place depended in large part on whether or not their organisations were able to access adequate resources to support them. These resources might be monetary (including financial support from government), but also included drawing on the time and expertise of external adult education providers and volunteers. Consequently, some educational activities taking place in their settings were long-term, ongoing projects, whereas others were ad hoc and time-limited. All interviewees described operating within a difficult funding climate which had a significant impact on the range of support and services they were able to provide (including, but not limited to, the educational activities they were able to offer). The following sections explore the impact of austerity on the range of educational activities supported by this group of third sector homelessness agencies. The accounts of the interviewees suggest that austerity has impacted on provision in these settings in two main ways: first, through the reduction in resources they are able to access to support such activities, and the way in which organisations have responded to such funding pressures, and second, through the impact that wider policies justified by the need to 'live within our means' have impacted on some of the most vulnerable people in our society.

Victims of the Shrinking Pots: Reducing Resources for Education in Homelessness Settings

Reflecting the lack of state-funded learning across the homelessness sector highlighted above, most organisations in which the study participants worked were not direct recipients of any sort of statutory skills funding. Given this, and that the provision of education and learning opportunities is not typically a primary aim of such organisations, recent cuts to statutory adult skills funding may appear to be of little significance to the homelessness sector. It is perhaps surprising then, that interview data reveal that the politics of austerity in adult education is felt in these contexts in a number of ways.

First, interviewees described a notable reduction in engagement and outreach work undertaken by local colleges and other external learning providers. Whilst many had hosted tutors from local education providers in the past, they were disappointed at the recent reduction or withdrawal of such support due to funding cuts:

> *We used to have the* [adult education provider] *in. They used to regularly do stuff at* [the organisation]. *I'm going back several years … particularly literacy classes … but all that funding's gone.* (Operational level worker, activity centre)

It is interesting to note that literacy support appeared to be the most common outreach activity previously undertaken—but whilst literacy and numeracy funding has supposedly been protected from the impact of austerity, this protection does not appear to extend to outreach work in these community settings. Relatedly, only one participant mentioned 'Skills for Life', one of the most significant adult education policies over the past few decades, reflecting that:

> All that concern with Skills for Life has gone … back then, you couldn't turn a corner without somebody telling you the stats about young male illiteracy levels and stuff like that. I don't hear it anymore. (Strategic level worker, activity centre)

There were some examples where organisations had been able to draw down Community Learning funds to directly provide learning opportunities. However, the specialist learning provider included within the sample explained how accessing funding which recognised the challenges working with their 'client group' was particularly difficult within the current funding climate:

> If we go to a hostel and two people show up, and the funding that we've used for that is based on a guided learning hour calculation … we've, you know, we can't … it's not sustainable for us. So we need to find funding that recognises how much it costs to do that well and that's a real struggle at the moment. (Strategic level worker, activity centre)

More generally, interviewees also felt that opportunities for learning within the wider community were becoming increasingly limited. Where respondents were supporting service users to identify learning opportunities outside of their organisation, several talked about restrictions on the courses available in their local areas. Most concerning was a lack of opportunities for 'older' learners:

If you're under 25, you've got a lot more options ... If I've got somebody who's 27, who would benefit so much – they don't get a look in. (Operational level worker, activity centre)

Interviewees also identified a lack of free or low cost learning opportunities, reflecting trends towards increasing consumerism in adult education and a tendency for lifelong learning to reproduce inequalities through the continued exclusion of those with least access to education (Bowl 2014; Field 2000). They also highlighted a decline in opportunities to attend night classes—this was particularly relevant for those homeless people who had volunteering commitments during the day and so were unable to take advantage of concessionary opportunities taking place in their local area at this time. Restrictions also extended to the types (subjects) of learning opportunities available.

[T]*here are a number other colleges who ... have found money to be able to fund courses but they tend to be the same old same old ... Want to do a level 2 in customer service? Want to do a level 2 in cleaning? Well no, we don't really - it's all a bit mundane!* (Strategic level worker, social enterprise)

Where there's a will there's a way: supporting education and learning activities through other means.

Homelessness organisations draw on a range of resources to support their work. Beyond statutory skills funding, interviewees described drawing on traditional third sector funding sources (for example large grant-making trusts and one-off grants from local authorities) to fund learning activities. Within the context of austerity a number of interviewees explained how they had needed to diversify their funding streams to keep their service running. More positively, in some instances new sources of funding had been used to support learning activities—a small minority of organisations sampled were successful in accessing funds designed to improve community health and well-being to provide learning opportunities for service users:

It amounts to maybe two or three hundred thousand quid over the last few years from health sources, that we've been able to use in relation to things around structured activities … like our [gardening] project, activities that will stimulate engagement … It's called health money, but it can be used for learning engagement. (Strategic level worker, activity centre)

Interviewees also explained how in the past they had been able to take advantage of free training from the National Health Service (NHS) for both staff and service users who were volunteering and hoping to work in the sector. Although this too had recently fallen victim to austerity:

[The NHS] *deliver training to any client that's working with clients in [local authority]. That's going to get cut … it's really good for them to have their mental health level 1, 2 and 3, for their stepping stones, for their learning, but that's not going to be available.* (Operational level worker, accommodation project)

In many instances though, it was the time donated by volunteers that was integral to the ongoing provision of learning activities. Several interviewees described the valuable role of volunteers in developing activities and helping service users to work towards their own educational goals through one-to-one support. Whilst highly valued by the organisations, a reliance on volunteers to support the ongoing provision of learning opportunities is perhaps at odds with the espoused importance of learning opportunities for homeless people by successive governments (Bowl 2014). Interviewees were conscious that both the quality and consistency of support provided by volunteers could not be guaranteed:

He is a volunteer. So again it's hit and miss. If [he] *doesn't want to come then we can't force him.* (Operational level worker, activity centre)

This was felt to be particularly problematic given that homeless learners could initially be reluctant to engage in education provision and had often been let down by the mainstream education system in the past.

Responding to Welfare Reform: The Wider Implications of Austerity on Education for Homeless Learners

The politics of austerity extends beyond cuts to public service expenditure. Interview data show how the wider implications of austerity (most notably, the major programme of welfare reform) also impact on the services offered by homelessness organisations as they responded to the needs of their service users, many of whom were struggling to adapt to a stricter and less generous welfare regime (Crisis et al. 2012; Batty et al. 2015). According to the accounts of the interviewees, welfare reform has impacted on the educational activities offered by homelessness services in several different ways. Some interviewees described needing to plan course provision around the conditions service users were expected to meet in order to access benefits. For example, provision was planned to allow for missed sessions and lateness in recognition of their service users' need to prioritise attending appointments at the job centre. This, it was felt, was not as well catered for in other 'mainstream' adult education settings such as local adult colleges.

> We definitely operate on the understanding that that's gonna happen and we have all sorts of things in place to make sure that doesn't derail things. (Managerial level worker, activity centre)
> It affects the attendance that we do have because they do have appointments on what they need to stick to. (Operational level worker, accommodation project)

Welfare reform also shaped the content of the activities offered by the organisations sampled. Whilst a range of educational activities had taken place in the past, a number of interviewees explained how increasing amounts of staff time were taken up by helping service users to learn about and understand benefit changes, and advocating on their behalf to challenge decisions made by the Department for Work and Pensions regarding their benefit claims:

There's an element of crisis work that has become a priority at times … the number of people in situations where they've been going for week after week without money … that kind of work has taken a priority over the last year or so. (Strategic level worker, activity centre)

This also involved putting in place or hosting training around improving digital skills in order to equip service users with the skills they need to navigate the new cost-saving 'digital by default' system for administering people's social security payments.

A Significant Change or Just More of the Same?

The above has highlighted two main ways in which austerity politics have impacted on adult education in third sector organisations supporting homeless adults. Austerity policies have impacted on the provision in these settings both directly, through the withdrawal of financial support to organisations of all kinds across the homelessness sector, and indirectly through the reduction of outreach activities in these settings conducted by professional adult educators. Wider policy shifts involving welfare retrenchment and a stricter social security regime often justified through rhetoric about the necessity of 'living within our means' has further impacted on educational activities in these settings, as resources are deployed towards 'crisis management' rather than broader, social investment activities designed to support service users towards social and economic independence in the longer term.

Yet whilst the scale of recent public spending cuts is unprecedented, and is undoubtedly having an impact on the services such organisations are able (or are needing) to provide, it might be argued that the place of adult education in these settings has not changed in any fundamental way as a result. Education in these settings has always occupied a precarious position. Whilst this reflects the fact that adult education is not typically a primary aim of such organisations, this also reflects established structures of social exclusion and longer term trends of an emphasis on education for employment above all else.

As a group, homeless people have consistently been identified as 'hard to help' and to be among those furthest away from the labour market so it is unsurprising that funding for skills support does not gravitate to these settings given the overwhelming focus on education for work. Furthermore, a lack of funding for 'older' adults (typically defined as those aged over 25) is a long-standing issue in adult education provision, which has been recognised by homelessness practitioners before the politics of austerity came into play—according to a survey of the homelessness sector in 2010 (pre-dating the politics of austerity), staff highlighted a lack of opportunities for those over the age of 25 (Homeless Link 2010). Despite policy rhetoric around the value and economic necessity of lifelong learning, for those who do not achieve at school or soon after, opportunities for learning and improving skills are limited. This is particularly the case for those unable to fund their own participation in adult education courses. As such, it could be argued that austerity politics amplifies longer term trends towards accreditation and instrumentalism which are hard to marry with the complex support needs of many homeless people.

Conclusion

As important providers of educational opportunities for homeless adults, understanding what provision in these settings looks like, and the range of factors which impacts on both the quality and quantity of this is an important area for policymakers, practitioners and researchers alike. Drawing on data from interviews with practitioners drawn from across the Greater Manchester homelessness sector, the above has explored the ways in which austerity politics has impacted on adult education in third sector organisations supporting homeless adults. It has demonstrated that when considering the impact of austerity politics on adult education (particularly that which takes place in non-specialised community contexts) it is important to look beyond education and skills policy. Cuts in a number of other public policy domains which are also subject to significant retrenchment have a cumulative impact on adult learners. It is also important to recognise that no major shift has taken place in these 'austere times'—community learning has always been poorly financed, and is not prioritised when homeless service users have (arguably) more pressing needs to address. Importantly, despite sporadic policy pronouncements about the importance of all adults participating in 'lifelong learning', statutory skills funding is still not making its way into specialist homelessness agencies in any significant way.

Recommendations for Policy and Practice

The research presented in this chapter took place in Greater Manchester, a large metropolitan county in the North West of England consisting of ten local authority districts. However, the findings are relevant for all those seeking to support those experiencing homelessness to access learning opportunities. The research has a number of implications for policy and practice. Below outlines several recommendations for stakeholders in government, the adult education sector and the homelessness sector.

For the Government

Despite sporadic policy announcements about the importance of ensuring homeless adults are given opportunities to engage in learning and develop their skills, a review of the Greater Manchester homelessness sector reveals a dearth of government funding in this area. Government must ensure that opportunities to participate in learning are adequately funded across the homelessness sector. Available funding must recognise the challenges involved in providing meaningful and sustainable learning opportunities for a group with multiple and complex needs, and build on existing provision which has been developed in response to service user needs and capabilities. Given increasing moves towards devolved skills funding, it is important that local government recognises its responsibilities in this area.

For the Adult Education Sector

Those administering skills funding at the local level should ensure that existing opportunities for community learning funding are effectively promoted to those working with homeless adults, and where necessary provide support with the application process. In addition, formal adult education institutions should ensure that relevant outreach opportunities are communicated clearly to the homelessness sector. Local colleges, universities and other learning institutions should also explore ways in which they could support adult education provision in homelessness and other community settings, for example through volunteer brokerage opportunities, thereby increasing the supply of trained volunteer skills tutors available in homelessness settings.

For the Homelessness Sector

Homelessness organisations should explore the ways in which existing activities can be used more effectively to develop learning opportunities for their service users, for example through the social enterprise activities available, service user involvement in newsletters and other aspects of the organisation. Opportunities for inter-agency collaboration should also be explored. For example, where organisations are unable to fund their own adult education activities, exploring the possibility of co-funding models, or promoting the activities provided by other similar organisations may offer ways to overcome this.

References

Amore, K., Baker, M., & Howden-Chapman, P. (2011). The ETHOS Definition and Classification of Homelessness: An Analysis. *European Journal of Homelessness, 5*(2), 19–37.
Anderson, I. (2010). Services for Homeless People in Europe: Supporting Pathways Out of Homelessness? In E. O'Sullivan, V. Busch-Geertsema, D. Quilgars, & N. Pleace (Eds.), *Homelessness Research in Europe*. Brussels: FEANTSA.
Barton, D., Appleby, Y., Hodge, R., Tusting, K., & Ivanic, R. (2006). *Relating Adults' Lives and Learning: Participation and Engagement in Different Settings*. London: NRDC.
Batty, E., Beatty, C., Casey, R., Foden, M., McCarthy, L., & Reeve, K. (2015). *Homeless People's Experiences of Welfare Conditionality and Benefit Sanctions.* London: Crisis.

Boeren, E. (2016). *Lifelong Learning Participation in a Changing Policy Context: An Interdisciplinary Theory*. London: Palgrave Macmillan.

Bowl, M. (2014). *Adult Education in Changing Times: Policies, Philosophies, Professionalism*. Leicester: NIACE.

Buckingham, H. (2010). *Hybridity, Diversity and the Division of Labour in the Third Sector: What Can We Learn from Homelessness Organisations in the UK?* (Working Paper 50). Third Sector Research Centre.

Castleton, G. (2001). The Role of Literacy in People's Lives. In J. Crowther, M. Hamilton, & L. Tett (Eds.), *Powerful Literacies*. Leicester: NIACE.

Crisis, Homeless Link, & St Mungo's. (2012). *The Programme's Not Working: Experiences of Homeless People on the Work Programme*.

Crowther, J., Maclachlan, K., & Tett, L. (2010). Adult Literacy, Learning Identities and Pedagogic Practice. *International Journal of Lifelong Education, 29*, 651–664.

DCLG. (2007). *Places of Change Programme: Application Guidance*. https://www.bipsolutions.com/docstore/pdf/19206.pdf. Accessed 6 May 2016.

DCLG/BIS. (2014). *New Support to Give Homeless People 'Basic Building Blocks' for Work*. https://www.gov.uk/government/news/new-support-to-give-homeless-basic-building-blocks-for-work. Accessed 6 May 2016.

DfEE. (2001). *Skills for Life: The National Strategy for Improving Adult Literacy and Numeracy Skills*. Nottingham: Department for Education and Employment.

Dumoulin, D., & Jones, K. (2014). *Reading Counts: Why English and Maths Skills Matter in Tackling Homelessness*. London: St Mungo's Broadway.

Dwyer, P., & Somerville, P. (2011). Introduction: Themed Section on Exploring Multiple Exclusion Homelessness. *Social Policy & Society, 10*(4), 495–500.

Field, J. (2000). *Lifelong Learning and the New Educational Order*. Stoke on Trent: Trentham Books, Ltd.

Fitzpatrick, S. (2005). Explaining Homelessness: A Critical Realist Perspective. *Housing, Theory and Society, 22*(1), 1–17.

Fitzpatrick, S., Kemp, P., & Klinker, S. (2000). *Single Homelessness: An Overview of Research in Britain*. York: Joseph Rowntree Foundation.

Fitzpatrick, S., Pawson, H., Bramley, G., Wilcox, S., & Watts, B. (2016). *The Homelessness Monitor: England 2016*. York: Joseph Rowntree Foundation.

Homeless Link. (2010). *Survey of Needs & Provision 2010 Services for Homeless Single People and Couples in England*. London: Homeless Link.

Homeless Link. (2012). *ETE & Accreditation: Meaningful Activities in Homelessness Services*. London: Homeless Link.

Homeless Link. (2015). *Support for Single Homeless People in England: Annual Review 2015*. London: Homeless Link.

Hough, J., Jones, J., & Rice, B. (2013). *Longitudinal Qualitative Research on Homeless People's Experiences of Starting and Staying in Work*. London: Broadway.

Luby, J., & Welch, J. (2006). *Missed Opportunities: The Case for Investment in Learning and Skills for Homeless People*. London: Crisis.

Neale, J. (1997). *Theorising Homelessness: Contemporary Sociological and Feminist Perspectives*. London: Routledge.

Olisa, J., Patterson, J., & Wright, F. (2010). *Turning the Key: Portraits of Low Literacy Amongst People with Experience of Homelessness*. London: Thames Reach.

Pleace, N., & Bretherton, J. (2014). *Crisis Skylight, an Evaluation: Year One Interim Report*. London: Crisis and University of York.

Reisenberger, A., Barton, D., Satchwell, C., Wilson, A., Law, C., & Weaver, S. (2010). *Engaging Homeless People, Black and Minority Ethnic and Other Priority Groups in Skills for Life*. London: NRDC.

Tett, L. (2010). *Community Education, Learning and Development*. Edinburgh: Dunedin Academic Press.

Wagner, D. (2012). *Confronting Homelessness: Poverty, Politics, and the Failure of Social Policy*. Boulder: Lynne Rienner Publishers.

9

Conclusions and Recommendations

Ellen Boeren and Nalita James

Introduction

The main aim of this book has been to present an account of how austerity has had an impact on the adult education sector in Britain, and to bring together chapters which are useful to those teaching and researching in the field, as well as policymakers and practitioners As discussed in the first part of this book, society is characterised by deep inequalities, the marginalisation of disadvantaged groups and too many people living in 'left behind' communities. While adult education could serve as a mechanism to increase social mobility and demonstrate society's social justice reflex, in recent years, the sector has not received the attention

E. Boeren (✉)
Moray House School of Education, University of Edinburgh, Edinburgh, UK
e-mail: Ellen.Boeren@ed.ac.uk

N. James
School of Education, University of Leicester, Leicester, UK
e-mail: nrj7@leicester.ac.uk

© The Author(s) 2019
E. Boeren and N. James (eds.), *Being an Adult Learner in Austere Times*,
https://doi.org/10.1007/978-3-319-97208-4_9

and support it deserves. Engagement with statistical and historical information in the first part of this book, including the use of data from the European Labour Force Survey and reflections on work by Raymond Williams, have demonstrated the ongoing inequality in adult education participation, and the need to reclaim the role of adult education as a way to engage in social change. Our introduction has explored the concept of austerity and the negative effects it has on those most in need of a wide range of support mechanisms to increase the quality of their lives.

The second part of the book has discussed five interesting pieces of research, carried out in relation to the situation of adult learners in the contexts of higher, further and community education. Perspectives from both adult learners and practitioners working in these education contexts have been discussed, based on in-depth engagement with evidence collected by the authors of these chapters. Three chapters focussed on the relationship between austerity and the situation of mature learners in higher education. One chapter focused on further education and a final one zoomed in on third sector organisations operating in the community to help homeless adults.

Arriving at the concluding chapter of the book, we will draw out some of the key insights and that have emerged across the chapters through a rich variety of lenses. Firstly, we synthesise the diverse perspectives and standpoints. The chapter will then end with recommendations for policy, practice and further research.

Theoretical and Political Perspectives

Ageism

One of the major themes discussed across the chapters, and particularly in the first part of the book, relates to the idea of ageism. Education policies nowadays only seem interested in serving young people, not adults and mature learners. In the chapters on higher education, it has been demonstrated that enrolment numbers for adult learners and part-time students have dramatically gone down in England, partly because of the introduction of higher fees. This has led to this group becoming rather invisible in the higher education landscape. Also in further education, as argued by Duckworth and Smith, there is a tendency of the college sector to focus on the 16–19 age group. While Sutton's chapter focusses on the isolation felt by mature learners, whether chosen or as a result of the age gap with the other students, the fact that there are fewer mature students in higher education nowadays anyway means that their reference peer group becomes smaller. The decreased attention for adult learners is also damaging for the stereotype that mature students are perceived as 'deficient', as explained by Meir. The ways in which mature students are seen as a group of students not worth investing in can have potentially have negative consequences for their confidence and identities, while their participation in education should in fact give them renewed chances to strengthen themselves in these areas. Such labels do not provide respect and dignity for adult student qualities, and can affect their expectations as well as negatively influence the actions of educators.

Not only do the chapters on higher and further education mentioned the lack of focus on older learners, Jones also highlights the lack of interest in adults above the age of 25 in her chapter on third sector community organisations active in the field of homelessness. While Boeren demonstrated that it is a general pattern across Europe for participation rates to decline by age, it is important to stress that age 25 is in fact the starting age for official adult education participation statistics collected by the European Commission. Not focussing on those age 25 and over, not only represses adult visibility in post-compulsory education, outside the initial schooling system, including further and higher education sector but is a strong indication of the disinterest in the sector rather than developing the position and privilege of adult learners. These chapters highlight how post-compulsory education culture and history have positioned adults as not being worthy of study, and few critical questions have been posed of the sector as it relates to adults.

Neo-Liberal Ideologies

Throughout the book, austerity has been clearly linked to neo-liberal education ideologies and Boeren, Clancy, Duckworth and Smith specifically mention the role of the OECD as a trendsetter in dominating an economic-oriented education policy agenda. Not only the OECD, but also the tones of the European Commission and the British austerity government clearly lean towards a 'learning for earning' perspective. Words and sentences like instrumentalism, managerialism, individualism, reductionism, performativity, gaming, the reproduction of social structures, the Westminster bubble, the Matthew effect,... have been regularly used throughout the chapters. Jones writes about the 'victims of the shrinking pots', but also acknowledges that the sector of community education has traditionally been underfinanced, and is thus a problem with a much longer history. Overall, the chapters have put a focus on the expectation of the adult learner as being individually responsible for his/her learning. Apart from the change in ideology globally, the British focus of this book has also demonstrated the strong turn to more managerial and economic approaches to adult education.

Wider Public Sector Cuts

Linked to the theme of austerity and neo-liberal education ideologies is the further impact of austerity on wider social policies. As demonstrated by Boeren, adult education participation rates tend to correlate with aspects like material deprivation and general life satisfaction. The United Kingdom has a rather average score for material deprivation compared to other countries in the EU-28 as demonstrated in Chapter 2. Clancy also focus on the general tendency to have lower participation rates in education and training among those living in the most deprived communities and neighbourhoods. Fraser and Harman, as well as Jones, also focussed specifically on the role of wider social policy austerity measures, such as general welfare and other public sector cuts, and how this is likely to have a knock on effect on adults' capacities to invest in post-compulsory learning activities. Duckworth and Smith further develop this line of thought through focussing on highlighting the role of education as contributing to stronger levels of social justice. Together with equality and inclusion, social justice in the wider society has been a very relevant theme of this book. It is apparent that even when government-funded institutions such as OFFA have made commitments to social mobility and the tackling of other inequalities, they have not been helped by the recent period of austerity. Further, austerity politics has led to reduced resources that organisations are able to access to support adult education in community settings. The wider implications of austerity (most notably, welfare reform) also impact on the services offered by organisations as they respond to the needs of their service users.

Transformative Power

On a more positive note, chapters throughout this book have also focussed on the transformative power of adult education. Clancy focussed on the role of residential adult education colleges, of which four are left in England. The chapters on higher education and further education zoomed in on experiences of adult learners and practitioners, providing evidence on the benefits participation can have in changing adult lives for the better. The chapter by Jones on homelessness education has also highlighted the positive role education can have in transforming the lives of adults living in this difficult situation. This theme on transformative power moves away from the focus on the constrained access to education that many experience, but provides insight on the role of adequate in-house support and sound pedagogical practices to apply by adult educators in order to strive towards positive participation experiences. Sutton discussed the increased risk for mature students in higher education to leave without the final degree qualification. This demonstrates that providing support to potential mature students to get into the system is not enough, but that support needs to continue during their participation process. Throughout the book, there is a focus on key words like hope, agency, confidence building and empowerment. In the introduction, we mentioned the EAEA's Manifesto for Adult Learning in the twenty-first Century, which apart from the focus on the enhancement of employment and career prospects, also includes the aims of increased active citizenship and social cohesion, equity and equality, as well as providing chances for adults to increase their life skills. Despite austerity coupled to neo-liberal education policies and wider public sector cuts, it has been stimulating to read stories about transformative experiences of adult learners in relation to these inclusive themes. Such an approach to education challenges the narrow content of authorized curricula, and hierarchical forms of power in the educational systems, and also highlights that educators can play a crucial role in helping adult learners work towards transformative learning.

Having discussed the major themes found across the chapters of this book, we now aim to translate these findings into a set of recommendations of policy and practice. This will be followed by suggestions for future research.

Recommendations for Policy and Practice

Change the Idea That Education Is Only Worth the Investment for Younger People

Ageism was the focus of our first theme. The idea that education should be for all, regardless of their background characteristics including age, has not been translated into practice. Widening participation initiatives focus on young people finishing school and mature learners have become a marginalised group in both higher and further education. Also in work on community education, this theme has been discussed. It is thus time for a new way of thinking among policy makers and make policy decisions accordingly. The economic and social impact of engaging in adult education play an important part on the individual and the wider economy, leading to better health, well-being and sociability. While it is understandable that the government wants to focus on getting everyone a good start in life, it is far from reality that everyone receives similar chances during childhood and teenage years.

The broken promises of social mobility and meritocracy need to be revisited. This includes rethinking the structures of compulsory education systems, but also through introducing a refocus on adult education. This should include second chance opportunities for adults who missed out first time round. From a social justice perspective, creating barriers limiting the access to education of adults older than 25 indicates the failure of striving towards equality and inclusion. Universities have a particular civic role to play to engage mature learners, become more aware of their continuing learning needs and of their strong potential to contribute to society.

Create Links Between the Education Sector and Other Public Sector Services

The declined participation in post-compulsory education among adults has been linked to reduced financial support for the sector. However, cuts in education should be seen in relation to wider austerity measures in other domains of social policy. A decreased overall budget demands an increased efficiency and effectiveness in order to maintain quality of provisions and social services. Moreover, as access to adult education has reduced, it is important that adults receive support and information from other services they use, for example health services or employment services. Practitioners working in these sectors can help adults on how to navigate their way through the available opportunities for education and training. Many of them might be unaware of existing opportunities or might not have thought of adult learning as a way to increase their chances in life. Especially in case of the most vulnerable adults in society, outreach activities need to be supported,-particularly long-term outreach in low participant areas. A greater emphasis in monitored adult WP targets could support HEIs to increase their outreach in communities, and/or provide a way of re-invigorating university-community education partnerships. In an ideal world, an increased budget would optimise these services. This recommendation on the further integration of services is relevant at the level of the United Kingdom as a whole, but would ideally also translate to initiatives of service providers working together in cities, towns and across local authorities. This will likely strengthen the success of reaching adults living in the surroundings of the available education and training opportunities.

Provide Educators with Training on Working with Adult Learners

The participation of adults in education and training can have transformative power, and help them in gaining higher levels of confidence and to create a stronger sense of agency. However, too often, mature learners are being stereotyped as deficient and work by widening participation offices focuses nearly exclusively on pupils in schools. If we want to reach a society in which truly everyone receives the chances to benefit from education, it is necessary that there are accessible learning pathways available for adult learners. This will require an effort from policy makers, as discussed above, but this strategy will also only work in practitioners working with adults have the appropriate level of knowledge and skills on how to deal with this specific group of learners. Their pedagogical practices and support will then hopefully prevent drop-out and dissatisfaction and lead to successful learning journeys. This recommendation also supports the view that experiences of adult learners can be varied and that stereotypical thinking about learners in this group is unlikely to be helpful to them. As such, there needs to be an adequate variety of support available for this group, ranging from flexible learning provisions through facilitating informal peer support between adult learners. The main implication for the practice of adult learning is that delivery can be contextualised by tutors so that it suits the unique goals and aspirations of each learner. This contrasts with the teaching of one size fits all programmes of learning, where all students study the same set of discrete and predefined skills regardless of their life experience, interests or educational goals. Engaging with the experiences of adult learners will help educators and those working in services like widening participation offices to increase their support for adult learners over time.

Be Open About the Benefits of Learning as an Adult Learner

While the benefits of learning have received considerable attention in the adult education literature, it is important to be critical on the often cross-sectional nature of this evidence. The majority of research in this area consists of snapshot studies, focussing on the experiences and facts and figures about learners at one single point in time. Data of the Labour Force Survey, used for monitoring purposes by the European Commission are also cross-sectional. A longitudinal follow-up on individuals is thus not possible. In fact, the United Kingdom is one of the few countries in Europe who have invested in longitudinal studies and HESA engages in large scale data collection among students and graduates as well. It is important to use evidence coming out of these data to create an accurate picture on what to expect as an adult learner, not only focussing on the economic and employment related benefits, but also on the effects it has on issues like social inclusion, social mobility and life satisfaction. It is not only important that administrations responsible for these data use them in a responsible way, but that research councils and other funding bodies provide opportunities to scholars to further exploit existing data and collect new primary data on the experiences and benefits of adult learning.

Having provided some recommendations for policy and practice, we now turn out attention to recommendations for future research.

Recommendations for Future Research

Undertake Research to Further Understand the Effects of Austerity Across Welfare Sectors and Underrepresented Groups

While relevant to the entire book, this recommendation was explicitly made by Harman and Fraser. It is important to see adult learning as part of the wider welfare state and to look deeper into the intersectionality between education, training and other sectors like employment services, as well as undertake an evaluation of the interventions intended to improve social mobility and inclusion. As suggested by Boeren, there aspects of social provision correlate with adult learning participation rates. While in an age of austerity it is recommended to use budgets in an efficient and effective way, as recommended above, it will also be useful to further investigate how this can best be done. Especially disadvantaged learners are expected to use a number of different services and it is important to further research the knowledge of practitioners about other services, including education, available for their clients. The chapter by Jones also highlights the need to document choices and experiences of under-represented groups. We need a more holistic picture of the meaning of adult education for individuals, institutions and communities.

Employ a Mix of Research Methods to Further the Understanding of Issues Relating to Adult Learners

Previous review studies in adult education have revealed the limited variety of research approaches being used in the field. Research in relation to adult learners, also in this book, tend to concentrate on smaller scale qualitative studies. While these are necessary to provide insight in-depth inside in the experiences of adult learners, it is recommended to make further use of existing large scale data as well. While a number of British longitudinal surveys exist, they are not often used by scholars active in adult education. Further exploitation of secondary datasets is recommended, especially at times in which research funding is hard to obtain.

Explore Issues of Adult Learning at Different Types of Institutions

Meir's recommendation can be widened to the rest of the book. Empirical evidence for her chapter was collected in one specific higher education institution. In fact, the higher education landscape in Britain is diverse. Research intensive Russell Group universities attract more students from privileged backgrounds, especially visible at the leading institutions Oxford and Cambridge. Post-1992 universities, formerly polytechnics which received university status in 1992 are more teaching-intensive and tend to attract more widening participation students. Further insights in how mature learners in these settings navigate through the system is being welcomed and results will have the potential to act as a framework for setting recommendations for the wider sector. Further investigation in exploring differences between institutions and initiatives undertaken in different geographical places should also be encouraged in relation to further education and community education. Further, as researchers we can play a role in challenging our own institutions on the policy and practice around adult education initiatives, recruitment strategies and pedagogical practices.

Explore the Impact of Brexit on Adult Learning

While harder to just at this current time, in the next few years, the effects of Britain leaving the European Union will become clearer. Vice-chancellors have warned that Brexit will have devastating effects on the higher education sector, large international companies are threatening to leave the country and to move their headquarters to the continent. While it has been suggested that low educated adults tended to have a higher likelihood to vote in favour of Brexit, it is also feared they are likely to experience the negative effects of Brexit. In the coming years, it will be important for scholars to monitor the situation of adult education and whether changes in wider social policies as a result of the move away from Europe will change the outlook of the sector. Since the Brexit vote, much emphasis has been placed on the training and retraining needs of people. However, nothing has changed. Adult education budgets are still being cut, outreach and community engagement work, and getting reluctant learners into education is side-lined. In times of austerity, the significance of this work should not be under-estimated, as it offers support and a place for communities to learn new skills together, as well reduce unemployment and inactivity by identifying and supporting people back into education as a pathway to work.

Final Remarks

The core aim of this book was to increase attention for adult education among academics, policy makers and practitioners, as well as prompt a new surge of interest in the challenges of adult education. This book has provided a critical account on the reduced attention for adult education in recent years. It has combined insights in the situation of British adult education from a European and historical perspective with voices from adult learners and practitioners working in higher, further and community education. It is hoped that this book will stimulate further discussions on the role of adult education in British society and will act as a tool to revisit some of the decisions that have been undertaken by policy makers in recent years, as well as better publicise what we know works in adult education as well as generate a renewed confidence and foster new advocates. Currently, a review of post-18 education in England is underway, under the leadership of Philp Augar. While the review will concentrate on areas like stronger diversifying between vocational and academic tracks, David Hughes, Chief Executive of the Association of Colleges, has put emphasis of seeing this review as a chance to look at the reshape of the entire post-18 sector, including tracks for those who want to learn while working or those who want to return to education at a later age. The review promises to focus on access and it will be interesting to see whether on this occasion, more attention will be paid to adult learners, on top of the traditional group of young widening participation students and that major barriers that have had a demonstrably negative impact on the participation of adult learners accessing education are removed.

Index

A
abuse 180
access 2, 4, 12–14, 25, 48, 56, 57, 59, 62, 67, 72, 73–75, 77–79, 82, 83, 90, 100, 101, 103, 104, 106, 123, 139, 142, 154, 155, 164, 167, 168, 172, 179, 183, 187, 188, 190, 192, 195, 203, 205, 210
Access to HE 13, 14, 103, 104, 106, 155, 167, 172
accreditation 23, 194
achievement 72, 139, 153, 155, 157, 162, 172, 173
active citizenship 3, 22, 204
Active Labour Market Policies 30
admissions criteria 12
Adult Education Survey 23, 25
age 5–7, 12, 27, 31, 32, 40, 50, 52, 59, 72, 74–76, 79, 81, 83, 97, 98, 100, 101, 103, 104, 106–109, 111–113, 115, 116, 118, 125, 152, 154, 194, 201, 204, 208, 210
age discrimination 101, 104, 107
ageism 200, 204
agency 8, 11–13, 58, 72, 76, 77, 98, 125, 127, 131–134, 141, 143–146, 152, 158, 161, 171, 196, 203, 206
alcohol 115, 180, 181, 183
All Parliamentary Group for Adult Education 83
anxiety 51, 66, 113, 141
apprenticeships 8, 37, 83, 84, 152, 155
aspiration 47, 52, 125, 134, 144
Association of College 8, 22, 83, 210
associationism 47

Index

austerity 1, 2, 6–12, 14, 15, 49, 53, 82, 123, 125, 144, 145, 151, 169, 173, 174, 179, 185, 186, 188–194, 199, 200, 202–205, 207–209

B

barriers 11, 55, 58, 59, 99, 101, 105, 107, 109, 117, 128, 158, 182, 183, 187, 205, 210
basic skills 4, 29, 181, 184
benchmarks 21, 74, 173
benefits 1, 3, 4, 7, 8, 14, 16, 25–27, 30, 67, 154, 167, 172, 173, 182, 183, 187, 192, 203, 207
benefits of learning 3, 25, 182, 207
BERA 160
biographical 125, 128
Birkbeck 72, 73, 78–80, 82, 87, 88
birth cohort studies 25
black and minority ethnic 74, 75
Bourdieu, Pierre 56, 57, 106
Brexit 34, 49, 50, 91, 209
Browne report 71
budget 10, 50, 83, 84, 88–90, 156, 205
bursaries 79–82, 88, 105

C

capabilities 181, 195
Cambridge 55, 56, 64, 209
capital 2, 6, 14, 26, 56–60, 64, 65, 136, 141, 153, 155, 158, 164, 170, 171
career 3, 5, 58, 63, 80, 87, 98, 100, 106, 125, 138, 139, 143, 164, 172, 204

chavs 49
choice 7, 10, 57, 99, 109, 111, 117, 118, 131, 133, 144, 157, 164, 169, 170
class 11–14, 41, 48, 49, 50–64, 66, 83–85, 87, 124–126, 129, 131, 135, 136, 138, 140–142, 144, 145, 154, 155, 158, 169, 170, 174
cohesion 3, 172, 204
community 2, 3, 12–14, 47, 48, 50, 53, 61, 62, 65–67, 82–86, 88–91, 97, 106, 139, 153, 154, 156, 157, 159, 160, 161, 165, 167, 171, 173, 179, 182–184, 187, 189, 190, 194–196, 200–205, 209, 210
community learning 48, 67, 83, 84, 156, 187, 189, 194, 195
competitiveness 9, 24, 124, 153
confidence 14–16, 57, 62, 64, 85, 89, 132, 133, 139, 140, 142, 143, 146, 163, 166–169, 171, 182, 184, 187, 201, 203, 206, 210
constraints 5, 146, 152, 153, 181
credit 6, 83
crisis 6, 7, 22, 71, 151, 181, 183, 184, 192, 193
curriculum 84, 154, 172
cuts 7–9, 11, 72, 82, 84, 89, 90, 151, 156, 167, 185, 188, 192–194, 202, 204, 205

D

debt 8, 80, 113
decommodification 33
deficit 47, 50, 75, 125, 136, 171

Deleuze, G. 126, 127, 129, 132, 138, 142, 144
democracy 3, 48–51, 66, 67, 153
deprivation 34–37, 154, 202
determinants 11, 22, 26–28, 30, 41, 56
disability(ies) 30, 52, 58, 75, 79, 81
disadvantaged 4, 5, 7, 12, 14, 25, 59, 66, 74–76, 88, 90, 91, 199, 208
dispossession 11, 47, 49
dispositions 57
diversity 57, 74, 79
drop-out 4, 98, 99, 101, 104, 105, 107, 206
drug 58, 181, 183
dyslexia 162, 167

EAEA 4, 203
earnings 57, 60, 86, 139, 202
economy 4, 7, 9, 10, 14, 29, 32, 34, 50, 52, 53, 99, 100, 104, 153, 156, 204
Education Maintenance Allowance (EMA) 59
elite 48, 49, 54–57, 60, 61
emotional capital 65, 170
employability 9, 52, 153, 155
employment 3–6, 22, 28–31, 34, 37–39, 41, 49, 50, 60, 83, 85, 90, 100, 101, 113, 117, 133, 134, 152, 167, 171, 172, 174, 183–185, 187, 193, 204, 205, 207
empower 152
empowerment 13, 161, 169, 203
engagement 2, 13, 16, 41, 53, 64, 65, 83, 88–90, 104, 143, 144, 160, 174, 182, 183, 188, 191, 196, 200, 209
equality 3, 48, 54, 55, 64, 74, 75, 100, 101, 123, 157, 203–205
equality act 100, 101
equity 3, 204
Esping-Andersen, G. 33
ethnicity 79, 81, 158, 170
Europe 4, 7, 9, 11, 21, 22, 26, 28, 29, 30, 201, 207, 209
excluded 3, 14, 15, 97, 112, 114, 136, 182, 183
experiences 2, 12, 13, 49, 62, 65, 98, 101, 107–110, 113, 114, 116–118, 123, 124, 126, 128–130, 132–134, 138, 140, 143, 145, 152, 158–163, 170, 171, 174, 175, 181, 203, 204, 206–208

fees 10, 12, 27, 37, 71, 73–75, 78–81, 88–90, 100, 102, 103, 124, 156, 201
fees cap 71
female 13, 125, 126, 139, 145, 146, 162
feminist 14, 143
financial hardship 79
Fircroft College 61, 63
first generation students 9, 37
formal learning 3, 23, 25, 89, 183
Foucault, M. 163
full-time 10, 12, 75, 77, 79, 100–103, 107, 118

Index

funding 6, 8, 12, 14, 15, 34, 52, 72, 74, 79, 82–84, 88, 90, 99, 101, 102, 123–125, 144, 152, 155, 156, 173, 174, 180, 183–185, 188, 189, 190, 194–196, 207, 208
funding tariffs 155
further education 2, 9, 10, 12, 14, 59, 83–85, 88, 105, 125, 132, 151, 152, 154–158, 161–168, 170–174, 200, 201, 203, 204, 209

G

GDP 34, 37, 38
gender 52, 79, 81, 117, 129, 131, 158, 170
gig economy 50, 53
glass ceiling 30
globalisation 153, 170
grammar schools 54
Greater Manchester 15, 179, 185, 186, 194, 195
grounded theory 128

H

hardship 6, 79
health 3, 7, 22, 27, 37, 53, 58, 78, 80, 114, 116, 117, 139, 140, 142, 157, 164, 167, 168, 172, 181, 183, 184, 190, 191, 204, 205
higher education 2, 4, 9, 12, 13, 22, 26, 37, 52, 55, 56, 58, 59, 61, 66, 67, 71–78, 81–85, 87, 88, 90, 91, 98–107, 123–127, 134, 135, 137–140, 143, 144–146, 152, 200, 201, 203, 208, 209
Higher Education Funding Council England (HEFCE) 12, 72, 74, 100, 102
HigherEducation Policy Institute (HEPI) 55
Higher Education Statistics Agency (HESA) 12, 72, 76, 77, 98, 102–105, 125, 207
Hillcroft College 63
historical 11, 48, 49, 60, 167, 171, 200, 210
history 2, 47–49, 53, 65–67, 72, 84, 108, 171, 172, 201, 202
homeless 14, 15, 179–186, 190–195, 200
hope 48, 49, 65, 67, 152, 153, 157, 162, 168, 170, 172, 175, 203
housing 7, 180, 181, 184
human capital 6, 153

I

identity 3, 52, 136–140, 144, 145, 160, 163
income 22, 50, 54, 56, 75, 79–82, 87, 91, 154
independent schools 54
in-depth interviews 15, 107
indicators 21, 33–35, 38, 41, 77, 173
individualism 123, 124, 139, 145, 169, 202
industry 152, 171, 172
inequality 5, 7, 11, 14, 21, 22, 24, 33, 54, 56, 57, 65, 124, 134, 152, 154, 155, 158, 170, 172, 182, 190, 199, 200, 203

informal learning 13, 23, 66
intergenerational 99, 152, 166
internationalisation 99
International Standard Classification of Education (ISCED) 23, 28
investments 5, 9, 11, 22, 25, 26, 27, 31, 34, 35, 37, 40, 41, 123, 193, 204
isolated 13, 98, 106, 109–112, 117, 144, 167
isolation 15, 53, 97, 98, 106, 107, 109–112, 114, 116–118, 182, 183, 201

J

job insecurity 38
Joseph Rowntree Foundation 49–50

K

knowledge dispossession 11, 47, 49
knowledge economy 14, 99, 153, 156

L

Labour Force Survey 11, 21–23, 25, 26, 28, 29, 31–33, 39, 200, 207
labour market 5, 11, 27, 30, 32, 34, 38, 154, 180, 194
learner identities 117
Leitch 10, 104
life experiences 13, 158
life satisfaction 35, 37, 41, 202, 207
literacy 6, 29, 38, 39, 52, 156–158, 165, 166, 181, 184, 187, 189

loan 59, 75, 80, 88, 155, 156
local authorities 6, 7, 63, 83, 84, 167, 180, 190, 191, 195, 206
localism 185
Local Education Authority 61
loneliness 106, 111

M

mainstream 14, 182, 183, 187, 191, 192
maintenance loans 80
managerialism 7, 15, 64, 202
marginalisation 5, 162, 199
marginalised 7, 15, 124, 174, 204
marketization 14
mass education 50, 51
Matthew effect 155, 202
mature students 3, 12, 13, 22, 74–78, 81, 82, 85, 87, 88, 90, 91, 97–118, 123, 124, 126, 201, 203
meritocracy 54, 169, 205
middle class 51, 54, 60, 135, 136
migration 4, 49
motivation 26, 107, 109, 117, 133, 135, 137, 139, 140, 143, 166, 167

N

narratives 13–15, 124, 125, 127, 129, 130, 134, 137–139, 144, 145, 155–161, 167, 169, 170, 172
national health service 7, 191
neighbourhood 6, 37, 77, 84, 85, 171, 202

neoliberal 2, 6–9, 52, 53, 57, 123–125, 133, 138, 144–146, 151, 153–156, 158, 165, 171, 173, 174
non-formal 13, 23–25, 48, 67, 89
non-traditional learner 59, 75
Northern College 62, 63
numeracy 6, 29, 52, 156, 181, 184, 187, 189

O

Office for Fair Access (OFFA) 12, 59, 74–77, 85, 91, 203
Open Method of Coordination 24
opportunities 1–5, 8, 9, 11, 15, 26, 29, 34, 41, 56, 57, 83, 85, 86, 89, 100, 104, 112, 134, 154, 156, 158, 163, 168, 169, 172, 182, 183, 186–191, 194–196, 205–207
oppression 131
Organisation for Economic Co-operationand Development (OECD) 5, 22–25, 29, 37, 38, 54, 173, 202
outreach 74, 76, 82, 84, 85, 88–90, 173, 187–189, 193, 196, 205, 209
Oxford 52, 55, 56, 61–64, 164, 209

P

participation 1–6, 8, 10–12, 14, 22–35, 37, 38, 41, 48, 55, 71, 72–79, 81, 83–88, 90, 91, 98–103, 108, 124, 125, 143, 144, 151, 155, 167, 182, 194, 200–206, 208–210

part-time 10, 12, 37, 59, 60, 71, 72, 74–77, 79, 80, 82, 85, 87, 89, 90, 100, 101, 103, 118, 125, 201
pedagogy 2, 63, 156–158
performativity 15, 173, 202
PIAAC 23, 25, 27, 38, 39
policy 2, 4, 6, 8, 10, 12–15, 24, 25, 30, 37, 41, 55, 57, 72–76, 84, 87, 90, 91, 98–100, 104, 105, 123, 142, 152–154, 160, 172–174, 179, 180, 182–185, 193–195, 199, 200, 202, 204–207, 209, 210
poor 8, 12, 49, 53, 55, 56, 64, 80, 86, 90, 106, 158, 162, 169, 174, 180, 195
poststructuralist 126
practice 2, 7, 11, 12, 15, 25, 73, 127, 131, 140–142, 144–146, 157, 161, 166, 167, 172, 175, 179, 183, 186, 195, 200, 203, 204, 206, 207, 209
pre-1992 university 98
precarious 7, 41, 49, 50, 65, 85, 180, 193
precarity 47, 53, 65
privatised 14
privilege 56, 57, 62, 64, 66, 124, 143, 154, 158, 169, 201, 208
professionalisation 15
prosperity 8
provision 6, 15, 22, 25, 33, 55, 73, 82–85, 87, 89, 99, 101, 152, 154, 172, 173, 179, 180, 182, 183, 186–188, 191–196, 205, 206, 208
public sector 7, 90, 202, 204, 205
public services 7, 84, 182

Q

qualifications 4–6, 10, 23, 26, 29, 57, 58, 62, 72, 75, 78–83, 85, 87, 89–91, 123, 124, 133, 134, 152, 172, 173, 181, 182, 203

R

race 51, 52, 131, 143
recession 6
recruitment 72, 74, 75, 78, 82, 86, 88–91, 100, 108, 146, 152, 160, 2099
reflexive 129, 130
refugee 88
Research and Development (R&D) 11, 34, 35, 40
residential colleges 48, 61–64, 66, 67
resilience 13, 14, 48, 65–67
resilient 65, 100
resistance 63, 126–128, 131, 132, 135, 145, 158
resources 9, 47, 48, 57, 58, 65, 67, 81, 160, 165, 169, 179, 180, 185, 187, 188, 190, 193, 203
responsibility 2, 6, 8, 9, 24, 48, 50, 60, 75, 98, 101, 105, 106, 110, 112, 116, 117, 124, 128, 130, 134, 144, 153, 167, 168, 181, 195
retention 25, 72, 78, 88, 90, 100, 101, 115, 116
retirement 27, 31, 100, 101
rhizomatic 127, 128, 138, 140
ripple effect 164, 167, 173
risk 4, 5, 22, 25, 98, 100, 124, 129, 203
Ruskin College 52, 61–63
Russell Group 55, 208

S

second chances 3, 58, 60, 82, 85, 91, 205
self-esteem 85, 89, 163, 171, 187
self-value 14
services 7, 30, 34, 86, 87, 88, 101, 180–188, 190–193, 195, 196, 203, 205, 206, 208
sexuality 52
single parent 82, 124
skills 4, 5, 8, 10, 16, 22, 23, 25, 27, 29, 30, 37, 41, 52, 57, 83, 87, 91, 100, 115, 138, 141, 152, 156, 164, 175, 181, 182, 184, 185, 187–190, 193–196, 204, 206
skills shortages 91
Skills, Training, Innovation and Employment (STRIVE) 184, 185
social class 52–55, 57, 83, 144, 145, 170, 174
social justice 47, 66, 76, 123, 124, 153, 174, 199, 203, 205
social mobility 11, 47, 50, 54, 56, 57, 59, 61, 91, 99, 153, 154, 171, 199, 203, 205, 207, 208
socio-economic background 13, 75
Standing Conference for University Teachers and Researchers in theEducation of Adults (SCUTREA) 2
stratification 14, 33, 153–155
student experience 59, 98
subjectivity 2, 124–127, 129, 132, 138, 142, 145, 146
Survey of Adult Skills 23, 25, 27, 38
sustainability 4
The Sutton Trust 56

T

taste 51, 57, 62, 64
Thatcherism 169
taxes 10
third-sector 14
tracking 40, 85
trade unions 62
traditional-aged students 98, 102, 106, 108, 111, 115, 118
transformation 5, 66, 134, 142, 143, 152, 157, 161, 168, 174, 175
transforming 14, 89, 203
transition 13, 78, 80, 106, 156

U

undergraduate 10, 12, 13, 77, 79, 97, 98, 100, 107, 125
under-represented groups 74, 81, 208
unemployed 9, 30, 31, 41, 52, 85, 167
UNESCO 5, 22–24
university 2, 6, 10, 13, 22, 55–57, 61, 62, 64, 67, 72–74, 77, 78, 79, 81–89, 91, 97, 98, 101, 102, 104–107, 109–112, 114–118, 123, 125, 137, 144, 156, 164, 205, 209
Universities and Colleges Union (UCU) 14, 156
University of Leeds 73, 84, 88

V

Vaughan Centre for Lifelong Learning 83

vocational 24, 27, 34, 83, 133, 152–155, 187, 210
vulnerable 6, 7, 116, 134, 154, 174, 188, 205

W

Workers Education Association (WEA) 64, 84, 85
welfare reform 15, 192, 203
welfare state 11, 22, 32, 35, 41, 207
well-being 3, 10, 35, 41, 157, 169, 172, 190, 204
White Paper on Higher Education 73, 99, 101
widening participation 12, 72–79, 81, 83, 87, 88, 90, 91, 99, 100, 101, 125, 144, 204, 206, 209, 210
Williams, Raymond 11, 47, 57, 60, 61, 62, 65–67, 200
women 13, 28, 30, 86, 100, 124–133, 135, 136, 140, 143–146, 158, 166, 181
working class 12, 13, 49, 50, 51, 57–63, 66, 84, 124, 125, 126, 135, 136, 140, 154
workplace 134
Widening Participation (WP) 125, 205

Z

zero hours' contracts 38, 50

Printed in the United States
By Bookmasters